REFL

DAILY PRAYER

ADVENT **2023** TO
EVE OF ADVENT **2024**

Church House Publishing
Church House
Great Smith Street
London SW1P 3AZ

ISBN 978 1 78140 395 2

Published 2023 by Church House Publishing
Copyright © The Archbishops' Council 2023

The opinions expressed in this book are those of the
authors and do not necessarily reflect the official policy of
the General Synod or The Archbishops' Council of the
Church of England.

Liturgical and commissioning editor: Peter Moger
Designed and typeset by Hugh Hillyard-Parker
Printed by CPI Group (UK) Ltd, Croydon CR0 4YY

What do you think of *Reflections for Daily Prayer*?

We'd love to hear from you – simply email us at

publishing@churchofengland.org

or write to us at

Church House Publishing, Church House,
Great Smith Street, London SW1P 3AZ.

Visit **www.dailyprayer.org.uk** for more
information on the *Reflections* series, ordering
and subscriptions.

Contents

In Memory of

The Revd Canon Anna Matthews
1978–2023

Anna was Vicar of St Bene't's Cambridge and
a regular contributor to *Reflections for Daily Prayer*.

Anna submitted her contribution to this volume
a few weeks before her sudden and tragic death
on 8 March 2023.

May she rest in peace and rise in glory.

Table of contributors

About the authors

Ally Barrett has worked in parish ministry, children's ministry and theological education, and is now Chaplain of St Catharine's College, Cambridge. She has published on baptism, weddings and all age preaching, and many of her hymns are published by Jubilate. She also paints, and has illustrated several books. In her spare time she enjoys improvisatory vegan cooking and feeding the ducks on the river Cam.

John Barton is Emeritus Oriel and Laing Professor of the Interpretation of Holy Scripture in the University of Oxford; and is now, in retirement, Senior Research Fellow, Campion Hall, Oxford. A priest in the Church of England, he assists in the parish of Abingdon-on-Thames, where he lives.

Gregory Cameron is the Bishop of St Asaph in the Church in Wales. A writer and occasional broadcaster, Gregory is also an artist and coin designer. He taught Old Testament and Canon Law in Cardiff University and is currently Chair of the Anglican Oriental Orthodox conversations. He enjoys interpreting and communicating the message of the Scriptures, and is excited about God's work in the Church today

Stephen Cottrell is the Archbishop of York. He was formerly Bishop of Chelmsford and is a well-known writer and speaker on evangelism, spirituality and catechesis. He is one of the team that produced *Pilgrim*, the popular course for the Christian Journey.

Andrew Davison is the Starbridge Lecturer in Theology and Natural Sciences in the University of Cambridge, and Fellow in Theology and Dean of Chapel at Corpus Christi College. His publications include *Why Sacraments?*, *Participation in God, Astrobiology and Christian Doctrine,* and *The Love of Wisdom: An Introduction to Philosophy for Theologians.*

Alan Everett is the vicar of All Saints West Dulwich in Southwark Diocese. To 2019, he was the vicar of St Clement Notting Dale and St James Norlands, in North Kensington, and, for 17 years before that, the vicar of St Michael and All Angels London Fields, in Hackney. His paintings can be viewed at alaneverett.com or on instagram at alaneverett.art.

Until his recent retirement, **Peter Graystone** worked for Southwark Diocese, helping South London churchgoers become more confident in what they believe, how they talk about it, and the way they live it out. He is the author of many books and reviews theatre for *The Church Times.*

4

Malcolm Guite is a life fellow of Girton College, Cambridge, a poet and author of *What do Christians Believe?; Faith, Hope and Poetry; Sounding the Seasons: Seventy Sonnets for the Christian Year; The Singing Bowl; Word in the Wilderness; Mariner: A voyage with Samuel Taylor Coleridge*, and *David's Crown: Sounding The Psalms*. He also writes the 'Poet's Corner' column for *The Church Times*.

Colin Heber-Percy is an Anglican priest serving in the Salisbury Diocese. Before ordination, he was a screenwriter. His films and works for television won many awards and are shown all over the world. He writes and publishes regularly on theology and philosophy. His recent publications include *Perfect in Weakness*, on the cinema of Andrei Tarkovsky, and the bestselling *Tales of a Country Parish* which was published last year to critical acclaim.

Chine McDonald is Director of Theos – the religion and society think tank. She was previously Head of Public Engagement at Christian Aid and is the author of *God is not a white man: and other revelations* (Hodder & Stoughton, May 2021). Chine contributes regularly to BBC religion and ethics programmes including *Thought for the Day*. She is vice-chair of Greenbelt Festival and a trustee of Christian Aid. Chine read Theology and Religious Studies at Cambridge University.

Rachel Mann is an Anglican priest, writer and scholar. Author of eleven books, including her debut novel, *The Gospel of Eve*, and the Michael Ramsey Prize shortlisted, *Fierce Imaginings*, she is Visiting Fellow at the Manchester Writing School. She regularly contributes to *Pause For Thought* on BBC Radio Two, as well as other radio programmes. More info: www.rachelmann.co.uk

Anna Matthews was vicar of St Bene't's, Cambridge from 2012 until 2023, prior to which she spent six years as a Minor Canon at St Albans Cathedral. Having a strong interest in vocations work and spirituality, she also served from 2012–19 as Director of Ordinands for the Diocese of Ely. Anna died in March 2023.

Nadim Nasser is an Anglican priest, and is the Director and Co-Founder of the Awareness Foundation and co-author of the Awareness Course. Born and raised in Lattakia, Syria, he studied theology at the Near East School of Theology in Beirut during the Lebanese Civil War. He has lectured at different universities in London and has appeared on TV and radio around the world. He is an author of two books, *The Culture of God* and *iJesus*.

5

Emma Parker is the Deputy Warden at Cranmer Hall and lectures in Preaching, Pastoral Care, Growing Faith in Children and Young People, and Spirituality. Prior to this she was the Priest in Charge of two parishes in East Durham. She has a PhD exploring Paul's concern for outsiders and the importance of 'outsider' opinion, and she loves running, gardening and being with her family (including two dogs!).

David Runcorn is a writer, speaker, spiritual director and theological teacher. He lives in Devon.

Jane Steen is the Bishop of Lynn in the Diocese of Norwich. She was consecrated in June 2021, having previously been Archdeacon of Southwark and, before that, Canon Chancellor of Southwark Cathedral and Director of Ministerial Education. Her one-time research looked at the use of seventeenth-century Anglican divines in Samuel Johnson's Dictionary. She is a member of the Church of England's Faith and Order Commission.

Angela Tilby is a Canon Emeritus of Christ Church Cathedral, Oxford, and Canon of Honour at Portsmouth Cathedral. She previously served in the Diocese of Oxford following a period in Cambridge, where she taught at Westcott House and was also vicar of St Bene't's Church. Before ordination she was a producer for the BBC, and she still broadcasts regularly.

Rachel Treweek is the Bishop of Gloucester and the first female diocesan bishop in England. She served in two parishes in London and was Archdeacon of Northolt and later Hackney. Prior to ordination she was a speech and language therapist and is a trained practitioner in conflict transformation.

Margaret Whipp is an Anglican priest and spiritual director based in Oxford. Her first career was in medicine. Since ordination in 1990, she has ministered in parish and chaplaincies and served in theological education. Her books include the *SCM Studyguide in Pastoral Theology* and *The Grace of Waiting*.

Lucy Winkett is Rector of St James's Church, Piccadilly. She contributes regularly to Radio 4's 'Thought for the Day', national press and radio, and is the author of *Our Sound is our Wound* (2010, Continuum) and *Reading the Bible with your Feet* (2021, Canterbury Press). Until 2010, she was Canon Precentor of St Paul's Cathedral in London, is a regular columnist for *The Church Times* and is a trustee of The National Churches' Trust.

About *Reflections for Daily Prayer*

Based on the *Common Worship Lectionary* readings for Morning Prayer, these daily reflections are designed to refresh and inspire times of personal prayer. The aim is to provide rich, contemporary and engaging insights into Scripture.

Each page lists the Lectionary readings for the day, with the main psalms for that day highlighted in **bold**. The collect of the day – either the *Common Worship* collect or the shorter additional collect – is also included.

For those using this book in conjunction with a service of Morning Prayer, the following conventions apply: a psalm printed in parentheses is omitted if it has been used as the opening canticle at that office; a psalm marked with an asterisk may be shortened if desired.

A short reflection is provided on either the Old or New Testament reading. Popular writers, experienced ministers, biblical scholars and theologians all contribute to this series, bringing with them their own emphases, enthusiasms and approaches to biblical interpretation.

Regular users of Morning Prayer and *Time to Pray* (from *Common Worship: Daily Prayer*) and anyone who follows the Lectionary for their regular Bible reading will benefit from the rich variety of traditions represented in these stimulating and accessible pieces.

This volume also includes both a simple form of *Common Worship* Morning Prayer (see inside front and back covers) and a short form of Night Prayer – also known as Compline – (see pp. 326–7), particularly for the benefit of those readers who are new to the habit of the Daily Office or for any reader while travelling.

Building daily prayer into daily life

In our morning routines, there are many tasks we do without giving much thought to them, and others that we do with careful attention. Daily prayer and Bible reading is a strange mixture of these. These are disciplines (and gifts) that we as Christians should have in our daily pattern, but they are not tasks to be ticked off. Rather they are a key component of our developing relationship with God. In them is *life* – for the fruits of this time are to be lived out by us – and to be most fruitful, the task requires both purpose and letting go.

In saying a daily office of prayer, we make the deliberate decision to say 'yes' to spending time with God – the God who is always with us. In prayer and attentive reading of the Scriptures, there is both a conscious entering into God's presence and a 'letting go' of all we strive to control: both are our acknowledgement that it is God who is God.

… come into his presence with singing.

Know that the Lord is God.
It is he that has made us, and we are his;
we are his people, and the sheep of his pasture.

Enter his gates with thanksgiving…

(Psalm 100, a traditional Canticle at Morning Prayer)

If we want a relationship with someone to deepen and grow, we need to spend time with that person. It can be no surprise that the same is true between us and God.

In our daily routines, I suspect that most of us intentionally look in the mirror; occasionally we might see beyond the surface of our external reflection and catch a glimpse of who we truly are. For me, a regular pattern of daily prayer and Bible reading is like a hard look in a clean mirror: it gives a clear reflection of myself, my life and the world in which I live. But it is more than that, for in it I can also see the reflection of God who is most clearly revealed in Jesus Christ and present with us now in the Holy Spirit.

This commitment to daily prayer is about our relationship with the God who is love. St Paul, in his great passage about love, speaks of now seeing 'in a mirror, dimly' but one day seeing face to face: 'Now I know only in part; then I will know fully, even as I have been fully known' (1 Corinthians 13.12). Our daily prayer is part of that seeing in a mirror dimly, and it is also part of our deep yearning for an ever-clearer vision of our God. As we read Scripture, the past and the future converge in the present moment. We hear words from long ago – some of which can appear strange and confusing – and yet, the Holy Spirit is living and active in the present. In this place of relationship and revelation, we open ourselves to the possibility of being changed, of being reshaped in a way that is good for us and all creation.

It is important that the words of prayer and Scripture should penetrate deep within rather than be a mere veneer. A quiet location is therefore a helpful starting point. For some, domestic circumstances or daily schedule make that difficult, but it is never impossible to become more fully present to God. The depths of our being can still be accessed no matter the world's clamour and activity. An awareness of this is all part of our journey from a false sense of control to a place of letting go, to a place where there is an opportunity for transformation.

Sometimes in our attention to Scripture, there will be connection with places of joy or pain; we might be encouraged or provoked or both. As we look and see and encounter God more deeply, there will be thanksgiving and repentance; the cries of our heart will surface as we acknowledge our needs and desires for ourselves and the world. The liturgy of Morning Prayer gives this voice and space.

I find it helpful to begin Morning Prayer by lighting a candle. This marks my sense of purpose and my acknowledgement of Christ's presence with me. It is also a silent prayer for illumination as I prepare to be attentive to what I see in the mirror, both of myself and of God. Amid the revelation of Scripture and the cries of my heart, the constancy of the tiny flame bears witness to the hope and light of Christ in all that is and will be.

When the candle is extinguished, I try to be still as I watch the smoke disappear. For me, it is symbolic of my prayers merging with the day. I know that my prayer and the reading of Scripture are not the smoke and mirrors of delusion. Rather, they are about encounter and discovery as I seek to venture into the day to love and serve the Lord as a disciple of Jesus Christ.

+ *Rachel Treweek*

Monday 4 December

Matthew 12.1-21

'Have you not read ...' (vv.3, 5)

Jesus asks his hearers if they are familiar with certain parts of the Bible. He would have known that they were, but he wants them to reconsider the passages' meaning. Usual interpretation gives way to something new when the Lord's Messiah stands on the earth.

Jesus often asks his followers to reassess normality. We are invited to see the world from his point of view, not ours. That is why Matthew gives us today's two episodes and a section from the prophet Isaiah. We are being asked to align ourselves with Jesus whose perspective is one of mercy, kindness, and healing. Jesus does not judge, or tell us that we lack these qualities, but Matthew's narrative reminds us that 'business as usual' sometimes crowds them out. Isaiah testifies that it is God's age-old purpose for us to treat each other justly, and gently. In naming the Gentiles (those not of God's chosen people, Israel), the prophet strikes a very contemporary note. God's chosen and beloved servant proclaims 'justice to the Gentiles', and there is no place for 'othering' each other.

During Advent, we can reflect on this truth. We prepare for God coming as a child, God who is not other than us, but God at one with us. We ready ourselves for new interpretations and new understanding of the Lord and of each other.

COLLECT

Almighty God,
give us grace to cast away the works of darkness
and to put on the armour of light,
now in the time of this mortal life,
in which your Son Jesus Christ came to us in great humility;
that on the last day,
when he shall come again in his glorious majesty
    to judge the living and the dead,
we may rise to the life immortal;
through him who is alive and reigns with you,
in the unity of the Holy Spirit,
one God, now and for ever.

Reflection by **Jane Steen**

Psalms **80**, 82 *or* **5**, 6 (8)
Isaiah 26.1-13
Matthew 12.22-37

Tuesday 5 December

Matthew 12.22-37

'... by your words you will be justified, and by your words you will be condemned' (v.37)

Words are formidable. From fairy tales to *Harry Potter*, words have power: the miller's daughter imprisoned by Rumpelstiltskin wins freedom by saying his name; Harry and his friends magic their way through Hogwarts by worded spells, not only by wands.

We do not live in these make-believe worlds, but our words matter. Words connect us – with each other, and with the world and the ideas we use them to describe. If our words are thoughtless, our link to others and the world will be thoughtless. If our hearts are not good, our speech is not good. In today's passage from Matthew, Jesus tells us that people will be forgiven every sin except blasphemy and speech against the Holy Spirit. Words, it seems, can matter even more than actions.

Perhaps that is why the Son of God comes to us as the Word of God. If our words matter, how much more God's. The Word for whom we prepare in Advent comes both to judge and to save, transforming our lives and our speech and himself bearing the judgement our casual talk deserves. As the seventeenth-century priest-poet, George Herbert wrote, imagining himself handing Christ a New Testament on Judgement Day:

> Let that be scann'd.
> There thou shalt find my faults are thine. ('Judgement', 1633)

Almighty God,
as your kingdom dawns,
turn us from the darkness of sin to the light of holiness,
that we may be ready to meet you
in our Lord and Saviour, Jesus Christ.

COLLECT

Wednesday 6 December

Matthew 12.38-end

'So will it be also with this evil generation' (v.45b)

This passage contains a hard saying: a person receives healing, yet the cause of suffering recurs and even worsens when 'the unclean spirit' returns, and not alone.

Whether or not we attribute disease to the work of evil spirits, the saying rings true: solutions we had hoped were permanent, are always temporary. Cured of disease, we will yet die. In his book, *Reconciliation*, Justin Welby describes the return of conflict after peace was brokered locally and regionally, but not nationally. Yet it is not, in the language of the passage, the evil spirit's return which is important. It is our freedom to choose.

Today's passage reminds us, that our choices have consequences. The people of Nineveh heard Jonah and chose to repent. The Queen of the South encountered Solomon's wisdom and chose to bless Israel's God. Others to whom Jesus spoke made no such choice. They met the Messiah and rejected him. Our choices are our own, but we are not absolved from their effects.

Despite this, the passage ends on a note of hope. Our circumstances, however difficult, need not always determine our actions. Anyone who does God's will belongs to Christ. Anyone who chooses the good can join the household of faith. Anyone, we might say, who refuses the spending and excess of a commercialised Christmas can take these weeks of Advent to prepare to greet Jesus.

COLLECT

Almighty God,
give us grace to cast away the works of darkness
and to put on the armour of light,
now in the time of this mortal life,
in which your Son Jesus Christ came to us in great humility;
that on the last day,
when he shall come again in his glorious majesty
    to judge the living and the dead,
we may rise to the life immortal;
through him who is alive and reigns with you,
in the unity of the Holy Spirit,
one God, now and for ever.

12 | *Reflection by* **Jane Steen**

Thursday 7 December

Matthew 13.1-23
'Listen!' (v.3b)

A lot of Christian history is in that one word, 'listen'. 'Listen!' says Jesus to the crowds. 'Listen,' wrote St Benedict, beginning his Rule some five hundred years later. 'Listen!' cried the unknown poet of 'The Dream of the Rood', telling the story of Christ in the voice of the cross, in eight century Britain. Listen!

Listening is much more than hearing. Listening is the way of the heart. Jesus' hearers cannot listen because their 'heart has grown dull'. Benedict's readers must 'incline the ear of [their] heart'. The 'Dream' poet contemplated the cross for a long time before his spirit heard its speech.

Listening is an art. It must be learned, not least by we who live in a noisy world. We are constantly hearing, but never listening. The piped music, the white noise of traffic, the bleeps and pings of phones: this plethora of sound stops our ears. But if we cannot listen, we perish.

The parable should shock us into listening and recognition. Do we fall away when the faith is hard? Are we choked by care and wealth? Questions of divine intent are irrelevant. Sentimentality about the seed falling on the path through no fault of its own, is misplaced. Advent hymnody rings out:

> Hark, a herald voice is calling;
> Christ is nigh, it seems to say.

We set time aside to ask, what diminishes our listening and dulls our hearts?

Almighty God,
as your kingdom dawns,
turn us from the darkness of sin to the
light of holiness,
that we may be ready to meet you
in our Lord and Saviour, Jesus Christ.

COLLECT

Friday 8 December

Matthew 13.24-43

'But he replied, "No"' (v.29)

In Charlie Mackesy's book, *The Boy, the Mole, the Fox and the Horse*, the Boy asks the Horse, 'What's the bravest thing you've ever said?'. The Horse replies, 'Help'. If anyone asked us, 'What's the hardest thing you've ever said?', the answer might be 'No'.

Jesus is adept at 'No'. He might not use the word, but he communicates its meaning. Sometimes, he cites Scripture. Or he might ask a question to which only one answer is possible. 'Who made me judge over you?' (Luke 12.14); clearly, no one.

The sower of good seed in today's parable was wise in saying, 'No'. Refusing to pursue the enemy or uproot the adversary's work saved valuable wheat for threshing. There are times for 'yes' (we remember Mary's response to Gabriel as Christmas approaches) but perhaps there are more times for 'no' than we realise.

'No' is a powerful word. It can stop us in our tracks, especially if we say it to ourselves. It allows us to refuse to engage, not to react in an expected way. It gives us back our freedom.

'No' is a good word to use in prayer. Held at the back of the mind, it comes into its own when we have ceased to pray and begun to think. 'No' acts as a mental circuit-breaker and allows us to return to the Lord.

COLLECT

Almighty God,
give us grace to cast away the works of darkness
and to put on the armour of light,
now in the time of this mortal life,
in which your Son Jesus Christ came to us in great humility;
that on the last day,
when he shall come again in his glorious majesty
    to judge the living and the dead,
we may rise to the life immortal;
through him who is alive and reigns with you,
in the unity of the Holy Spirit,
one God, now and for ever.

14   *Reflection by* **Jane Steen**

Saturday 9 December

Matthew 13.44-end

'The kingdom of heaven...' (vv.44, 45, 47)

Today's reading reminds us of the Four Last Things traditionally associated with this Advent season: death, judgment, heaven and hell. Slightly out of order, we begin with heaven.

The heavens open at Jesus' baptism (Matthew 3). The temple curtain rips at his death, revealing the Holy of Holies (Matthew 27). Barriers between God and humanity fall away. Earth can access heaven. But these apocalyptic moments differ from today's vignettes of the kingdom of heaven, in which the kingdom is not so much a place as an action or effect.

The kingdom of heaven is unpredictable. It might come as happened-upon treasure or after a lifetime's searching. Contact with the kingdom is utterly transformative. The finder of treasure and merchant of pearls relinquish everything for its sake. And it is indiscriminate – a net gathering up 'every kind' (v.47), with the righteous and the evil separated only at 'the end of the age'.

This kingdom of heaven seems very different from a ripped curtain and open heavens, but the connection lies in the Beatitudes. Jesus speaks there of the characteristics of kingdom living, such as humility, hunger for righteousness, mercy, and purity of heart. These enable us to live in heaven's kingdom now and to behold our God hereafter (Matthew 5.8). Until then, we set our hearts on the values of kingdom, always searching, always open to surprise, always renouncing whatever distracts us from God.

Almighty God,
as your kingdom dawns,
turn us from the darkness of sin to the
light of holiness,
that we may be ready to meet you
in our Lord and Saviour, Jesus Christ.

COLLECT

Monday 11 December

Psalm **44** *or* 27, **30**
Isaiah 30.1-18
Matthew 14.1-12

Matthew 14.1-12

'... he feared the crowd' (v.5)

In this second week of Advent, Herod's story illuminates another Last Thing: judgment.

Church wall paintings depicting judgment were once common. From the eleventh-century master working in Houghton-on-the-Hill in Norfolk to Michelangelo adorning the Sistine Chapel, artists have conjured vivid images of the Last Judgment. Humanity's sins come home to roost and fear overtakes us as punishment is meted out, in pictures designed to call us to repentance. But perhaps it is not like that. Perhaps fear is the problem, rather than judgment.

Herod put John in prison because he feared the crowd too much to execute him. But Herod's fear is deeper. He fears because he knew he had done wrong to take his brother's wife. And so, Herod acts unjustly, first in imprisoning John and then in putting him to death. God, we might say, does not need to judge Herod; he judges himself.

Fear always impacts judgment. We are afraid, we make a poor decision, we fear the results, our next decision is worse, and soon, there is a vicious circle which we cannot escape.

God's judgment is different. God knows what we have done amiss, but God has no fear to provoke punishment; of what, after all, could God be afraid? We pray, in the words of a Pentecost prayer, for 'a right judgment in all things' because we ask nothing less than to be like God, motivated not by fear but by love.

COLLECT

O Lord, raise up, we pray, your power
and come among us,
and with great might succour us;
that whereas, through our sins and wickedness
we are grievously hindered
in running the race that is set before us,
your bountiful grace and mercy
may speedily help and deliver us;
through Jesus Christ your Son our Lord,
to whom with you and the Holy Spirit,
be honour and glory, now and for ever.

| *Reflection by* **Jane Steen**

Psalms **56**, 57 *or* 32, **36**
Isaiah 30.19-end
Matthew 14.13-end

Tuesday 12 December

Matthew 14.13-end

'We have nothing...' (v.17)

Sometimes, 'we have nothing' is true. People lack shelter. The land drowns. There is hunger and death. Such tragedies belie the disciples' words. 'We have nothing', they say, when the One through whom all things were made stands before them.

Their 'we have nothing' is powerful. It limits the disciples but liberates Jesus. 'We have nothing, we can do nothing, let them buy their own food' is juxtaposed with taking, blessing, breaking, giving. They feel they have nothing; he knows himself to possess everything.

This feeding foreshadows the Last Supper and the Church's Eucharist. But it also reverses and fulfils the Tempter's challenge: 'command these stones to become bread'. We notice the differences. Here is no command, only compassion. Here is no reliance on self but only on God, blessed for the loaves. Here not one, but many, may eat.

The limiting or liberating possibilities of 'we have nothing' shed light on another Advent Last Thing: hell. In a well-known story, the eternal banquet is laid only with metre-long chopsticks. In hell, where all try to feed themselves, all have nothing. In heaven, all feed each other and are satisfied. Belief that 'we have nothing' can limit or liberate.

Today, we make any perceived lack liberating and not limiting, increasing our reliance on God, and praying for all who truly have nothing.

Almighty God,
purify our hearts and minds,
that when your Son Jesus Christ comes again as
judge and saviour
we may be ready to receive him,
who is our Lord and our God.

COLLECT

Reflection by **Jane Steen** | 17

Wednesday 13 December

Psalms **62,** 63 *or* **34**
Isaiah 31
Matthew 15.1-20

Matthew 15.1-20

'... for the sake of your tradition' (v.3)

Traditions – familiar practices handed down over time – shape our sense of how things should be, holding us in customary patterns. Today's reading cautions against traditions that have become ends in themselves. 'Why do your disciples break the tradition of the elders?' the Pharisees demand of Jesus. His reply reminds both them and us that tradition can replace the very faith it should foster.

Advent is replete with traditions, carols and wreaths among them, punctuation marks in our busy lives, signs of significance. 'The bells of waiting Advent ring' wrote John Betjeman and in this season, it is the waiting which matters. But we have become a hasty people, with short attention spans, and we too often waste the waiting. Christmas is coming, and these precious weeks of spiritual preparation are lost in a rush of readying and wrapping.

We are not the first people to find the outer practice of religion distracting from its true purpose. Perhaps that is why the Psalmist writes so lyrically of the importance of waiting on God, and not rushing into action: 'On God alone my soul in stillness waits; from him comes my salvation' (Psalm 62.1). We remember that so often, God speaks to our hearts when we cease from busy-ness and attend to him, and we set aside thoughts of the future to focus on the present. As the poet R.S. Thomas puts it in his poem 'Kneeling', 'The meaning is in the waiting'.

| COLLECT | O Lord, raise up, we pray, your power and come among us, and with great might succour us; that whereas, through our sins and wickedness we are grievously hindered in running the race that is set before us, your bountiful grace and mercy may speedily help and deliver us; through Jesus Christ your Son our Lord, to whom with you and the Holy Spirit, be honour and glory, now and for ever. |

Reflection by **Jane Steen**

Psalms 53, **54**, 60 *or* 37*
Isaiah 32
Matthew 15.21-28

Thursday 14 December

Matthew 15.21-28

'Even the dogs eat the crumbs that fall from their masters' table'
(v.27)

Is this encounter with the Canaanite woman a turning point for Jesus? He came for his own people ('the lost sheep of the house of Israel'), yet the Gentile woman's demon-possessed daughter receives healing.

Jesus' priority is unsurprising. The Bible is clear about the primacy of God's chosen people in salvation. Gentiles will come to the God of Israel, but through the people of Israel (Zechariah 8.23). More surprising to us is the woman's acceptance of the derogatory term 'dog'. We might wonder how this affected her, just as we might consider how negative portrayal impacts our own lives. This woman showed both humility and courage. She accepted Jesus' language in humility, more focused on her daughter than on herself. Out of her love, she pressed on courageously.

We can be curious about Jesus' reaction to her. As Zechariah foretold, a Gentile found God's mercy through a Jew. But perhaps this Gentile also showed this Jew his role before God: sparking the fulfilment of Zechariah's prophecy in him, focusing his ministry and self-understanding. We cannot know if she did. But we can remember the Jewishness of the Jesus for whom we prepare during Advent and, as we do so, repent the unspeakable horrors inflicted on Jesus' people in his name and seek restored and regenerative relationships with all people.

Almighty God,
purify our hearts and minds,
that when your Son Jesus Christ comes again as
judge and saviour
we may be ready to receive him,
who is our Lord and our God.

COLLECT

Friday 15 December

Psalms 85, **86** *or* **31**
Isaiah 33.1-22
Matthew 15.29-end

Matthew 15.29-end

'... he sat down' (v.29)

Matthew often tells us that Jesus sat down: on a mountain, by a lake, in a boat. St Augustine detected a graceful pause before Jesus spoke in chapter five (5.1). We notice the same pause here. Jesus sits. Then people come and he cures them.

To sit down should be to remain. We hurry even seated in our cars. 'I sat on a bench, waiting for something. / An angel perhaps' wrote Mary Oliver. She saw none, 'because / I didn't stay long enough'. But when the Son of God came among us, he sat, stayed, remained. That is the mystery of the Incarnation for which Advent readies us: God with us, God remaining, God sitting down.

We are told that too much sitting is bad for us. We should get up, walk around a bit more – like Jesus. He seems always at it, criss-crossing the land, teaching, feeding, healing. But remember too his sleeping in the storm-tossed boat (Matthew 8.24). Being God, he was at rest in God. So in today's reading, he acts powerfully while seated, his pose directing us to his, and our, right repose.

Two weeks of Advent are yet left to us. 'You have made us for yourself, O Lord, and our hearts are restless until they rest in you' wrote Augustine. We renounce our restlessness, resolving to remain with the Lord.

COLLECT

O Lord, raise up, we pray, your power
and come among us,
and with great might succour us;
that whereas, through our sins and wickedness
we are grievously hindered
in running the race that is set before us,
your bountiful grace and mercy
may speedily help and deliver us;
through Jesus Christ your Son our Lord,
to whom with you and the Holy Spirit,
be honour and glory, now and for ever.

Reflection by **Jane Steen**

Psalm **145** *or* 41, **42**, 43   **Saturday 16 December**
Isaiah 35
Matthew 16.1-12

Matthew 16.1-12

'... the signs of the times' (v.3b)

We, who have two thousand years of Christianity behind us, easily interpret Jesus' words about the sign of Jonah. Three days in the belly of the whale and release to life parallel Jesus' three days in the tomb and his resurrection. It's easy for us, but it must have been very obscure at the time.

Signs are all around us, but we miss their significance. Jesus berates not only the Pharisees and the Sadducees but also his own disciples when, like us, they take what is literal and miss the metaphor. Today's reading reminds us that the world is not an instruction manual, with all its meaning on the surface. It is a rich revelation of the glory of God, if only we will look.

We are familiar with this depth in the sacraments of our faith. An outer substance (like bread) leads us to an inner and sacred reality (Christ's body). Pauline Stainer's 'Carol' shimmers with this mystery of inseparable sign and significance:

> O white under white
> of the Christchild laid
> like a tear, like a tear
> in a stem of glass
> *sancta*
> *sancta simplicitas.*

Around us, Christmas decorations increasingly abound. If their outer brightness causes us to consider the state of our heart before God, returning to him in repentance and love, our Advent will go well, and our Christmas joy be deepened.

Almighty God,
purify our hearts and minds,
that when your Son Jesus Christ comes again as
judge and saviour
we may be ready to receive him,
who is our Lord and our God.

COLLECT

Reflection by **Jane Steen**   21

Monday 18 December

Psalm **40** *or* **44**
Isaiah 38. 1-8, 21-22
Matthew 16.13-end

Matthew 16.13-end

'But who do you say that I am?' (v.15)

At the heart of this conversation are questions of identity. Who is Jesus? Simon's God-inspired answer to this question shines a light on his own identity too; in claiming Jesus as Messiah, he gains a new name, Peter, 'the rock'. But it soon becomes clear that he has not understood Jesus' identity at all. In denying Jesus' future suffering he earns himself a new, troubling title, Satan, the tempter.

This is not the first time that Jesus has been tempted by the thought of a life and ministry without suffering. His time in the wilderness (Matthew 4.1-11) involved just such temptations, with Satan promising, among other things, that 'you will not dash your foot against a stone'. No wonder Peter's reaction provokes, in return, such a harsh rebuke.

Jesus understands that his suffering is both an inevitable aspect of his incarnation and necessary for his work of salvation. His encounters with 'Satan' are, in a sense, rehearsals for what is to come, and so are crucial moments in his psychological journey to the cross.

It is in the light of who Jesus is that Peter comes to grasp his own identity, but it is who Peter is, complete with his awkwardly blurted-out misunderstandings, that helps Jesus articulate his own identity and show what this means to those who take up their cross and follow him. Asking 'Who is Jesus?' will always invite us to reflect, 'Then who am I?'

COLLECT

O Lord Jesus Christ,
who at your first coming sent your messenger
to prepare your way before you:
grant that the ministers and stewards of your mysteries
may likewise so prepare and make ready your way
by turning the hearts of the disobedient to the wisdom of the just,
that at your second coming to judge the world
we may be found an acceptable people in your sight;
for you are alive and reign with the Father
in the unity of the Holy Spirit,
one God, now and for ever.

| *Reflection by **Ally Barrett***

Psalms **70**, 74 *or* **48**, 52
Isaiah 38. 9-20
Matthew 17.1-13

Tuesday 19 December

Matthew 17.1-13

'It is good for us to be here' (v.4)

Peter, in his compulsion to speak when others might keep silent, so often draws our attention to the surprising quality of God's presence in the world. The transfiguration story offers several revelations of who God is in Christ. In the shining cloud and the appearance of Moses and Elijah, the disciples catch a glimpse of the Jesus' eternal nature, and his glory. Through the voice from heaven, they learn that at the heart of the Godhead is perfect love. And in the midst of their terror, Jesus' 'do not be afraid' puts that love into action, reminding the disciples to focus on the work that is before them once they return to the plain, continuing to participate in God's loving purposes.

Jesus' command not to speak about these revelations allows the disciples to reflect on what has happened and to understand the whole multifaceted picture; it will take time to reconcile the vision of Jesus' heavenly nature with the wandering Rabbi they already know: this process begins on the walk down the mountain.

Peter is right, though: it is good for us to be here. In this season of the year there might be more moments than usual in which we ascend the mountain and glimpse the glory, becoming overwhelmed with the love. We will need to reconcile these with those times when we are surrounded by human need and must find Christ at ground level by continuing his work.

God for whom we watch and wait,
you sent John the Baptist to prepare the way of your Son:
give us courage to speak the truth,
to hunger for justice,
and to suffer for the cause of right,
with Jesus Christ our Lord.

COLLECT

Wednesday 20 December

Matthew 17.14-21

'How much longer must I be with you?' (v.17)

Remaining faithful through times of suffering and trauma is not easy. The young boy who Jesus heals has been tormented not only by the illness itself, but by the danger it puts him in—the fire and the water—and his father is desperate for a cure that Jesus' disciples could not provide.

Jesus's criticism of their lack of faith in the face of this young boy's suffering seems harsh, but even as he rails against his friends, he still reassures them of something crucial: he is *with them*: 'How much longer must I be with you?' he asks, perhaps more in exasperation than in anger.

In Isaiah 43.2 we find comfort in the idea of a God who walks with his children through fire and water, flames and flood, promising 'I will be with you'. In the incarnation, this vision becomes flesh and blood: Jesus is *Emmanuel*, God with us, dwelling with us, pitching his tent among our own (John 1.14). And today's passage is emblematic of what Jesus came to do: entering into humanity's suffering, while also bringing relief and healing; wondering at our lack of faith, while offering us glimpse after glimpse of the immeasurable love and power of God; teaching us by word and action that hope is real and tangible. This is what it means for him to 'be with' us.

COLLECT | O Lord Jesus Christ,
who at your first coming sent your messenger
to prepare your way before you:
grant that the ministers and stewards of your mysteries
may likewise so prepare and make ready your way
by turning the hearts of the disobedient to the wisdom of the just,
that at your second coming to judge the world
we may be found an acceptable people in your sight;
for you are alive and reign with the Father
in the unity of the Holy Spirit,
one God, now and for ever.

| *Reflection by* **Ally Barrett**

Psalms **76**, 97 *or* 56, **57** (63*)
Zephaniah 1.1 – 2.3
Matthew 17.22-end

Thursday 21 December

Matthew 17.22-end

'Then the children are free' (v.26)

While still a child (Luke 2.49), Jesus referred to the Temple as 'my Father's house' and later encouraged his disciples to call God 'Father' when he taught them to pray (Luke 11.2; Matthew 6.9). Jesus is clear that just as he can call God 'Father' so can his disciples and followers. Paying the temple tax, then, is a choice, not an obligation, for as children of God they are indeed wholly free.

Jesus' bizarre instructions to Peter must have left the latter more baffled than usual, but at least they offer him a way out that demonstrates not only Jesus' power, but also his sense of humour. First, by performing the miracle of the coin in the fish's mouth, he shows his mastery over the natural world and, by extension, over everything else as well; should he refuse to pay there is nothing that anyone could do about it. Second, Jesus shows his friends that his conflicts with the religious authorities are calculated, part of a bigger plan; he is not above picking his battles. And third, the miracle ensures that the temple tax is paid by none other than God himself.

But Jesus' choice to resolve this dilemma with a miracle to avoid a conflict, while continuing to remind Peter that he will suffer and die by human hands and refuse to save himself, must have been the hardest part of this message for Peter to grasp.

God for whom we watch and wait,
you sent John the Baptist to prepare the way of your Son:
give us courage to speak the truth,
to hunger for justice,
and to suffer for the cause of right,
with Jesus Christ our Lord.

COLLECT

Friday 22 December

Psalms 77, **98** *or* **51**, 54
Zephaniah 3.1-13
Matthew 18.1-20

Matthew 18.1-20

'Let such a one be to you as a Gentile and a tax-collector' (v.17)

The parable of the lost sheep can be read as a simple story of inclusion, welcoming the lost home, returning those who have gone astray to the safety of the fold. The advice about resolving differences in the Church, though it begins with approaches to reconciliation, could be read as advice about how to exclude, when exclusion is needed – 'let such a one be to you as a Gentile and a tax collector' – were it not for the fact that Jesus included tax collectors among his friends and disciples and spent considerable time not only with Gentiles, but also foreigners, women, lepers, and any number of other 'outsiders'.

So what is happening here? Jesus is not advocating an 'anything goes' approach to communal identity, but rather is redefining what constitute the boundaries, or rather, the centre. The flock's identity is based not on the fence around the pasture, but on the shepherd who calls his sheep, and their willingness to hear his voice and follow him home. The offer of membership in the community that genuinely has Jesus as its defining character (v. 20) must remain open to any who embrace what that identity means. Verses 18-19 therefore become an outworking of the Christly character that is at the heart of the Church, rather than a statement of human authority. What kind of communities, then, do we create in Jesus' name? And who would he have us welcome?

COLLECT

O Lord Jesus Christ,
who at your first coming sent your messenger
to prepare your way before you:
grant that the ministers and stewards of your mysteries
may likewise so prepare and make ready your way
by turning the hearts of the disobedient to the wisdom of the just,
that at your second coming to judge the world
we may be found an acceptable people in your sight;
for you are alive and reign with the Father
in the unity of the Holy Spirit,
one God, now and for ever.

| *Reflection by* **Ally Barrett**

Psalm **71** *or* **68**
Zephaniah 3.14-end
Matthew 18.21-end

Saturday 23 December

Matthew 18.21-end

'Not seven times, but, I tell you, seventy-seven times' (v.22)

What we do not only reflects who we already are, but also helps shape who we are becoming. Once we have practised forgiveness seventy-seven times there is a good chance that the habit of showing mercy is ingrained – or at least that we have stopped counting and started realising that grace does not have a limited budget.

This passage, though, is about more than encouraging mercy. It is about acknowledging that our own mercy, our own acts of forgiveness, our own graciousness, all flow from our experience of being shown mercy, being forgiven, receiving grace upon grace. We all, at some time or another, have hurt our neighbours and grieved the heart of God, and all of us have been in need of mercy. In the life, death, and resurrection of Jesus Christ we see how God meets this deep human need.

The economy of mercy commended here is challenging in its truthfulness but hopeful in its abundance. It involves a 'reckoning' in which the extent of our debt is made visible. It involves the realisation that we cannot, in our own power alone, mend what we have broken. It recognises our longing to be reconciled. It demands a solidarity with one another that calls out any injustice that would disrupt this wondrous way of ordering our relationships. And it is, above all, an invitation to participate in the divine economy of grace.

God for whom we watch and wait,
you sent John the Baptist to prepare the way of your Son:
give us courage to speak the truth,
to hunger for justice,
and to suffer for the cause of right,
with Jesus Christ our Lord.

COLLECT

Monday 25 December
Christmas Day

Psalms **110**, 117
Isaiah 62.1-5
Matthew 1.18-end

Matthew 1.1-18

'He did as the angel of the Lord commanded him' (v.24)

This passage describes Joseph as righteous (v.19), but his unwillingness to expose Mary to the 'public disgrace' that would have been dealt to a woman found to have committed adultery (and how else would the pregnancy be explained?) reveals that Joseph is more than righteous. Justice and righteousness explain Joseph's intention to divorce her in accordance with the law; only compassion can explain his determination to protect her not just from disgrace, but potentially from death by stoning.

The remainder of the reading shows us that we can add 'courageous', 'obedient' and 'faithful' to our understanding of Joseph's character. His willingness to be part of the divine plan revealed by the angel, treating Jesus as his own son, saves Mary (and their marriage). But his decision has much more far-reaching consequences: it also ensures that Jesus is legally born into the Davidic line. The promise of the prophets (v.23) now makes sense in the context of the genealogy included at the start of the chapter. The purposes of God have always been worked out in the world through the courage, obedience, compassion and righteousness of very ordinary, yet extraordinary people, whom God calls to participate in the work of salvation. This, too, is how 'God is with us'. In both Mary and Joseph we learn what it looks like to say 'yes' to God's will in a way that was – and still is – world-changing.

COLLECT

Almighty God,
you have given us your only-begotten Son
to take our nature upon him
and as at this time to be born of a pure virgin:
grant that we, who have been born again
and made your children by adoption and grace,
may daily be renewed by your Holy Spirit;
through Jesus Christ your Son our Lord,
who is alive and reigns with you,
in the unity of the Holy Spirit,
one God, now and for ever.

| *Reflection by* **Ally Barrett**

Tuesday 26 December
Stephen, deacon, first martyr

Acts 6

'Full of grace and power' (v.8)

The need for deacons emerges from a conflict between Greek and Jewish Christians, and a particular concern that as the Church grows, it remains sustainable as a community in which nobody – especially the most vulnerable – should have their needs neglected. Caring for widows was deeply ingrained in Jewish culture, so resourcing the extension of this care to the Hellenists was a powerful symbolic statement about communal identity. The deacon's work is therefore not just 'waiting at tables' but is presented as pastoral, practical, compassionate, fostering justice, building unity, and offering care. It expresses something utterly foundational about how the Christian community saw itself. No wonder the Twelve felt that they must look for wise, spiritually gifted and respected individuals to fulfil this new role in the Church – the role of the deacon would be demanding and complex, requiring sensitivity and boldness, and essential to the Church's ongoing growth and flourishing.

The deacons were appointed in order to free up the preachers and teachers for their work of spreading the word of God, and the Church clearly grew as a result. But it is from Stephen's work of loving service, in which the vulnerable are given back their worth and dignity, that his astonishing witness to the gospel in word and deed would spring. Stephen embodies how evangelism, pastoral care, and fostering community can be woven together in a life of Christian witness.

COLLECT

Gracious Father,
who gave the first martyr Stephen
grace to pray for those who took up stones against him:
grant that in all our sufferings for the truth
we may learn to love even our enemies
and to seek forgiveness for those who desire our hurt,
looking up to heaven to him who was crucified for us,
Jesus Christ, our mediator and advocate,
who is alive and reigns with you,
in the unity of the Holy Spirit,
one God, now and for ever.

Reflection by **Ally Barrett**

Wednesday 27 December

John, Apostle and Evangelist

Psalms **21**, 147.13-end
Exodus 33.12-end
1 John 2.1-11

1 John 2.1-11

*'Beloved, I am writing you no new commandment,
but an old commandment' (v.7)*

The 'new commandment' must surely be the one Jesus gave to his disciples the night before he died, that they should love one another as he loved them (John 13.34). Here that same command is explicitly extended to everyone who claims belief in Jesus, and therefore the 'one another' is now similarly expanded, treating as family the whole community of the faithful (vv. 9-10). As the command to love increases, so do our opportunities to fail, through sin, though we are assured that the grace of God in Christ is still more than enough for our restoration and reconciliation (v.2). This vast scope of God's grace reflects John 3.16, with its confidence in God's love for the *entire world* (the Greek word in both passages is 'cosmos').

'Abiding', then, is more than looking to Jesus as a moral example, it means becoming the branches that receive their nourishment from the vine (John 15.5), becoming so full of God's love that there is no room for hatred towards others. This is a vision of the kind of relationship with God that Christ makes possible in the miracle of the incarnation: through Jesus we can experience such a profound union with God that love overflows into all our words and deeds – we become the instruments of God's outpouring of love in the world. This is indeed a very old commandment, for its roots lie in God's loving act of creation itself.

COLLECT

Merciful Lord,
cast your bright beams of light upon the Church:
that, being enlightened by the teaching
of your blessed apostle and evangelist Saint John,
we may so walk in the light of your truth
that we may at last attain to the light of everlasting life;
through Jesus Christ your incarnate Son our Lord,
who is alive and reigns with you,
in the unity of the Holy Spirit,
one God, now and for ever.

| *Reflection by* **Ally Barrett**

Psalms **36**, 146
Baruch 4.21-27
or Genesis 37.13-20
Matthew 18.1-10

Tuesday 28 December
The Holy Innocents

Matthew 18.1-10

'Whoever becomes humble like this child is the greatest in the kingdom of heaven' (v.4)

Later in his Gospel, Matthew reminds us to see Christ in those in need (25.40, 45). Here, we are to look at the children in our midst as if they were Christ himself, and we are warned that there are dire consequences for us when we fail in this. Of course, it was the idea that a child in his realm was a king, a potential rival, is what terrified Herod, leading to his massacre of the innocents.

The context of this passage is the discussion among the disciples about greatness and status and it suggests that it is the child's humility that is key, which places these verses alongside others where Jesus speaks of the last being first, such as Matthew 20.16 and Mark 10.31. The reversal of first and last reads like a threat if we are the 'first' who are benefitting from systems that leave the 'last' at risk of harm. The heart of Jesus' teaching here is how we understand and exercise our power. Do we use it in a way that may hurt those less powerful, or do we seek ways to uphold and protect the vulnerable?

Above all, we are exhorted to embrace humility. Herod could not grasp that greatness in the kingdom has nothing to do with earthly status and everything to do with the reality that being fully known by and beloved of God (v. 10), like the child, is more than enough.

COLLECT

Heavenly Father,
whose children suffered at the hands of Herod,
though they had done no wrong:
by the suffering of your Son
and by the innocence of our lives
frustrate all evil designs
and establish your reign of justice and peace;
through Jesus Christ your Son our Lord,
who is alive and reigns with you,
in the unity of the Holy Spirit,
one God, now and for ever.

Reflection by **Ally Barrett**   31

Friday 29 December

Colossians 1.1-14

'... as you bear fruit in every good work and as you grow in the knowledge of God' (v.10)

This beautiful opening to the letter to the Colossians weaves together a cornucopia of themes relating to discipleship, and presents them all as interconnected, inseparable from one another. There can be no tension here between faith and works, or between faith and understanding, for in the life of discipleship everything is inextricably intertwined; everything is an expression of the believers' rootedness in God though Jesus Christ.

Three times the writer uses the image of bearing fruit, with echoes both of the command to fruitfulness (Genesis 1.28), and the vine and the branches (John 15.5). Here, fruitfulness relates particularly to growth in understanding, wisdom and knowledge of God (v. 10) and comprehension of the grace of God (v. 6). This connection has been developed through the centuries of Christian thought, including most famously by St Anselm (1033-1109), who coined the phrase 'faith seeking understanding' and whose writing weaves together philosophy, theology, prayer, and praise. Neither Anselm nor the letter to the Colossians intended to imply that faith needs to be replaced by something more intellectual. Rather, the point is that faith and wisdom, understanding and good works, are all bound together in the life of the Christian disciple. The gospel hope generates love (vv.4, 8) but living out this love, especially in times of challenge (v.11), requires an ongoing process of discernment, that our actions may truly reflect God's will (v.10).

COLLECT

Almighty God,
you have given us your only-begotten Son
to take our nature upon him
and as at this time to be born of a pure virgin:
grant that we, who have been born again
and made your children by adoption and grace,
may daily be renewed by your Holy Spirit;
through Jesus Christ your Son our Lord,
who is alive and reigns with you,
in the unity of the Holy Spirit,
one God, now and for ever.

| *Reflection by* **Ally Barrett**

Saturday 30 December

Colossians 1.15-23

'Through him God was pleased to reconcile to himself all things'
(v.20)

Whoever wrote this letter, whether Paul or someone else, sent the church in Colossae one of the most astonishing and beautiful theological poems in the Christian tradition. The way that Jesus is presented here is a key reason for questioning the epistle's authorship: the author's understanding of who Jesus is would feel more at home in the Gospel according to St John. We recognise here the pre-existent Son of God, the one through whom all things were made (John 1.3), and through whom we can come to know God fully (John 14.9). And, like John's prologue, this description of Christ is no dry theological statement, but an outpouring of praise. The Colossians are offered these remarkable words expressing awe and wonder both at who Jesus is, and at what he accomplished through his life, ministry, death and resurrection.

The point here is that God's nature is understood not only in who God is, eternally, but also in what God does, in relationship with creation and with us. The overarching theme is reconciliation, which the writer treats on both a cosmic and on a very personal level. The awe and wonder reflect the astonishing reality and depth of God's love for us, and the hope this offers. We need not be estranged from God: the transcendent, eternal creator of all things has come to us, and opened his arms to draw us into his divine embrace.

God our Father,
whose Word has come among us
in the Holy Child of Bethlehem:
may the light of faith illumine our hearts
and shine in our words and deeds;
through him who is Christ the Lord.

COLLECT

Reflection by **Ally Barrett**   33

Monday I January

Naming and Circumcision of Jesus

Psalms **103**, 150
Genesis 17.1-13
Romans 2.17-end

Romans 2.17-end

'You that teach others, will you not teach yourself? (v.21)

There is no hypocrisy like religious hypocrisy. Paul berated those who demanded obedience to high moral principles but did not live up to the standards they expected of others. In particular, he turned his attention to Jews who had been circumcised (the outward sign of their religion) but were not obedient to the Law (the inward sign of their religion). The difference between people's professed faith and their actions was being observed and mocked by outsiders. It shamed God. It still does, wherever it is found.

There is no pride like religious pride. Paul's words must have shocked his Jewish readers. Pride in the Law that God had given them had held them together through centuries of hardship. They had come to believe that merely fulfilling the rituals of their religion was sufficient to confirm their status as God's uniquely privileged people. But that was not true of all. Some recognised their need for forgiveness and found it in the good news of Jesus.

There is no freedom like religious freedom. Belonging to God was no longer the exclusive entitlement of any one nation. Because of the death and resurrection of Jesus a transformation had taken place which offered grace worldwide. A butterfly had taken wing. And any rituals that were for show rather than for love of God had been left behind like the discarded chrysalis.

COLLECT

Almighty God,
who wonderfully created us in your own image
and yet more wonderfully restored us
through your Son Jesus Christ:
grant that, as he came to share in our humanity,
so we may share the life of his divinity;
who is alive and reigns with you,
in the unity of the Holy Spirit,
one God, now and for ever.

34 | *Reflection by* **Peter Graystone**

Psalms **18.1-30**
Ruth I
Colossians 2.8-end

Tuesday 2 January

Colossians 2.8-end

'Why do you live as if you still belonged to the world?' (v.20)

Nothing less than Jesus is what you need. The phrases 'in him' and 'with him' pound through this passage like the relentless pulse of a drum and bass track. They express the totality of our identification with Christ. Having discovered the best possible way to experience life, we have fullness of life 'in him'. In a spiritual sense that suggests utter commitment, we are circumcised 'in him'. With our past put behind us we are buried 'in him'. Living a new life we are raised 'in him'. How have these things helped us find the relationship with God that the human soul is hardwired to seek? Because 'in him the whole fullness of deity dwells bodily'.

Nothing more than Jesus is what you need. Through the life, death and resurrection of Christ, God has done all that is required to be freely and joyfully at one with him. The moment a human being suggests that we need to do something additional, the boundlessness of the grace of God is thrown into question and our life will be diminished. Legalism can add nothing. That's why Paul dismissed new moon festivals and food restrictions. Mysticism can add nothing. That's why Paul dismissed obsession with angels and trances. Asceticism can add nothing. That's why Paul dismissed the notion that the body is an evil thing that needs to be pitilessly denied anything that would give it pleasure.

Heavenly Father,
whose blessed Son shared at Nazareth
the life of an earthly home:
help your Church to live as one family,
united in love and obedience,
and bring us all at last to our home in heaven;
through Jesus Christ our Lord.

COLLECT

Wednesday 3 January

Psalms **127**, 128, 131
Ruth 2
Colossians 3.1-11

Colossians 3.1-11

'Set your minds on things that are above' (v.2)

Here is a fact. Because Jesus died, God regards the former version of me as having died, and now sees me as one with Jesus. Here is another fact. Because Jesus rose from the dead, he guarantees life for me beyond this existence. A third fact. When Jesus returns in glory, everyone will see that I share his glorious life.

And here is the logical consequence of these three facts. It is utterly inappropriate for me to think or behave as though none of these things is true.

The long list of wrong ways to think or behave is so depressing because it is so mundane. If it were gangsters and drug dealers whose sins were listed here, I could keep this passage at arm's length. But this is recognisable, ugly behaviour that I usually persuade myself I can get away with it because it won't land me in jail. That might have seemed acceptable once, writes Paul, but it is totally out of place for someone who is now at one with Jesus.

Those who first heard Paul's letter read to them in Colossae would have understood his reference to getting dressed and undressed. Part of the ceremony that surrounded the baptism of a new believer was laying aside old clothes and putting on new clothes. The outward change of appearance was evident to all. An inward change of demeanour needed to be equally evident.

COLLECT

Almighty God,
who wonderfully created us in your own image
and yet more wonderfully restored us
through your Son Jesus Christ:
grant that, as he came to share in our humanity,
so we may share the life of his divinity;
who is alive and reigns with you,
in the unity of the Holy Spirit,
one God, now and for ever.

| *Reflection by* **Peter Graystone**

Psalms **89.1-37**
Ruth 3
Colossians 3.12 – 4.1

Thursday 4 January

Colossians 3.12 – 4.1

'Do everything in the name of the Lord Jesus' (3.17)

The life, death and resurrection of Jesus have broken down every barrier that divides human from human. But it's unrealistic to think that there will never be occasions when Christians are at odds with one another. Paul offers four ways of dealing with those difficulties.

Let the forgiveness of Christ be passed on. So do not prolong grudges. Let the peace of Christ rule (the word used in verse 15 means to be the referee). So pursue harmony. Let the word of Christ decide. So scrutinise his teaching. Let the name of Christ be honoured. So come before him in shared thanksgiving.

Although Paul's instructions about relationships appear antiquated at first sight, they seem different if we put ourselves in the shoes of those who first heard them. A wife had no privileges and could be divorced and made destitute at whim. Imagine how she feels when she discovers that her Christian husband now has duties toward her. A child had no rights and could be subjected to abuse in the name of parental discipline. Imagine how she reacts when she discovers that her Christian father now has responsibilities toward her. A slave was expendable property and didn't even own the clothes he wore. Imagine how he responds when he discovers that his Christian master now has obligations toward him. What might Paul say to the women, children and slaves of our generation to have the same liberating impact?

Heavenly Father,
whose blessed Son shared at Nazareth
the life of an earthly home:
help your Church to live as one family,
united in love and obedience,
and bring us all at last to our home in heaven;
through Jesus Christ our Lord.

COLLECT

Friday 5 January

Colossians 4.2-end

'Complete the task' (v.5)

Of all the people from whom the Christians of Colossae wanted to hear news, surely the one for whom they had the greatest heart was Epaphras. They had never met Paul. It was Epaphras, a citizen of Colossae, who had originally told them the good news of Jesus Christ, and he went on to become a companion of Paul. It must have encouraged them deeply to know that Epaphras was 'wrestling in his prayers' for them.

What does it mean to wrestle in prayer? Paul explains at the beginning of the chapter. It's persistent, requiring devotion. It's alert. It's thankful (the sixth time Paul has mentioned this in his short letter). And it's specific (there is nothing vague about Paul's requests for the church's prayers). It's hard work. There are no short cuts in prayer. Those who love deeply pray deeply.

'Complete the task,' Archippus was told. Time was not on the Colossians' side. Within a year of Paul's letter arriving, an earthquake struck the town. According to the historian Tacitus it was entirely destroyed in AD61 and never rebuilt. I wonder what Archippus' task was, and whether he completed it. Centuries later a new town was built on top of the ruin. It is called Honaz, and it's famous for wrestling. How ironic! As a new year gets underway, what is the task which God is calling you to complete? Treat it as urgent.

COLLECT

Almighty God,
who wonderfully created us in your own image
and yet more wonderfully restored us
through your Son Jesus Christ:
grant that, as he came to share in our humanity,
so we may share the life of his divinity;
who is alive and reigns with you,
in the unity of the Holy Spirit,
one God, now and for ever.

| *Reflection by* **Peter Graystone**

Psalms **132**, 113
Jeremiah 31.7-14
John 1.29-34

Saturday 6 January
Epiphany

John 1.29-34
'This is the Son of God' (v.34)

A lamb and a dove. How strange that the immense power of God to save should be represented by images of such gentleness.

The lamb had a rich role in the Old Testament. The lamb killed at the first Passover had saved Jewish households and allowed them to escape slavery. The servant described in Isaiah 53.7 was 'like a lamb that is led to the slaughter' and led the nation to escape the consequences of its wrongdoing. But Jesus is described by John the Baptist as incomparably more: 'The Lamb of God who takes away the sin of the world.' He is younger than John, but eternally older, and his work will have consequences throughout eternity.

The dove was the sacrificial offering of a woman if she was too poor to offer a lamb. The bird was the first sign of fragile hope when, olive leaf in beak, it returned to Noah after the flood subsided. But the dove that John witnessed descending on Jesus was a sign of his absolute divinity – the Holy Spirit of God himself indwelling and empowering him. Jesus submitted to being baptised by John, but the baptism he offers is boundlessly greater because it is nothing less than the baptism of the Holy Spirit.

The ironies are great, but the Christian faith is entirely characterised by strength manifested through weakness. John recognised it. The salvation of the world was at hand.

O God,
who by the leading of a star
manifested your only Son to the peoples of the earth:
mercifully grant that we,
who know you now by faith,
may at last behold your glory face to face;
through Jesus Christ your Son our Lord,
who is alive and reigns with you,
in the unity of the Holy Spirit,
one God, now and for ever.

COLLECT

Reflection by **Peter Graystone** | 39

Monday 8 January

Psalms **2**, 110 *or* **71**
Genesis 1.1-19
Matthew 21.1-17

Genesis 1.1-19

'God saw that it was good' (v.4)

In the beginning there was not a multitude of quarrelling gods. There was not an abstract force. There was not a chance set of circumstances. Instead there was a personal God who, for personal reasons which are inscrutable but pregnant with love, chose to utter the cosmos into existence. And that – oh yes – is good!

As well as being a description that is breathtakingly simple and beautiful, the first chapter of the Bible is notable for revealing to us how the world was not created. It confounds beliefs that were prevalent at the time of its composition, and challenges many of today's conjectures about time and space. Our world is not of itself divine (as pantheism might suggest), but a creation by God. It is not godless (defying atheism). Impersonal forces do not dictate events (in other words, astrology is poppycock). Material things, such as your body with all its sensual pleasures, are not intrinsically evil (a view which, in the form of gnosticism, was a live issue in the early Christian years and refuses to go away). And most wonderfully, despite all the misery that nihilism has caused through the centuries, existence is not meaningless.

Once there was God. Then there was God and also the universe. Now there is God, the universe, and also you and me. The wonder of it is staggering. Stay just where you are and stagger for a while.

C O L L E C T

Eternal Father,
who at the baptism of Jesus
revealed him to be your Son,
anointing him with the Holy Spirit:
grant to us, who are born again by water and the Spirit,
that we may be faithful to our calling as your adopted children;
through Jesus Christ your Son our Lord,
who is alive and reigns with you,
in the unity of the Holy Spirit,
one God, now and for ever.

Reflection by **Peter Graystone**

Psalms 8, **9** *or* **73**
Genesis 1.20 – 2.3
Matthew 21.18-32

Tuesday 9 January

Genesis 1.20 – 2.3

'God saw everything that he had made' (1.31)

Look at your Bible – not the words, but the actual book. Black ink on white paper, soft paper against a hard cover, monochrome text beside a coloured wrapper. Pattern and variety are the joyous evidence of God's delight in his creation.

The opening words of the Bible abound in the same structure and diversity. Day is separated from night, light from dark, water from land, sentient beings from inert objects, work from rest. The light of day one is partnered with the sun and stars of day four. The water and air of day two teem with fish and birds on day five. The land and vegetation of day three are vitalised by animals and humans on day six.

Here is the foundation of what scientists now call ecology. Humans, animals, plants and minerals are in delicate balance, a single community within creation. The role that God has given to humans in this is clear. They are to take charge of it. But the words used in verse 28 can be interpreted in a stewardly or exploitative way. We can use our power to tend the planet's resources or to exhaust them for our short-term benefit. In this generation we find ourselves confronting the possibility that human beings may go the way of the dinosaurs. The survival of humankind depends entirely upon the way we choose to occupy the space that God has allocated to us in his magnificent creation.

Heavenly Father,
at the Jordan you revealed Jesus as your Son:
may we recognize him as our Lord
and know ourselves to be your beloved children;
through Jesus Christ our Saviour.

COLLECT

Wednesday 10 January

Psalms 19, **20** *or* **77**
Genesis 2.4-end
Matthew 21.33-end

Genesis 2.4-end
'The breath of life' (v.7)

God bestows extravagant gifts on humans. He gives away things that are his by right. He gives the honour of naming things. He gives the responsibility of cultivation. He gives the privilege of conserving the environment. He gives the delight of human company. (The word helper, used to describe the relationship of a woman to a man, is the same word that is used repeatedly to describe God's relationship with Israel.)

All these things are healing qualities. Humans have the capacity to be part of God's work to heal the earth. It once seemed that sea otters had been hunted to extinction for their pelts until a tiny colony was found in Alaska and helped, cub by cub, into a substantial population. Then on Good Friday 1989 the Exxon Valdez spilled eleven million gallons of oil into Prince William Sound and killed twelve thousand in twenty-four hours. Work resumed to re-establish the otter population, and it has been restored to its former numbers. However, it took twenty-four years.

Time is not on our side if we are to heal our damaged earth. We now have the knowledge of good and evil. We now have the understanding of life. The trees are crying out to us and we must change. We must know this. Our children must know this. Our neighbours must know this. Our leaders must know this. This is the last ditch. This is where we turn and fight.

COLLECT

Eternal Father,
who at the baptism of Jesus
revealed him to be your Son,
anointing him with the Holy Spirit:
grant to us, who are born again by water and the Spirit,
that we may be faithful to our calling as your adopted children;
through Jesus Christ your Son our Lord,
who is alive and reigns with you,
in the unity of the Holy Spirit,
one God, now and for ever.

| *Reflection by* **Peter Graystone**

Psalms **21**, 24 *or* **78.1-39***
Genesis 3
Matthew 22.1-14

Thursday 11 January

Genesis 3

'Knowing good and evil' (v.22)

On the television news evil announces itself unmistakeably with drones and bombs. In fantasy fiction evil is recognisable because it's ugly, scaly and rides a dragon. But in most of our everyday lives, evil is mundane and slips past our defences with indirect suggestions and wheedling questions.

Eve finds herself thinking, 'Surely God's instructions didn't apply to these circumstances.' That sounds like something one might say ten seconds before a porn site opens up. Then Eve is made to doubt whether God is entirely truthful: 'I assure you that you will not die.' That's the talk of someone offering to share their drugs. And Eve wonders whether God's motivation is to be trusted or if God is just preventing her from achieving her potential: 'You could be like God.' That echoes down the centuries in the mind of anyone who prioritises money or power in their worldview. If we don't recognise evil for what it is, the snake is still hissing.

The result for the humans was that their relationship with God broke and they now knew they had something to hide. Their relationship with each other broke as they tried to wriggle out of the blame. Their relationship with the earth broke and they were banished from the place where work, rest and play were an equal and stress-free joy. Even their own self-image broke and they literally didn't like what they saw in themselves.

Heavenly Father,
at the Jordan you revealed Jesus as your Son:
may we recognize him as our Lord
and know ourselves to be your beloved children;
through Jesus Christ our Saviour.

COLLECT

Friday 12 January

Psalms **67**, 72 *or* **55**
Genesis 4.1-16, 25-26
Matthew 22.15-33

Genesis 4.1-16, 25-26

'Am I my brother's keeper?' (v.9)

The seventeenth-century theologian Blaise Pascal describes humankind like this: 'How chaotic and what a mass of contradictions, and yet what a prodigy… He is the glory and the scum of the universe.' Such is Cain, capable of triumphs and unspeakable acts, a murderer and yet the architect of a great city (v.17). He is internally conflicted, 'a restless wanderer on the earth' (v.14, NIV). He yearns for God because God's absence is unbearable, and yet he dreads him: 'I shall be hidden from your face.' He is the twenty-first-century mortal, grieving the difference between what is and what might have been. His name means 'possessed'.

It isn't entirely clear why Abel's offering was acceptable and Cain's wasn't. Maybe it was to do with the quality of what they presented. Maybe there was something deep-down wrong in Cain's attitude. Certainly it anticipates the need for a blood sacrifice in God's plan for the redemption of the world through Jesus. God's first approach to Cain is compassionate – he receives assurance of a second chance and a warning that temptation unopposed is a menacing beast. But Cain opens the door to the animal within. When God asks for a second time, 'What have you done?' Cain lies like his father before him. But even then, God protectively marks him. Endlessly loving both to Cain and to his twenty-first-century successors, God longs for them to be his possession once more.

COLLECT
Eternal Father,
who at the baptism of Jesus
revealed him to be your Son,
anointing him with the Holy Spirit:
grant to us, who are born again by water and the Spirit,
that we may be faithful to our calling as your adopted children;
through Jesus Christ your Son our Lord,
who is alive and reigns with you,
in the unity of the Holy Spirit,
one God, now and for ever.

| *Reflection by* **Peter Graystone**

Psalms 29, **33** *or* **76**, 79
Genesis 6.1-10
Matthew 22.34-end

Saturday 13 January

Genesis 6.1-10

'The wickedness of humankind was great' (v.5)

The start of chapter 6 is, in all honesty, difficult to understand. What is clear is that it's chaotic, in dramatic contrast to chapter 1. Sexual abuse is rampant. Life is lived with no regard to God or the way God designed the world to thrive. 'Sons of god' (v.6) might refer to pagan priests or supernatural beings, but whoever they are the titanism of their offspring is disturbing. Anarchic powers have been let loose in a godless culture.

Two things characterise God's response to this mayhem – grief and grace. An unimaginable change has taken place. The men and women of God's good creation, in whom he took such delight, have so anguished him that he now regrets ever bringing them into existence. But his grace will not let his grief have the last word. Through one family, that of Noah, a new hope and a new life are going to be possible.

What was it about Noah that set him apart from the rest of humankind? He was righteous and his accord with God had that devoted closeness which had featured in God's initial relationship with Adam and Eve – it is described as walking together. The quality of Noah which we most need to emulate is his obedient trust in the Lord. So great was that faith in God to navigate the direction of his days that he would later stake his life on an ark which had no rudder.

Heavenly Father,
at the Jordan you revealed Jesus as your Son:
may we recognize him as our Lord
and know ourselves to be your beloved children;
through Jesus Christ our Saviour.

COLLECT

Monday 15 January

Psalms 145, **146** *or* **80**, 82
Genesis 6.11 – 7.10
Matthew 24.1-14

Genesis 6.11 – 7.10

'Put the door of the ark in its side' (6.16)

What are we to make of this story? Like many of the stories in Genesis it's an archetypal narrative involving us all, operating at the deepest level. From the time we played with toy arks as children, to the days when, as adults, we fear for the fate of the world, as we see the waters rising and we return to this story of somebody's divinely inspired efforts to save what could be saved.

But as Christians we also inherit a many layered re-reading and re-imagining of this story in the light of Christ. St Augustine, for example, dwells richly on it in *The City of God*. Perhaps his Christian re-imagining of it can help us with ours. For him the ark is the City of God, gathered in, tempest-tossed, but still alive, ready to begin a new story, a new creation. And he goes further, in an inviting intimacy. He notices that the proportions of the ark, are also those of the human body, and therefore of Christ's body, then he adds:

> 'And its having a door made in the side of it certainly signified the wound which was made when the side of the Crucified was pierced with the spear; for by this those who come to Him enter; for thence flowed the sacraments by which those who believe are initiated.'

There indeed is an ark in which all of us are gathered, saved, and carried to a new beginning.

COLLECT

Almighty God,
in Christ you make all things new:
transform the poverty of our nature by the riches of your grace,
and in the renewal of our lives
make known your heavenly glory;
through Jesus Christ your Son our Lord,
who is alive and reigns with you,
in the unity of the Holy Spirit,
one God, now and for ever.

46

*Reflection by **Malcolm Guite***

Psalms **132**, 147.1-12 *or* 87, **89.1-18**   **Tuesday 16 January**
Genesis 7.11-end
Matthew 24.15-28

Genesis 7.11-end

'In the six hundredth year of Noah's life' (v.11)

St John Chrysostom, one of the most celebrated preachers of the Early Church, has an interesting reflection on this passage. He notes that when we heard of Noah's age, before the building of the ark, he was five hundred, and wonders if it took a hundred years to build. But he's not interested in the timescale for its own sake, he's interested in mercy and grace. He compares this story with the story of Nineveh, whose repentance averted disaster. Perhaps, he speculates, God gave Noah such a slow project because he wanted to give the world a chance to change, before it was too late, a whole century! Reading Chrysostom, I reflected on our own climate crisis. How long have we got for the radical change, the *metanoia*, we need to turn things around? How many years have we wasted?

Some say the first article pointing to climate change was in 1896 when Swedish chemist Svante Arrhenius suggested that carbon dioxide concentrations in the atmosphere might affect earth's climate via the greenhouse effect, in which case our century of opportunity is already up. But most scientists agree that the first modern warning, and the basis for many other papers, was published by Manabe and Wetherald in 1967, so perhaps we've still got a little under half that century of grace to turn things around.

Whatever the case, this story certainly lets us know that it is not just ourselves, but every other creature, the whole web of life, that depends upon our repentance.

Eternal Lord,
our beginning and our end:
bring us with the whole creation
to your glory, hidden through past ages
and made known
in Jesus Christ our Lord.

COLLECT

Reflection by **Malcolm Guite**   47

Wednesday 17 January

Psalms **81**, 147.13-end *or*
119.105-128
Genesis 8.1-14
Matthew 24.29-end

Genesis 8.1-14

'There in its beak was a freshly plucked olive leaf' (v.11)

Now the story turns from death to resurrection, from the death of the old creation to the birth of the new. The hint is in the verse 'And God made a wind blow over the earth, and the waters subsided' (v.1) with its conscious echo of the earlier Genesis verse 'the Spirit of God (*ruach*) moved upon the face of the deep' (Genesis 1.2), for the Hebrew *ruach*, like the Greek *pneuma*, is always wind, *and* spirit, *and* breath.

So for Christian readers, the appearance of the dove makes perfect sense. As Alcuin beautifully put it:

'The dove of the Holy Spirit... flies down to Noah after the Flood as to Christ after baptism, and, with the bough of restoration and light, announces peace to the world.'

Again Christ and the Ark are linked, this time by the mission of the Spirit. The Anglo-Saxon poet and priest Alcuin sees the dove as the symbol of peace, as the olive is of mercy, The *eleison*, in *Kyrie eleison* derives from the Greek word for oil, specifically olive oil. So for Christians this moment of the dove returning with the olive branch foreshadows the heavens opening and the dove descending on the Lord's anointed. And this is not just an event 'out there and back then,' but an event that includes us now. We are all in one sense, together in an ark, and in another we stand in and with Christ as the dove descends, and we too receive, as Alcuin says, 'restoration, light and peace'.

COLLECT

Almighty God,
in Christ you make all things new:
transform the poverty of our nature by the riches of your grace,
and in the renewal of our lives
make known your heavenly glory;
through Jesus Christ your Son our Lord,
who is alive and reigns with you,
in the unity of the Holy Spirit,
one God, now and for ever.

| *Reflection by* **Malcolm Guite**

Psalms **76**, 148 *or* 90, **92**   **Thursday 18 January**
Genesis 8.15 – 9.7
Matthew 25.1-13

Genesis 8.15 – 9.7

'So Noah went out' (8.18)

At last, after a year of confinement, they came out of the ark. Chrysostom tries to imagine what that confinement must have been like:

'This righteous person experienced an infinity of afflictions and anxieties, by the privation of air and the vicinity of so many animals: in the midst of all this his spirit remained unshakable... as well as his faith in God.'

Unlike Chrysostom, we don't have to imagine such claustrophobic confinement, for in one sense we have all been through it, in the Covid lockdowns we endured. For those with gardens it was easier, but for many millions, confined in tower blocks, perhaps, like Noah locked in with fractious families or restive pets, it was a deep privation, and for all of us, there was, in Chrysostom's words, 'an infinity of afflictions and anxieties'.

But Noah and his family stepped out, as we did, into a new beginning, and the echoes of Genesis 1 and 2 are unmistakeable: 'for in his own image God made humans.' And they begin their new life, as we should begin ours, with worship.

Even with this fresh start God foresees that we will fall again into sin, but, for the Christian, all that talk of the shedding of human blood, with its echo of the Cain and Abel story, also points forward to the One whose shed blood will be the sacrifice that redeems all.

Eternal Lord,
our beginning and our end:
bring us with the whole creation
to your glory, hidden through past ages
and made known
in Jesus Christ our Lord.

COLLECT

Friday 19 January

Psalms **27**, 149 *or* **88** (95)
Genesis 9.8-19
Matthew 25.14-30

Genesis 9.8-19

'... and with every living creature' (v.10)

Now we come to that key biblical word: covenant. Later in Genesis we will witness the particular covenant with Abraham and his descendants, but it must always be set within this more primal covenant God makes with the whole of humanity and with 'every living creature'. Whatever claims we may subsequently make about special covenants with a chosen people, with a Church or even a whole religion, they are only particular aspects of this primal covenant with the whole of humanity, whatever their faith, and with every living creature whether useful to humanity or not. In this story we have learned that we are all in the same boat, and in this reading, we learn that we are all in the hands of the same God.

And the sign of that universal covenant is the rainbow, which has rightly become a universal symbol well beyond its origin story. Of course, it fits perfectly into its original context for the rainbow appears when the sun has at last come through even as the last rain falls, but for that very reason it is a symbol of promise and hope. The hymn writer George Matheson understood this entirely when he wrote:

> 'I trace the rainbow through the rain
> and feel the promise is not vain
> that morn will tearless be.'

Those who also find in the rainbow a symbol of diversity and inclusion are right to do so, for this rainbow covenant included all creation.

COLLECT

Almighty God,
in Christ you make all things new:
transform the poverty of our nature by the riches of your grace,
and in the renewal of our lives
make known your heavenly glory;
through Jesus Christ your Son our Lord,
who is alive and reigns with you,
in the unity of the Holy Spirit,
one God, now and for ever.

| *Reflection by* **Malcolm Guite**

Psalms **122**, 128, 150 *or* 96, **97**, 100
Genesis 11.1-9
Matthew 25.31-end

Saturday 20 January

Genesis 11.1-9

'Therefore it was called Babel' (v.9)

At the funeral sermon of Bishop Lancelot Andrewes, who gave us much of the magnificent language of the King James Bible, it was said that he knew so many languages 'that he could have served as interpreter general at the confusion of tongues.' But it is Andrewes' own commentary on this story, in a Pentecost sermon, that should be celebrated. It was traditional, he pointed out, to say that the blessing of Pentecost was a reversal of the curse of Babel, that where there was a confusion of tongues there was now a universal understanding. But this is not quite true, says Andrewes, God did something far better than a mere reversal.

If Babel had been put into reverse, then at Pentecost all those people, with their many languages would suddenly have understood classical Hebrew. They would have had to forget their 'mother tongues, with all their diversity of sound and culture, and be conformed to one tongue', and the Church would have been monoglot, monocultural, a towering edifice of linguistic and cultural domination, the very thing for which the tower of Babel was cast down. But God did something better, he blessed and delighted in the linguistic and cultural diversity of that gathering, he affirmed that everybody's mother tongue and native culture was a blessed vehicle for Christian truth. He risked translation. Of course he did, says Andrewes, for he had already made the greatest translation of all, when the Word was made flesh.

Eternal Lord,
our beginning and our end:
bring us with the whole creation
to your glory, hidden through past ages
and made known
in Jesus Christ our Lord.

COLLECT

Reflection by **Malcolm Guite** | 51

Monday 22 January

Psalms 40, **108** *or* **98**, 99, 101
Genesis 11.27 – 12.9
Matthew 26.1-16

Genesis 11.27 – 12.9

'... to the land that I will show you' (12.1)

After the first all-inclusive blessings, the gifts of creation in Adam and Eve and the covenant with all living things after the flood, Genesis now focuses down on particular names and family trees. We zoom in as it were, on the story of Abraham. But this is still Genesis, the book of beginnings, and three great faiths all trace a beginning to this story.

Two striking things attend this beginning: that Abram was already seventy-five when the adventure started, and that he didn't know where he was going. In that respect God's call was rather like Gandalf turning up on Bilbo's doorstep and sending him off on his adventure. Comfortably middle-aged, well settled and established, his first response is 'No adventures today, thank you'. Yet, he does set off, and paradoxically, leaving everything behind and braving the unknown, he becomes who he really is.

So it is with Abram and Sarai, who will, in the course of their adventures, become their true selves so radically that they receive new names.

So it was with Peter, and so it is with us. For we too are pilgrim people, but pilgrims without maps, only the assurance that Abram had: 'I will show you.' But God shows us the next step only once we are actually on the road. If Paul later calls Abraham the father of faith, it is not faith as credal box-ticking, but faith as radical trust.

COLLECT

Almighty God,
whose Son revealed in signs and miracles
the wonder of your saving presence:
renew your people with your heavenly grace,
and in all our weakness
sustain us by your mighty power;
through Jesus Christ your Son our Lord,
who is alive and reigns with you,
in the unity of the Holy Spirit,
one God, now and for ever.

52 | *Reflection by* **Malcolm Guite**

Psalms 34, **36** *or* **106*** *(or* 103)
Genesis 13.2-end
Matthew 26.17-35

Tuesday 23 January

Genesis 13.2-end

'Separate yourself from me' (v.9)

For the Israelites, those who, centuries later, came to call themselves 'the Children of Abraham' and to inhabit the land over which he wandered, it must have been extraordinarily moving to hear this story of their ancestor, with all its familiar and carefully remembered place names. They must have thrilled to the romance of their backstory, their prequel. For Christians too, it is resonant, for it is the beginning of that concentration and particularity which leads to Christ.

That concentration begins with this separation of peoples, this moment of dividing and diminishment, or it might be said, distillation, which makes up the Old Testament narrative: the tale of a series of diminished or concentrated remnants. So now, Abram is divided off from Lot, soon Ishmael and Isaac will be divided. The narrative will concentrate on Isaac, then of his sons Esau and Jacob, on Jacob, and, of his many children, on Joseph.

The motif will be repeated again and again: Gideon going forward with only a remnant of his men. Only David, the runt of the litter, chosen for kingship. Only the remnant of Israel returning from exile, until only one strand of the seed of the promise to Israel is concentrated in one Person, and in him – this tiny, particular remnant of the seed of promise – does the promise becomes universal and all God's promises find their yes in Christ.

God of all mercy,
your Son proclaimed good news to the poor,
release to the captives,
and freedom to the oppressed:
anoint us with your Holy Spirit
and set all your people free
to praise you in Christ our Lord.

COLLECT

Wednesday 24 January

Psalms 45, **46** *or* 110, **111**, 112
Genesis 14
Matthew 26.36-46

Genesis 14

'King Melchizedek of Salem brought out bread and wine' (v.18)

This is extraordinary. Amongst this confusing flurry of kings, variously in alliance and at war, and after Abram's heroic rescue-raid, as he catches his breath in the King's Valley, there suddenly appears a king who is altogether different, for he is not only a king but also 'a priest of God most high', and he comes bearing bread and wine.

Now in the whole Old Testament dispensation there is an absolute separation of priesthood and kingship, they are of different families and castes, with this one extraordinary exception, the priest-king, whose name means 'king of righteousness' and who comes from a place whose name means 'peace' is only mentioned once again in the Old Testament when Psalm 110 prophesies of the coming Messiah: 'Thou art a priest forever after the order of Melchizedek.'

For the Early Church this mysterious priest-king offering Abram the elements of communion was surely a foreshadowing of Christ, and that is the reading of Genesis we find in Hebrews 7, responding to the same mystery: 'Without father or mother, without genealogy, without beginning of days or end of life, resembling the Son of God, he remains a priest forever.' (v.3)

What do we make of it now? Perhaps to look for grace in unexpected places, from unexpected people. The stranger at our door may bear or be the sacrament for us. Might we treat them as generously as Abram did Melchizedek?

C O L L E C T

Almighty God,
whose Son revealed in signs and miracles
the wonder of your saving presence:
renew your people with your heavenly grace,
and in all our weakness
sustain us by your mighty power;
through Jesus Christ your Son our Lord,
who is alive and reigns with you,
in the unity of the Holy Spirit,
one God, now and for ever.

Reflection by **Malcolm Guite**

Psalms 66, 147.13-end
Ezekiel 3.22-end
Philippians 3.1-14

Thursday 25 January
Conversion of Paul

Ezekiel 3.22-end
'I fell on my face' (v.23)

God seems to be in the habit of knocking people off their high horses so as to set them on their feet. As with Ezekiel so with Saul becoming Paul. Like Saul, Ezekiel is overwhelmed by the glory of the divine presence and falls to the ground. And like Paul, the first stage of his recovery is paradoxically a kind of dependency and confinement. Ezekiel is bound with mortal cords and cannot speak, Paul is blinded and must be led by the hand, spending three days in darkness neither eating nor drinking.

Perhaps both these impetuous leaders had to learn something of wisdom and humility from the experience of disability and dependence. Certainly, the paradox of strength in weakness became the hallmark of Paul's teaching, indeed his whole life embodied the paradoxes of the gospel. I tried to list some of them in a poem once:

> An enemy whom God has made a friend,
> A righteous man discounting righteousness,
> Last to believe and first for God to send,
> He found the fountain in the wilderness.
> Thrown to the ground and raised at the same moment,
> A prisoner who set his captors free,
> A naked man with love his only garment,
> A blinded man who helped the world to see,
> A Jew who had been perfect in the Law,
> Blesses the flesh of every other race
> And helps them see what the apostles saw –
> The glory of the Lord in Jesus' face.

(from Sounding the Seasons)

Almighty God,
who caused the light of the gospel
to shine throughout the world
through the preaching of your servant Saint Paul:
grant that we who celebrate his wonderful conversion
may follow him in bearing witness to your truth;
through Jesus Christ your Son our Lord,
who is alive and reigns with you,
in the unity of the Holy Spirit,
one God, now and for ever.

COLLECT

Reflection by **Malcolm Guite**   55

Friday 26 January

Genesis 16

'The angel of the Lord found her' (v.7)

This is an appalling story, and yet, if we will look closely, it offers some healing, some surprise, some redress. One might expect the narrative to have dismissed Hagar, this suffering servant, this surrogate mother, just as easily as Sarai and Abram did. Not so. The narrative follows her as she stumbles alone into the desert, pregnant, vulnerable, rejected. And she is led, she knows not how, surely by the hidden angel, to a spring of water.

Muslims, who venerate this as one of their own origin stories, pay close attention: their much-maligned word *Sharia*, means 'a path to water', so vital to a desert people, and their law, like that of the children of Israel, was meant to show a path through life that brings us to the source and sustenance of life itself. So Hagar found her *Sharia*, and there the angel of the Lord blessed her, and told her to call her son by a name that means 'God will hear'. The blessing she receives echoes directly the covenant blessing given to Abraham.

The early Christians were not afraid to notice this, and Chrysostom writes:

> 'As she bore the race of the righteous, she was honoured by the appearance of an angel... See the goodness of the Lord who does not disdain anyone, even the slave or the servant... without looking at the difference of the ranks, but at the disposal of the soul.'

COLLECT

Almighty God,
whose Son revealed in signs and miracles
the wonder of your saving presence:
renew your people with your heavenly grace,
and in all our weakness
sustain us by your mighty power;
through Jesus Christ your Son our Lord,
who is alive and reigns with you,
in the unity of the Holy Spirit,
one God, now and for ever.

56 | *Reflection by* **Malcolm Guite**

Psalms **68** *or* 120, **121**, 122
Genesis 17.1-22
Matthew 27.1-10

Saturday 27 January

Genesis 17.1-22

'I will bless him' (v.20)

And so the covenant comes – the distinct calling of a chosen people, whose token and demarcation is to be circumcision, the little ritual death that is to be the sign of this new belonging. We flinch at the mutilation just as we are repelled by the casual assumption that there will be slaves. Is there anything for us here?

Well first I think we should note that the slaves too are to be circumcised. They too, whatever their racial origin, are to be completely included in the covenant, they too will be his people and he will be their God. We may no longer have slaves, though modern slavery is rife, but who are the people we look down on? Who are the people we exclude as unfit for our own little holy covenants? God will have them counted in.

And the second thing to note is that even as God makes this covenant with Abraham, now newly named, he affirms Ishmael too: 'I will bless him and make him fruitful'.

One covenant, one blessing, does not exclude another. I must follow and flourish in the community of faith in which God has set me, delighting in all its traditions and particularities, but it is not for me to presume, that God does not lavish his blessing on communities to which I do not belong.

God of all mercy,
your Son proclaimed good news to the poor,
release to the captives,
and freedom to the oppressed:
anoint us with your Holy Spirit
and set all your people free
to praise you in Christ our Lord.

COLLECT

Reflection by **Malcolm Guite**   57

Monday 29 January

Psalms **57**, 96 *or* 123, 124, 125, **126**
Genesis 18.1-15
Matthew 27.11-26

Genesis 18.1-15

'When Abraham saw them, he ran...' (v.2)

Old age is not for wimps. Disappointment and loss, declining vigour of mind and body, cast dismal shadows on the stoutest of souls. However euphemistically we speak of the senior years, we know that this season rarely comes without some measure of tragedy and struggle. How refreshing, then, to meet an older person whose eyes still dance with youthful optimism.

Old Abraham positively skips along with eagerness. On first sight of his mysterious visitors, he runs towards them, bending low with reverence, then rushing around to instruct, present, and serve a feast of lavish hospitality. For him, there is no begrudging this unexpected intrusion on a quiet life. Instead, he greets with open arms the passing strangers who arrive at his door.

It's a beautiful story, crafted over countless years of telling and retelling. As hearers, we know that Abraham and Sarah are entertaining angels unawares. It is easy for us to smile at Sarah's bemusement, recognising in her questioning, perhaps, the shaky condition of our own faith.

'Is anything too wonderful for the Lord?' (v.14) After decades of delay in the fulfilment of God's promise, who knows what scars were left on Abraham's hundred-year-old soul? How remarkable, then, that he could still respond wholeheartedly to this fresh invitation of faith – hitching up his dusty old robes to race towards God's future.

COLLECT

God our creator,
who in the beginning
commanded the light to shine out of darkness:
we pray that the light of the glorious gospel of Christ
may dispel the darkness of ignorance and unbelief,
shine into the hearts of all your people,
and reveal the knowledge of your glory
in the face of Jesus Christ your Son our Lord,
who is alive and reigns with you,
in the unity of the Holy Spirit,
one God, now and for ever.

| *Reflection by* **Margaret Whipp**

Psalms **93**, 97 *or* **132**, 133
Genesis 18.16-end
Matthew 27.27-44

Tuesday 30 January

Genesis 18.16-end

'Abraham remained standing before the Lord' (v.22)

Stories of Abraham are celebrated in all the great monotheistic religions. He is revered as a great man of prayer in Jewish tradition, always interceding on behalf of the whole fragile world. In the 'Quran likewise, Abraham stands as a towering figure of faith, described as 'forbearing, tender-hearted, and oft-turning to Allah'.

Today we get a glimpse into the inner dynamics of Abraham's prayer life, eavesdropping on a conversation of staggering intimacy and boldness. Not only does Abraham have privileged access to stand before the Lord, but he is even granted a disclosure of God's own private thoughts, 'Shall I hide from Abraham what I am about to do?'

Such favoured friendship with the Lord brings its own responsibility. Like God, Abraham must grapple with the horrific problems of unfaithfulness and evil in the world, haggling with the Almighty to plead the cause of mercy. The fate of Sodom offers a small, local example of a larger and perennial theological argument, encountered by believers of every generation, 'Shall not the judge of all the earth do right?' (v.25, AV). 'If you desire the world to endure, there can be no strict justice,' wrote Rabbi Levi, 'While if you desire strict justice, the world cannot endure. Yet – you hold the cord by both ends.'

Do we trust the grace of God enough to gaze unflinchingly on the evil of our world and still plead for mercy?

God of heaven,
you send the gospel to the ends of the earth
and your messengers to every nation:
send your Holy Spirit to transform us
by the good news of everlasting life
in Jesus Christ our Lord.

COLLECT

Reflection by **Margaret Whipp** | 59

Wednesday 31 January

Psalms **95**, 98 *or* **119.153-end**
Genesis 19.1-3, 12-29
Matthew 27.45-56

Genesis 19.1-3, 12-29

'Lot's wife... became a pillar of salt' (v.26)

Striking geological landmarks often bear curious names, recalling the story of some local legendary character. Within the British islands we may know the fanciful Old Man of Hoy, the Giant's Causeway, and the Sleeping Giant of Arran. Generations of Israelites must have pointed out the tall salt stack overlooking the Dead Sea with its anthropomorphic features – 'Remember Lot's wife!' (Luke 17.32)

Neither Lot nor his unnamed wife come out very well in this story. They seem to have settled all too comfortably in a city whose violent ways cried out for censure to the heavens. In marked contrast to Abraham's eagerness and generosity, Lot's response to the angelic visitation is constrained, uncertain, and riven with compromise. Even when the angels are hurrying to save his life, Lot lingers on the threshold: he and his womenfolk have to be dragged out from danger by the hand.

The image of a pillar of salt is a terrifying metaphor for human recalcitrance. Unbending and frozen to the spot, Lot's wife stands for everything in our hearts which has lost impetus, through complacency, or stubbornness, or fear.

Of course, the tragedy is that salt can be such a beneficial thing when it is free-flowing and available for use. In our response to the invitations of another new day, can we pray for a willing, supple, and generous heart?

COLLECT

God our creator,
who in the beginning
commanded the light to shine out of darkness:
we pray that the light of the glorious gospel of Christ
may dispel the darkness of ignorance and unbelief,
shine into the hearts of all your people,
and reveal the knowledge of your glory
in the face of Jesus Christ your Son our Lord,
who is alive and reigns with you,
in the unity of the Holy Spirit,
one God, now and for ever.

| *Reflection by* **Margaret Whipp**

Genesis 21.1-21

'The Lord dealt with Sarah as he had said...' (v.1)

There is a steady pulse of repetition in the way today's story is told. Read a few verses aloud – in the way that these ancient stories were meant to be shared – and you will feel their reassuring rhythm of a promise gloriously fulfilled.

'The Lord dealt with Sarah as he had said
and the Lord did for Sarah as he had promised.
Sarah conceived and bore Abraham a son in his old age
at the time of which God had spoken to him.' (vv.1-2)

In case we don't grasp the immediate force of this event, the storyteller's artful reiteration drums its significance into our consciousness. God is faithful in his promise. God has been faithful to his word. God is always faithful to his people. Like the strains of a favourite song, or the recollection of an old family story, these words of faith work deep grooves of consolation into our corporate memory.

The people of Israel knew what it meant to draw on such comfort. Through many a wilderness and terrible existential crisis, their trust in God's constancy would be tested beyond imagining. Centuries later, Christians join to praise the same God. Hailing the steadfastness of 'Abraham's God and mine', we too gain strength and courage from the 'Ancient of everlasting days and God of love'.

What might be your soul's song of praise for this new day?

God of heaven,
you send the gospel to the ends of the earth
and your messengers to every nation:
send your Holy Spirit to transform us
by the good news of everlasting life
in Jesus Christ our Lord.

COLLECT

Friday 2 February

Presentation of Christ
in the Temple

Psalms **48**, 146
Exodus 13.1-16
Romans 12.1-5

Exodus 13.1-16

'When... your child asks you, "What does this mean?"...' (v.14)

Bright-coloured rituals, handed on from generation to generation, are one of the great attractions of religious faith. It is a lovely thing to see children and adults, wide-eyed with wonder, holding up their flaming candles for the annual blessing at a Candlemas service.

What it all means is impossible to convey in a few short words. Rich layers of memory and celebration that shape a whole community of faith are not easily compressed into neat verbal formulae. Far better to act out in movement and liturgy the deep intuitions which they enshrine.

Just like our ancient forebears, we pick up the cadences of a living faith through sedimented rhythms of liturgical time. As earth turns slowly towards the coming spring, we bless the wax of summer bees and kindle once more our little candles of hope – the Light of Christ held out for the world.

Our expressions of worship have come a long way from their fearful precursors in animal, and even human, blood sacrifice. Demands for the 'purification' of women after childbirth have also retreated into the shadows of liturgical history. In the Light of Christ, we are set free to celebrate the gift of new life without shame or fear.

Our best instincts lie in constant need of purification. But a healthy memory of luminous faith is a priceless inheritance to place in our children's hands. Happy Candlemas!

COLLECT

Almighty and ever-living God,
clothed in majesty,
whose beloved Son was this day presented in the Temple,
in substance of our flesh:
grant that we may be presented to you
with pure and clean hearts,
by your Son Jesus Christ our Lord,
who is alive and reigns with you,
in the unity of the Holy Spirit,
one God, now and for ever.

Reflection by **Margaret Whipp**

Psalm 147
Genesis 23
Matthew 28.16-end

Saturday 3 February

Genesis 23

'I am a stranger and an alien residing among you' (v.4)

Bereavement is a time of unique human vulnerability. Sarah's death at the end of a long life marks a major turning point in our story. For her family, it is the loss of a wife and mother; while, for the clan of Abraham, Sarah's death marks the loss of a great matriarchal spirit whose life embodied the fulfilment of a glorious promise.

Emerging from the tent of mourning Abraham cuts a poignant figure, the flimsiness of his life exposed like never before, to plead for a burial place in a land of strangers. There is a pitiable tone to his request: broken by grief, he presents himself as no more than a resident alien, exiled from his homeland and people. Yet the dignity of this sorrowing elder is unmistakeable; he is a 'mighty prince' who can still show himself to be a highly persuasive negotiator.

And where is God in this all too human story of inheritance and loss? Curiously, there is no mention in this passage of the Lord whose presence has been such an intimate and reassuring constant in the life of Abraham and Sarah. Perhaps, from our own experiences of the numbness of grief, we can identify with this foggy sense of absence.

In this darkest of times, a costly transaction secures for the people of Abraham their first foothold of land in Canaan. Quietly and faithfully, God is working to fulfil the promise of a lifetime.

Almighty God,
by whose grace alone we are accepted
and called to your service:
strengthen us by your Holy Spirit
and make us worthy of our calling;
through Jesus Christ your Son our Lord,
who is alive and reigns with you,
in the unity of the Holy Spirit,
one God, now and for ever.

COLLECT

Monday 5 February

Psalms 1, 2, 3
Genesis 29.31 – 30.24
2 Timothy 4.1-8

Genesis 29.31 – 30.24

'May the Lord add to me another son!' (v.24)

Being present at the birth of a baby is a thrilling experience. TV favourites like *Call the Midwife* capture the essential magic and intensity of this most primal human drama. At the culmination of mounting crisis, with one last push and a loud cry, a child is born!

Today's passage takes us deep into the messy world of maternity, sparing none of the conflict and cruelty that sometimes hides behind a happy ending. There are those who seem to have it easy, while others struggle with the stigma of barrenness. Envy, fear, and shame bring out the worst of manipulative behaviours, from bitter sibling rivalry to a seamy kind of surrogacy not so far removed from *The Handmaid's Tale*. Strong passions are at work.

An underlying theology is also at work. It is not particularly sophisticated, but it is punchy and important. There is one giver of life who is God alone. So much is powerfully acknowledged in the pious names given to each of Jacob's children.

Perhaps there is a salutary reminder in these ancient tribal tales that the gift of life – for individuals and families, as for nations and species – is never ultimately ours to command. Today we might recall the humbling words of our General Thanksgiving prayer, 'We bless you for our creation, preservation, and for all the blessings of this life.'

COLLECT

Almighty God,
you have created the heavens and the earth
and made us in your own image:
teach us to discern your hand in all your works
and your likeness in all your children;
through Jesus Christ your Son our Lord,
who with you and the Holy Spirit reigns supreme over all things,
now and for ever.

| *Reflection by* **Margaret Whipp**

Psalms **5**, 6 (8)
Genesis 31.1-24
2 Timothy 4.9-end

Tuesday 6 February

Genesis 31.1–24

'I am the God of Bethel...' (v.13a)

The story moves on to follow Jacob on his travels. This crafty young man has a habit of getting himself into bitter scrapes. In an earlier chapter, he had left his home country in Canaan after a dispute with his brother Esau. Now he finds himself in conflict again with his father-in-law Laban in the land of Paddan-Aram.

It is here that God meets up with him. In his hour of trouble, Jacob is receptive to God's call and prompting, hearing the voice of the Lord through a dream, 'I am the God of Bethel, where you anointed a pillar and made a vow to me. Now... return to the land of your birth' (v.13).

This profoundly mystical experience brings stability and direction to the wayward Jacob. The Lord takes him back to one of those touchstone moments in his own life when he was assured of God's faithfulness and concern. It was at Bethel that Jacob had been overawed by the nearness of God's presence, marking the sanctity of the moment with a very personal vow of commitment (28.10-22).

In our own winding pilgrimage through life there are graced times and places where the loving kindness of God comes extraordinarily close. We do well to remember these Bethel-experiences. Whatever later times of confusion might arise they maintain a vital touchstone of what truly matters most.

Almighty God,
give us reverence for all creation
and respect for every person,
that we may mirror your likeness
in Jesus Christ our Lord.

COLLECT

Wednesday 7 February

Psalm **119.1-32**
Genesis 31.25 – 32.2
Titus 1

Genesis 31.25 – 32.2

'The Lord watch between you and me...' (v.49)

Another journey is marked by another sacred pillar. Jacob is in full flight from his father-in-law and former employer, taking with him Laban's daughters and grandchildren and a substantial chunk of his material wealth.

There are two sides to this hurried getaway. On the one hand, Jacob is following a divine invitation to return to his own people and country. On the other hand, he has despoiled and outwitted a respected tribal leader and the patron of his own good fortune. What to Jacob seems like justifiable plunder looks to Laban like daylight robbery. And, unknown to both of them, Rachel has also spirited away her own father's household gods.

Fear and tension crackle through this fast-moving story as we move towards an angry showdown at the place called Mizpah. Here Jacob and Laban meet, face to face with their own partial truths and polished evasions.

Instead of killing each other at this point, they set up a shared boundary marker. It is telling that even the name given to this heap of stones is different for the two men: they bring two different perspectives and two different languages (v.47). But they unite in a commitment to refrain from further violence.

What is notable in this rapprochement is the invocation of God as witness (v.49). Perhaps there are difficult boundary areas in our own lives where we need God's help to keep us from bringing harm to others and ourselves.

COLLECT | Almighty God,
you have created the heavens and the earth
and made us in your own image:
teach us to discern your hand in all your works
and your likeness in all your children;
through Jesus Christ your Son our Lord,
who with you and the Holy Spirit reigns supreme over all things,
now and for ever.

| *Reflection by* **Margaret Whipp**

Psalms 14, **15**, 16
Genesis 32.3-30
Titus 2

Thursday 8 February

Genesis 32.3–30

*'... you have striven with God and with humans, and have
prevailed' (v.28b)*

The story of Jacob wrestling the angel is one of the most famous
dramas in the Hebrew scriptures. Its haunting themes have been
richly explored in art and sculpture, psychology and literature.
Something primal and powerful reverberates down the ages in this
nocturnal battle of the titans.

The shadowy setting for this scene is profoundly evocative. The river
Jabbok plunges steeply from the east of the Jordan, cutting deep
ravines through the hill country. Jacob, with his wives and flocks and
children, must traverse this challenging terrain to return to his
homeland and people. With Laban behind him, and his estranged
brother Esau ahead of him, he reaches a physical and metaphorical
crossing point. Alone in the night, Jacob joins an intense spiritual
battle with his angel.

Before this midnight struggle he is Jacob the trickster and supplanter,
outmanoeuvring his rivals by the sheer power of his wits. But now he
is up against an opponent who will not release him. Skin on skin, he
must wrestle for his very life – and something must give way. With
one last wrench, Jacob breaks free with both a new dignity and a
painful limp.

Jacob's manly combat ends with the dawn of new day. From this
point on, the hero knows himself to be wounded and vulnerable but
is named by God a worthy prince – 'Israel'.

Almighty God,
give us reverence for all creation
and respect for every person,
that we may mirror your likeness
in Jesus Christ our Lord.

COLLECT

Reflection by **Margaret Whipp** | 67

Friday 9 February

Psalms 17, **19**
Genesis 33.1-17
Titus 3

Genesis 33.1–17

'... and they wept' (v.4)

Many years have passed since Jacob's youthful flight from Canaan. Through artful storytelling we have traced the slow maturation of his faith and character to the point where he stands ready to re-enter the promised land of his fathers.

Stories of the hero's return abound in narrative history. A young adventurer, bruised and humbled after many ordeals, faces the final challenge of meeting and coming to terms with his own people and origins. It is a journey of wisdom, atonement, and ultimate blessing.

Jacob's approach to his brother Esau is beautifully choreographed. Every gesture communicates deference and goodwill, showering his former rival with gifts and bowing low before his presence. Jacob's desire is to return in peace; and his earnest prayer is to avert any lingering malice (vv.10-12). But apprehension builds as Esau bears down on him with four hundred men. Can any honourable reconciliation be possible?

In the event, the two men meet with tenderness and mercy, falling on each other's neck with tears of brotherly recognition. Perhaps the grace of years has wrought a softening of attitude, a facility for compromise, a willingness to live and let live.

In the Hebrew scriptures Jacob and Esau stand for so much more than two troubled siblings, representing for us the tangled fortunes of great nations and their age-old conflicts. Let us pray for all who work long and hard to bring peace in our fearful world.

COLLECT

Almighty God,
you have created the heavens and the earth
and made us in your own image:
teach us to discern your hand in all your works
and your likeness in all your children;
through Jesus Christ your Son our Lord,
who with you and the Holy Spirit reigns supreme over all things,
now and for ever.

| *Reflection by* **Margaret Whipp**

Psalms 20, 21, **23**
Genesis 35
Philemon

Saturday 10 February

Genesis 35

'God... has been with me wherever I have gone' (v.3b)

Today's reading brings completion to the rich and meandering narrative of the patriarchs Abraham, Isaac and Jacob. It is a chapter of poignant contrasts in which we see the return of Jacob to his own land, the birth of a precious younger son, and the deaths of his wife Rebekah, preceded by that of her old nurse Deborah, and followed by that of his father Isaac.

In his poem 'Little Gidding', T.S. Eliot evokes those timeless places 'where prayer has been valid'. As the cycle of generations presses onward, Jacob returns to such a place at the shrine of Bethel. He remembers his earlier vow to build there an altar for prayer and sacrifice if 'he shall come again to his father's house in peace' (28.22).

Now in reflective mood, Jacob calls to mind the many mercies he has received from the Lord's hand. Bearing eloquent testimony to God's faithfulness down the years, he shares with his household his personal gratitude for God's answer in the day of distress and his constant presence through his long and weary sojourn in a foreign land (v.3).

In moving response, the good Lord appears once more at the shrine to reaffirm the covenant of blessing for Jacob-Israel, for his offspring, and for countless future peoples. The wheels of history may be turning: but the unfailing grace of God promises a continuing hope for the future. As it does in every generation.

Almighty God,
give us reverence for all creation
and respect for every person,
that we may mirror your likeness
in Jesus Christ our Lord.

COLLECT

Reflection by **Margaret Whipp** | 69

Monday 12 February

Galatians 1

'Deserting... and turning to another gospel' (v.6)

Lent begins in a couple of days. It is good to think about that in advance, not letting it catch us unawares. Lent is the season of preparation for Easter, and we will get the most out of that if we take a moment to prepare for it too. Perhaps ask yourself today, 'What do I want from the season that lies ahead?'

For most of the next two weeks, the lectionary presents us with Paul's Letter to the Galatians, which makes for good Lenten reading. There is a certain astringency to Galatians which suits the season, and a presentation of what, for Paul, stands at the heart of the gospel. Lent is a good time to try something new – some new form of prayer, or service, or Bible reading – but it is also a time to return to the centre and foundation of the faith. In other biblical books we read, 'Stand at the crossroads, and look, and ask for the ancient paths' (Jeremiah 6.16) or 'Return to your stronghold, O prisoners of hope' (Zechariah 12.9). Paul's challenge about returning, and not straying is more combative: 'if anyone proclaims to you a gospel contrary to what you received, let that one be accursed' (Galatians 1.9).

Perhaps, in the days to come, try concentrating on the central themes of Christianity, which we can take for granted, but which support everything else about it.

COLLECT | Almighty Father,
whose Son was revealed in majesty
before he suffered death upon the cross:
give us grace to perceive his glory,
that we may be strengthened to suffer with him
and be changed into his likeness, from glory to glory;
who is alive and reigns with you,
in the unity of the Holy Spirit,
one God, now and for ever.

| *Reflection by* **Andrew Davison**

Tuesday 13 February

Galatians 2.1-10

'... the freedom we have in Christ Jesus' (v.4)

As I said yesterday, Galatians makes for good Lenten reading material, which begins tomorrow. The letter's message of holding fast to the faith is appropriate for this time of year, and there can be more than a little grit to the letter, but it is also good reading for Lent because it is about freedom as much as anything else. We see that in today in the reference to 'the freedom we have in Christ'.

The freedom Paul has in mind is one that comes from recognising that our salvation rests with God and not with what we might or might not have achieved. This freedom is not meant as an excuse for living selfishly or without concern for right and wrong, but rather as something that turns us towards others (Galatians 5.13). As the Church of England's preface for the Eucharist during Lent has it,

> Through fasting, prayer and acts of service
> you bring us back to your generous heart.
> Through study of your holy word
> you open our eyes to your presence in the world
> and free our hands to welcome others.

There are many ways of keeping Lent, but one suggestion is to apply ourselves, day by day, to thinking about what we need to be freed for and from, both for our own greater joy, and so as to be more available to love and serve others.

Holy God,
you know the disorder of our sinful lives:
set straight our crooked hearts,
and bend our wills to love your goodness and your glory
in Jesus Christ our Lord.

COLLECT

Wednesday 14 February

Ash Wednesday

1 Timothy 6.6-19

'... take hold of the life that really is life' (v.19)

The message of Lent is simple enough: 'take hold of the life that really is life.' The Greek for 'take hold' has a direct and earthy sense to it. It often means, literally, to grasp or seize something, and hold it tight. It can also mean 'take possession', in the sense of laying hold to a legal claim. Although there is nothing here to grasp with our hands, the message is to be as urgent about the faith, and the gospel, and the true life it offers, as if the seizing really were physical.

The imagery concerning hands is also there in the preceding verses, about the 'uncertainty of riches,' and the importance of being 'generous, and ready to share'. Recent neuroscience and psychology have underlined how much our thinking and language are based in our bodily experience and interaction with the world around us. One way to meditate on this passage – to 'get to grips with it', we might say – especially if there is no-one else around, might even be to enter into it with action or posture: miming or adopting a pose, such as opening and closing our hands, in some parts of holding firm (in relation to God and 'true life') and, in others, of letting go or sharing (in relation to what possessions we might enjoy). It is sometimes good to read the Bible with our whole body.

COLLECT

Almighty and everlasting God,
you hate nothing that you have made
and forgive the sins of all those who are penitent:
create and make in us new and contrite hearts
that we, worthily lamenting our sins
and acknowledging our wretchedness,
may receive from you, the God of all mercy,
perfect remission and forgiveness;
through Jesus Christ your Son our Lord,
who is alive and reigns with you,
in the unity of the Holy Spirit,
one God, now and for ever.

Reflection by **Andrew Davison**

Psalm **77** *or* **37***
Genesis 39
Galatians 2.11-end

Thursday 15 February

Galatians 2.11-end

'... not by the works of the law but through faith in Jesus Christ'
(v.16)

Paul leaves us in no doubt that he is getting to the heart of the matter. He tells us that no one stands right with God or is put right with God (is 'justified') by doing the works of the law. Paul says that three times in a single verse, 'not by the works of the law but through faith in Jesus Christ... not by doing the works of the law, because no one will be justified by the works of the law' (v.16).

Historically, not least in the Protestant traditions, the great contrast here was thought to be between human actions and human faith: not 'works of the law', but 'faith in Jesus Christ'. Recent scholarship has highlighted an additional depth, so that what the NRSV translates here as 'faith *in* Jesus Christ' could be rendered 'the faith *of* Jesus Christ'. In that case, the contrast would not so much be between two things which belong to us – our faith *versus* our works of the law – but between anything at all that might originate with us, and what belongs to Christ, or between anything that we might do, and what Christ has done for us.

Especially if the 'faith in Jesus Christ' interpretation is the more familiar understanding for you, perhaps dwell today on the other: remembering that the message of grace is that Christ stands for us, and is faithful even when we are not.

Holy God,
our lives are laid open before you:
rescue us from the chaos of sin
and through the death of your Son
bring us healing and make us whole
in Jesus Christ our Lord.

COLLECT

Friday 16 February

Galatians 3.1-14

*'Having started with the Spirit, are you now ending
with the flesh?' (v.3)*

Completion stands at the heart of the Passion story and the doctrine
of redemption. 'It is finished!' says Christ upon the cross, or
'completed!' – 'accomplished!' A variant of that word features in
one of Paul's outbursts of astonishment and grief in today's reading:
'Are you so foolish? Having started with the Spirit, are you now
ending with the flesh?' Or, as we might also translate it, 'Although
the Spirit started things off, are you now confident that the flesh will
bring things to completion?'

Paul is not down on the flesh. Christ redeemed us in and by his body.
Paul also writes that 'the life I now live in the flesh' (Galatians 2.20).
It is just that Paul no longer measures his life according to his own
actions or human accomplishments ('the flesh'), but by 'faith in the
Son of God [or faith in the faithfulness of Christ], who loved me and
gave himself for me'.

In this part of Galatians, 'flesh' is a problem because it stands for
confidence in our own actions. For the Galatians, that was notably
confidence in one particularly human action, namely circumcision.
As we make our way through Lent, Paul's challenge is for us to ask
how we try to justify ourselves to God, rather than accepting and
receiving God's justification of us by Christ.

COLLECT

Almighty and everlasting God,
you hate nothing that you have made
and forgive the sins of all those who are penitent:
create and make in us new and contrite hearts
that we, worthily lamenting our sins
and acknowledging our wretchedness,
may receive from you, the God of all mercy,
perfect remission and forgiveness;
through Jesus Christ your Son our Lord,
who is alive and reigns with you,
in the unity of the Holy Spirit,
one God, now and for ever.

| *Reflection by* **Andrew Davison**

Psalm 71 *or* 41, **42**, 43
Genesis 41.1-24
Galatians 3.15-22

Saturday 17 February

Galatians 3.15-22

'Now a mediator involves more than one party; but God is one'
(v.20)

This is one most enigmatic sayings in all of Paul's letters. Writing in 1865, Bishop Lightfoot estimated '250 to 300' interpretations of it, not thinking much of most of them. Paul might be out to elevate the gospel over the law, since the law came through mediators, but the gospel from God directly, in Christ. Alternatively, the idea may be that mediations need to be negotiated and depend on the behaviour of both parties, while the grace of God in Christ has a glorious unilateral character to it: the gospel is so much more about God's faithfulness than it is about ours.

Alternatively, another commentator (Hans Dieter Betz, 1989) suggests that Paul's idea is that 'redemption requires conformity to the oneness of God.' On that, we can conclude with a magnificent passage from Augustine:

> Distracted and clinging to many things, it was necessary… that those same many things should join in proclaiming the One that should come… that, freed from the burden of many things, we should come to that One, and should love that One who, without sin, died in the flesh for us… that we should be justified by being made one in the one righteous One… and through Him as mediator, reconciled to God, cling to the One, feast upon the One, and remain one.

Holy God,
our lives are laid open before you:
rescue us from the chaos of sin
and through the death of your Son
bring us healing and make us whole
in Jesus Christ our Lord.

COLLECT

Reflection by **Andrew Davison** | 75

Monday 19 February

Galatians 3.23 – 4.7

'... all of you are one in Christ Jesus' (v.28)

In a justly celebrated line, Paul writes that 'There is no longer Jew or Greek, there is no longer slave or free, there is no longer male and female; for all of you are one in Christ Jesus.' The foundation for this is set out immediately before, namely membership of a new family, in which these diverse people 'all [become] children of God'. This new birth or adoption – here Paul speaks in terms of the latter – sets the running for all who belong to this family, trumping the accidents of natural birth.

The idea is also important in John's Gospel: 'to all who received him, who believed in his name, he gave power to become children of God, who were born, not of blood or of the will of the flesh or of the will of man, but of God' (John 1.13). As we might put it, the waters of baptism turn out to be thicker than blood.

The Church has taken its time in learning this lesson. That is an understatement. Even the great Augustine, commenting on our passage in one of his less impressive moments, wrote that although 'the unity of faith' teaches us 'that there are no such distinctions', nonetheless, 'within the orders of this life they persist', and in such matters it is best 'to avoid offence to others'. Surely, we are called to something more subversive than that!

COLLECT

Almighty God,
whose Son Jesus Christ fasted forty days in the wilderness,
and was tempted as we are, yet without sin:
give us grace to discipline ourselves in obedience to your Spirit;
and, as you know our weakness,
so may we know your power to save;
through Jesus Christ your Son our Lord,
who is alive and reigns with you,
in the unity of the Holy Spirit,
one God, now and for ever.

| *Reflection by* **Andrew Davison**

Psalm **44** *or* **48**, 52
Genesis 41.46 – 42.5
Galatians 4.8-20

Tuesday 20 February

Galatians 4.8-20

'... enslaved to beings that by nature are not gods' (v.4)

Taken by itself, this phrase could just about mean enslavement to fictional or imagined gods, precisely by following fictions. However, this is not the first time that Paul has mentioned supernatural beings in Galatians. Yesterday, we read 'we were enslaved to the elemental spirits of the world.' Paul surely therefore sees these beings as real, but counterfeit in comparison with the one God: they are more like angels, or the spirits of places, and seem of an evil character.

Pentecostal theology takes this sort of reference seriously. Elsewhere in Christianity, denial of angels and demons is not so prevalent as was a generation ago, but much academic theology still passes over these passages as something of an embarrassment, or at least strictly subordinate to a theology of justification, faith, grace, law, and so on. The tide might be turning. For a taste of Paul with these matters stressed and urgent, David Bentley Hart's recent translation of the New Testament is worth reading.

Looking on the wastes of twentieth-century history, Karl Barth insisted that we are bound to come under one power or another, and that this makes being under Christ good news. It belongs to 'divine mercy' that Christ should bring us under his 'lordship', because in that he 'delivers us from all other lordships' – including those 'beings' in Galatians – excluding once and for all their capacity to threaten us.

COLLECT

Heavenly Father,
your Son battled with the powers of darkness,
and grew closer to you in the desert:
help us to use these days to grow in wisdom and prayer
that we may witness to your saving love
in Jesus Christ our Lord.

Wednesday 21 February

Galatians 4.21 – 5.1

'Hagar is Mount Sinai in Arabia and corresponds to the present Jerusalem' (v.25)

Here is Paul reflecting on a familiar story from the Book of Genesis. For anyone who likes their biblical interpretation sober, scholarly, and solidly grounded in the text, this passage is an eye-opener, even something of a scandal. Anyone who thinks the goal is to get back to something like the intention of the author, or what the first readers would have made of it, is not going to like this way to read Genesis.

Paul's method is allegory, where various parts of a story are taken to stand for (Paul says 'corresponds' to) something else. Allegory would become an important way to read the Bible, especially after the influence of the theological tradition coming out of Alexandria in Egypt in the early days of the Church, where allegory was as much in evidence among Jewish writers as Christian ones. Allegory would be influential for centuries to come, and here is Paul up to it too. How do we know when to take it seriously? After all, we could use an allegory to make almost any text mean anything.

A rule sprang up that we should not read any passage of the Bible in this 'non-literal' way when it can be justified by the literal reading of some other passage. Christians are forever drawing on the Bible to make creative allusions. (If you are using Common Worship Daily Prayer, look at the canticle refrains.) You may do it yourselves. When is that legitimate, and when are we playing fast and loose? It's responsible whatever what we're saying is in accord with how the point is covered, more straightforwardly, elsewhere in the Bible: which is how Paul uses allegory here.

COLLECT

Almighty God,
whose Son Jesus Christ fasted forty days in the wilderness,
and was tempted as we are, yet without sin:
give us grace to discipline ourselves in obedience to your Spirit;
and, as you know our weakness,
so may we know your power to save;
through Jesus Christ your Son our Lord,
who is alive and reigns with you,
in the unity of the Holy Spirit,
one God, now and for ever.

Reflection by **Andrew Davison**

Psalms **42**, 43 *or* 56, **57** (63*)   **Thursday 22 February**
Genesis 42.18-28
Galatians 5.2-15

Galatians 5.2-15

'... the only thing that counts is faith working through love' (v.6)

We have read a good deal so far in Galatians about various words or categories that history has strongly associated with Paul, and rightly so: faith and works, grace and law. With today's reading, a fifth word bursts onto the scene, one that we should recognise as being as equally central to Paul's lexicon as any of the others, namely *love*.

One of the seemingly great disagreements in the New Testament is between Paul, elevating faith over works, and James, writing that works are what makes faith real. With talk of 'faith working through love', however, as Bishop Lightfoot put it, those words 'bridge over the gulf which seems to separate the language of St Paul and St James. Both assert a principle of practical energy, as opposed to a barren, inactive theory.'

The problem is perhaps that we treat faith in a more cognitive and individual way than what it intended in either the Old Testament or the New. Consider Abraham, the great paradigm of faith. His faith was, above all, trust in God. Unlike self-justifying works, it was all about God. And yet that trust wasn't purely internal, or about assenting to ideas. It is seen in leaving his home, and in raising the knife to sacrifice his son. Precisely because faith is most of all trust, it is inseparable from love.

Reflection by **Andrew Davison**   79

Friday 23 February

Psalm **22** *or* **51**, 54
Genesis 42.29-end
Galatians 5.16-end

Galatians 5.16-end

'There is no law against such things' (v.23)

Paul's Letter to the Galatians has its grumpy moments, but if the mood is often tense, that is because of Paul's love for the Galatians, and his fears about what they stand to lose. The tone is often fraught, but then along comes one of the sunniest passages in the whole of the Bible: the list of the fruit of the Spirit.

Just as, yesterday, love emerged as the final answer to the relation of grace and works, so these fruits lift us out of theological wrangles about the role and status of the law, since 'there is no law against such things.' Paul's contrast is between flesh and spirit. It's important to recognise that this is not a judgement on the body as such, or some denigration of materiality. 'Flesh' and 'Spirit' are two ways of living in its entirety. There is a led-by-the-Spirit way of being a bodily creature, and a 'fleshly' way of being abstractly spiritual and disdainful of creation.

Although the word 'grace' does not feature in the reading today, it lies at the heart what is going on here. By grace, God truly gives us what he gives – such as these fruits – and, in that, they do not spring from our own efforts or deserving, but from God's gracious gift.

COLLECT

Almighty God,
whose Son Jesus Christ fasted forty days in the wilderness,
and was tempted as we are, yet without sin:
give us grace to discipline ourselves in obedience to your Spirit;
and, as you know our weakness,
so may we know your power to save;
through Jesus Christ your Son our Lord,
who is alive and reigns with you,
in the unity of the Holy Spirit,
one God, now and for ever.

Reflection by **Andrew Davison**

Saturday 24 February

Galatians 6

'Bear one another's burdens' (v.2)

If we were looking for a contradiction in the New Testament, we seem to find one here: 'Bear one another's burdens' (v.2), but 'all must carry their own loads' (v.5). Something interesting must be going on. Here are three suggestions from various commentaries.

First, the 'burdens' in v.2 seem to be associated with sin and temptation (v.1). If so, then we do well to be pastorally generous with others, but strict with ourselves. 'Do not judge', Christ says, but, he adds, be aware that you will be judged by God.

Second, the words in the two verses are different. Usage varies, but burden' in v.2 puts the emphasis on heaviness and weight. In contrast, while the 'load' in v.5 is certainly not easy, it seems to be the sort of burden that we all have to carry in daily life. As elsewhere, therefore, Paul is keen to stress that Christian charity is no excuse for shirking one's everyday responsibilities (2 Thessalonians 3.10).

Finally, we might notice that in v.5 Paul seems to be simply repeating some well-worn Greek maxim, praising the sort of self-sufficiency familiar to any Stoic philosopher. On the other hand, v.2 looks of Paul's own making. As elsewhere, Paul does not disparage Greek wisdom, but the newness of love offers the yet 'more excellent way' (1 Corinthians 12.31) than anything known before.

Heavenly Father,
your Son battled with the powers of darkness,
and grew closer to you in the desert:
help us to use these days to grow in wisdom and prayer
that we may witness to your saving love
in Jesus Christ our Lord.

COLLECT

Reflection by **Andrew Davison**

Monday 26 February

Hebrews 1

'Long ago...' (v.1)

No 'Paul, a servant of Jesus Christ... to all God's beloved' or 'Paul, called to be an apostle of Christ... to the Church of God'. No introduction, no greeting, no indication that this is an epistle at all. Instead we are plunged straight into a theological treatise on the cosmic Christ.

Who wrote the Epistle to the Hebrews? God alone knows. So says Origen, writing in the mid third century. Origen suspects it might have been written by Clement, the third Bishop of Rome (c.35–100). And to whom is this letter addressed? 'To the Hebrews' is a later Christian best guess, based on the way the text draws so extensively on Old Testament sources and seeks to reveal Christ as their fulfilment.

And this lacing together of past and present, of 'long ago' to 'these last days', is our key to the text, and to our understanding of Hebrews' Christology. Christ is a 'reflection', a turning back, a perfect mirroring of God's glory; he is an exact 'imprint', a fixing of God's very being in the now; and he 'sustains all things' into the future. His throne 'is for ever and ever', embracing all time.

The 'Epistle to the Hebrews' sets out to remind us: the Bible is a book, bound, with a spine. It tells one story, beginning, middle and end: Christ. This is not for Hebrews then or Gentiles now. It is for all. For ever.

C O L L E C T	Almighty God,
	you show to those who are in error the light of your truth,
	that they may return to the way of righteousness:
	grant to all those who are admitted
	    into the fellowship of Christ's religion,
	that they may reject those things
	    that are contrary to their profession,
	and follow all such things as are agreeable to the same;
	through our Lord Jesus Christ,
	who is alive and reigns with you,
	in the unity of the Holy Spirit,
	one God, now and for ever.

| *Reflection by* **Colin Heber-Percy**

Psalm **50** *or* **73**
Genesis 44.1-17
Hebrews 2.1-9

Tuesday 27 February

Hebrews 2.1-9

'Pay greater attention' (v.1)

Attention costs. We have to pay for it. Or do we? Like so much else in our world, attention has become a transaction. Our attention is valuable, measured these days in clicks, likes and shares.

But the word in the Greek of Hebrews that is translated here as 'pay attention to' is actually better rendered as 'hold to' or 'attend to' or even 'devote oneself to'. We are called to hold fast that which we have heard, lest we 'drift away'. This message is a life preserver. Not something for which we pay, but something which has been thrown to us, and for us. It is salvation.

In Matthew's Gospel, when Peter steps out of the boat he notices the wind and waves. Frightened, he starts to sink (Matthew 14.28-33). Think of the storms and travails in our own lives. We feel we are sinking. Perhaps we feel ourselves drifting away. Peter cries out, and Jesus takes him by the hand.

We are unable to win the salvation to which we are called, or pay for it or merit it, but we can see it in the saving action of Jesus Christ, walking towards us.

To be saved is first to be spent; to be found we must have been lost. Recognising that we are adrift and unable to save ourselves is the first step. 'Lord, save me!' (Matthew 14.30).

And hold fast.

Almighty God,
by the prayer and discipline of Lent
may we enter into the mystery of Christ's sufferings,
and by following in his Way
come to share in his glory;
through Jesus Christ our Lord.

COLLECT

Wednesday 28 February

Hebrews 2.10-end

'... to become like his brothers and sisters' (v.17)

Six and a half thousand hymns written in one lifetime is an extraordinary feat. But this is the final tally of human hymnal, Charles Wesley (1707–88). While most of his hymns are now forgotten, many are still cherished. Think of 'Love divine...' or 'And can it be...' But arguably the best loved of all is 'Hark! The herald angels sing'.

Perhaps it was Monday's reading from Hebrews, with its reference to angels as 'spirits in divine service' (Hebrews 1.14) that has put me in mind of Wesley's carol. The line, 'veiled in flesh, the Godhead see' is taken by many to be unorthodox. They say it implies a divine Christ hidden behind the human Jesus, that Jesus of Nazareth is God's disguise. But what if the revelation *is* the veil, is made possible *by* the veil? After all, a screen separates, but it also displays. And a cinema without a screen, without a veil, would be useless. Jesus is not God's disguise, but God's self-disclosure.

Wesley's line suggests we can see the godhead only when it is veiled, *because* it is veiled. Likewise, for the writer of Hebrews, incarnation is identification. The deity becomes like us 'in every respect'. Flesh and the thousand natural shocks it is heir to, becomes the means whereby we are saved through God's atoning action in Christ Jesus.

We are saved, not from sufferings, but '*through* [his] sufferings'. He suffered – in the flesh – for us.

COLLECT

Almighty God,
you show to those who are in error the light of your truth,
that they may return to the way of righteousness:
grant to all those who are admitted
    into the fellowship of Christ's religion,
that they may reject those things
    that are contrary to their profession,
and follow all such things as are agreeable to the same;
through our Lord Jesus Christ,
who is alive and reigns with you,
in the unity of the Holy Spirit,
one God, now and for ever.

Reflection by **Colin Heber-Percy**

Psalm **34** *or* **78.1-39***
Genesis 45.1-15
Hebrews 3.1-6

Thursday 29 February

Hebrews 3.1-6

'... we are his house' (v.6)

Tucked into the courtyard of San Pietro in Montorio on the Gianicolo in Rome is the Tempietto, the Little Temple. Designed by Bramante in the early sixteenth century, the Tempietto is supposed to be built over the site of St Peter's crucifixion. It is tiny, more sculpture than building, a dummy run for Bramante's big commission – St Peter's basilica. Despite its being so small, and so hard to find, the Tempietto is a masterpiece of Renaissance Italian architecture.

The most significant feature of the building is also the most immediately obvious: it is perfectly circular, which means no aspect of this temple is more important than any other. Nothing is obscured behind an imposing façade. There is no backstage. No cheap seats. No grand apartments, no servants' quarters. No forgotten corners.

In his letter to the Ephesians, Paul talks of us being 'built together spiritually into a dwelling-place for God' (Ephesians 2.22). We are called to be built into a living, unified whole. This is not a temple we enter; we *are* the temple, his house. And as such, we are a circle, like the Tempietto, with Christ as the keystone, holding us together as 'holy partners in a heavenly calling'.

Walls divide. And in a wall, the stones or bricks are often all the same. In this circle, there are no dividing walls; and each stone – each 'partner', each Peter – is cut and dressed to serve a unique loving purpose.

Almighty God,
by the prayer and discipline of Lent
may we enter into the mystery of Christ's sufferings,
and by following in his Way
come to share in his glory;
through Jesus Christ our Lord.

COLLECT

Friday 1 March

Hebrews 3.7-end

'... as long as it is called "today"' (v.13)

You are reading these words today. How could it be otherwise? And yet I am writing these words to be read on a day that will be 'today' only for a brief twenty-four hours sometime in my future. Our passage for this twenty-four hours is concerned with history and time. We are urged to 'hold our first confidence firm to the end'. From yesterday, through today, and into tomorrow.

But this holding must not become a hardening. Hardening is related to sinfulness and rebellion and unbelief. Instead, we are called to 'hear his voice' and to remain obedient. Elsewhere, Paul commands us to 'stand firm and hold to the traditions which you were taught' (2 Thessalonians 2.15). And our word 'tradition' means – at its Latin root – to hand over, to hand on, or to surrender.

To hold today to the faith tradition of our ancestors does not mean we are backward looking. Precisely the opposite. We do not look back *to* the past, we look out *from* the past. For God 'has put a sense of past and future into [our] minds, yet [we] cannot find out what God has done from the beginning to the end' (Ecclesiastes 3.11). To try to find out, to put God to the test is to break the terms of our surrender, and to harden.

In faith, and as partners of Christ we live today. And it is always today.

C O L L E C T

Almighty God,
you show to those who are in error the light of your truth,
that they may return to the way of righteousness:
grant to all those who are admitted
    into the fellowship of Christ's religion,
that they may reject those things
    that are contrary to their profession,
and follow all such things as are agreeable to the same;
through our Lord Jesus Christ,
who is alive and reigns with you,
in the unity of the Holy Spirit,
one God, now and for ever.

　Reflection by **Colin Heber-Percy**

Psalms 3, **25** *or* **76**, 79
Genesis 46.1-7, 28-end
Hebrews 4.1-13

Saturday 2 March

Hebrews 4.1-13

'... his rest is still open' (v.1)

'Busy' is often our stock answer to the question, 'How are you?' or 'How are things?' We take pride in our being busy. It suggests we are wanted, in demand, and unavailable. A busy phone line means our call cannot be answered. 'All our operators are busy right now…'

To be busy is to be restless. And, as Augustine prays in the opening chapter of his *Confessions*, 'our hearts are restless till they rest in you.' In our restlessness and distraction, we are operators, conformed to the business of the world.

Our ancestors, as the writer of Hebrews makes clear, were not listening, were disobedient, and therefore failed to find rest. In short, they had closed themselves to the good news that comes to us and offers rest.

We think of rest as taken or earned. But here rest is *entered*. Paradoxically, to enter this rest takes effort. There are six days before the Sabbath, but those six days find their point and their end in rest. Likewise, our efforts and our toil make sense only with rest as their reward.

The call in this passage is to make every effort to remain faithful and obedient to the promised rest that is the meaning of our lives, our sole purpose and end.

If busy is closed, rest remains open. Ultimately, we are never restless. Our call will be taken, and heard.

Almighty God,
by the prayer and discipline of Lent
may we enter into the mystery of Christ's sufferings,
and by following in his Way
come to share in his glory;
through Jesus Christ our Lord.

COLLECT

Reflection by **Colin Heber-Percy**   87

Monday 4 March

Hebrews 4.14 – 5.10

'... a great high priest' (4.14)

In my early twenties I attended a church where the vicar would use this passage as an invitation to confession: 'Seeing we have a great high priest who has passed into the heavens...' After one service, I approached the vicar and asked, 'Who is this great high priest?' I imagined some eminent prelate had recently gone to their reward. The vicar looked at me. 'Jesus,' he said. 'Jesus is our great high priest.' What? I had never imagined Jesus as a high priest. And truth be told, I still don't, or not often.

We tend to think of Jesus as a baby in a manger, or as an inspired and itinerant teacher, as a charismatic leader, innocent victim of oppression or/and as the Messiah, Christ, Son of God. But a priest? Surely, as representatives of religious and temporal authority, the priests are those whom Jesus comes to confront with their hypocrisy and worldly values? How can we think of him as 'one of them'?

But priesthood, as defined in this passage, is sacrificial and vocational; it demands obedience and 'reverent submission'. So Jesus is not just a priest, but the very model and measure of a universal and cosmic priesthood. That we are unable to attain to the perfection of this model is the point. We don't have to. He has 'in every respect been tested, as we are' so that *through him* we may 'receive mercy and find grace'.

COLLECT

Almighty God,
whose most dear Son went not up to joy
    but first he suffered pain,
and entered not into glory before he was crucified:
mercifully grant that we, walking in the way of the cross,
may find it none other than the way of life and peace;
through Jesus Christ your Son our Lord,
who is alive and reigns with you,
in the unity of the Holy Spirit,
one God, now and for ever.

| *Reflection by* **Colin Heber-Percy**

Tuesday 5 March

Hebrews 5.11 – 6.12

'... unskilled in the word of righteousness' (5.13)

Is righteousness a skill we can learn, a faculty we can train? We are used to thinking of Christianity as having less to do with our understanding, however dull it may be, and more to do with faith and love. There is a danger in this: that we make our faith fluffy in an effort to render it palatable for all, more widely appealing and 'relevant'.

Writing in the seventeenth century, Brother Lawrence says in *The Practice of the Presence of God* that 'We must know before we can love.' Knowledge or understanding is a prerequisite.

A new member of a Bible study group confessed to me recently that she felt uncomfortable after an evening meeting. 'You're all so much further on in your faith than I am,' she said. I found myself trying to allay her fears by suggesting there is no 'further on' in faith, that we are all learning all the time. While this may not be false, there was, I now suspect, a hint of disinguousness in my answer.

Because, according to Hebrews, we *can* progress – by diligence, practice, and imitation – from infancy to maturity, from milk to solid food. And we do this through attention to the teaching, through learning, through knowing stuff.

By ducking difficult questions and skirting complexities we may be in danger of watering down 'the word of righteousness' and our theological tradition, offering milk when the world is hungry for solid food.

Eternal God,
give us insight
to discern your will for us,
to give up what harms us,
and to seek the perfection we are promised
in Jesus Christ our Lord.

COLLECT

Reflection by **Colin Heber-Percy** | 89

Wednesday 6 March

Psalm **38** *or* **119.105-128**
Genesis 49.1-32
Hebrews 6.13-end

Hebrews 6.13-end

'... behind the curtain' (v.19)

When Dorothy pulls aside the curtain in Oz's throne room she finds, not a mighty wizard, but an ordinary bloke with a microphone. Faith in the wizard turns out to be 'smoke and mirrors'; it is groundless.

When we swear an oath, we swear on that which is greater than ourselves. That which is greater than us acts as surety, as guarantor, as ground. But, as St Anselm puts it, 'God is that than which nothing greater can be conceived.' So who underwrites God's promise? God, according to our passage. Is this not like Baron Munchausen pulling himself out of the swamp by his own hair? Or me pulling myself up by my bootstraps? If I draw the curtain aside, will I find something Oz-ish, unsupported and arbitrary? Smoke and mirrors?

While 'all things are possible with God' (Matthew 19.26; Mark 10.27), there remains a class of actions not open to God (or any other agent). These are not actions which, as a matter of fact, God cannot perform; they are things logically impossible, like constructing a circle that has corners.

God is not true to his word; God *is* the truth. So 'it is impossible that God would prove false'. For God's promise to prove false would be for God not to be God. This is not a proof, but a promise. A promise *as person* preceding us and entering 'the shrine behind the curtain'.

C O L L E C T	Almighty God, whose most dear Son went not up to joy but first he suffered pain, and entered not into glory before he was crucified: mercifully grant that we, walking in the way of the cross, may find it none other than the way of life and peace; through Jesus Christ your Son our Lord, who is alive and reigns with you, in the unity of the Holy Spirit, one God, now and for ever.

Reflection by **Colin Heber-Percy**

Genesis 49.33 – end of 50
Hebrews 7.1-10

Thursday 7 March

Hebrews 7.1-10

'... without genealogy' (v.3)

Surely Melchizedek is a walk on, a supporting artist, an extra? Apart from this fleeting, two verse passage from Genesis (14.18-20) to which the writer of Hebrews refers, only one other mention of Melchizedek occurs in the Old Testament. In Psalm 110 we find, 'You are a priest forever according to the order of Melchizedek.' And that's it. So what does the writer find in these brief glimpses of an obscure King of Salem that is so vital?

Psalm 110 is the most cited psalm in the New Testament (mainly here in Hebrews). Glorying in the victory of God's priest-king, the psalm was taken by Christians from the earliest days to tell of Christ's coming in judgement and power.

Whereas Matthew and Luke in their Gospels are keen to provide a genealogy for Jesus, establishing him as a scion of the house of David, the writer of Hebrews places that which is superior outside of history. Melchizedek's authority rests in his being 'without father, without mother, without genealogy'. Melchizedek comes to occupy a transcendent position, beyond time and space, in virtue of his having no history. No 'begats' precede him or follow him; he is lineage-less.

This shadowy extra in the narrative of scripture turns out to be the threshold between God and the world, between transcendence and immanence, between promise and fulfilment. And Christ is the one who steps across that threshold.

Eternal God,
give us insight
to discern your will for us,
to give up what harms us,
and to seek the perfection we are promised
in Jesus Christ our Lord.

COLLECT

Friday 8 March

Psalm **22** *or* **88** (95)
Exodus 1.1-14
Hebrews 7.11-end

Hebrews 7.11-end

'... approach God' (v.19)

How do we approach God? Through the law, or through the Life? Presenting the argument of Hebrews as a dichotomy like this does a deep disservice to the text, and raises the spectre of antisemitism that has had disastrous consequences throughout European history. In short, Hebrews does not rehearse an argument against Judaism, but within Judaism.

A superficial and specious reading of Hebrews might suggest the author points to a turning over of the Temple, an abandoning of the old dispensation, and an abrogation of the law. Rather than advocating severance or schism, however, the writer talks of change. 'When there is a change in the priesthood, there is necessarily a change in the law.' This is not inevitably a total break with tradition or the law, but a new way of belonging to that tradition and abiding by that law.

In fact, Hebrews out-conserves the conservatives by attesting to the validation of Christ Jesus' priestly ministry according to the order of Melchizedek. The Epistle to the Hebrews offers, not something radically new, but something radically old, and better: a 'better hope', a 'better covenant'.

How do we approach God? Through a better hope, a saving promise. And this will demand our relying, not on priests to offer gifts and make sacrifices on our behalf 'day after day' but by relying today and always on him, the high priest who offered himself as sacrifice once for all.

COLLECT

Almighty God,
whose most dear Son went not up to joy
    but first he suffered pain,
and entered not into glory before he was crucified:
mercifully grant that we, walking in the way of the cross,
may find it none other than the way of life and peace;
through Jesus Christ your Son our Lord,
who is alive and reigns with you,
in the unity of the Holy Spirit,
one God, now and for ever.

Reflection by **Colin Heber-Percy**

Psalm **31** *or* 96, **97**, 100
Exodus 1.22 – 2.10
Hebrews 8

Saturday 9 March

Hebrews 8

'... a sketch and shadow' (v.5)

A few years ago, at an exhibition of Raphael's drawings, I was captivated by a sketch of the resurrection. People's bodies, tumbling away from the tomb like victims in an explosion, express shock, wonder, and fear. The deft sketch was made on a discarded piece of paper into which a compass point had previously been pressed. Turning over the page, Raphael used the compass's puncture hole as the inspiration and focus of his new composition. The empty hole in the page, like the empty tomb, becomes like a singularity at the heart-start of a Big Bang. 'I am about to do a new thing; now it springs forth, do you not perceive it?' (Isaiah 43.19).

What was obsolete disappears by being turned over, like a page, what was damaged becomes the entry point for the faultless. It would be hard to find a better illustration of the meaning of the resurrection, or the message of Hebrews with its call for us to recognise the transcendence of Christ, our high priest who has 'now obtained a more excellent ministry.'

The 'sketch and shadow' of this world with its laws and temples and traditions is suddenly and explosively pierced with 'a new covenant', a new truth. There is no longer need for teaching or for the law to command 'Know the Lord' for we have been turned over, and what was damage is now blessing, what was an end is now a beginning.

Eternal God,
give us insight
to discern your will for us,
to give up what harms us,
and to seek the perfection we are promised
in Jesus Christ our Lord.

COLLECT

Reflection by **Colin Heber-Percy**

Monday 11 March

Psalms 70, **77** *or* **98**, 99, 101
Exodus 2.11-22
Hebrews 9.1-14

Hebrews 9.1-14

'Christ came as a high priest of the good things...' (v.11a)

The Letter to the Hebrews is charged with powerful imagery. Jesus is both great high priest and Son of God. This theologically exciting vision of Christ can be intimidating. Then a phrase which draws one deeper into mystery: 'Christ came as a high priest of the good things that have come'. For all the highly ritualised and cosmic language which speaks of Jesus entering once for all into the holy place to obtain eternal redemption with his blood, we can rest in the knowledge that he is the priest of the good things. What might they be? Surely these are the things which flow out of restored relationship and intimacy with God: forgiveness and friendship; refreshed love and hope, and the breaking down of all that might separate us from the love of God.

Indeed, the offer of intimacy with God himself, in and through Jesus, is the greatest thing. Through Christ we are invited to re-enter and renew our place as people of gift: we are invited to recognise that all we have comes from God and the only appropriate response is thanksgiving and praise. For in Christ, we are not separated from the good things of God, but discover that such good things are our abiding dwelling place. For all the high falutin language, Christ's love calls us home. We discover that our home is found in our dwelling-place with God.

COLLECT

Merciful Lord,
absolve your people from their offences,
that through your bountiful goodness
we may all be delivered from the chains of those sins
which by our frailty we have committed;
grant this, heavenly Father,
for Jesus Christ's sake, our blessed Lord and Saviour,
who is alive and reigns with you,
in the unity of the Holy Spirit,
one God, now and for ever.

| *Reflection by* **Rachel Mann**

Psalms 54, **79** *or* **106*** *(or* 103)
Exodus 2.23 – 3.20
Hebrews 9.15-end

Tuesday 12 March

Hebrews 9.15-end

'He is the mediator of a new covenant...' (v.15a)

Many scholars have suggested that Hebrews was written to a group of persecuted Jewish Christians tempted to give up following Jesus. If that view has been questioned in recent scholarship, one cannot avoid how Jesus is seemingly presented as the one who supersedes the Jewish gift of law and covenant. He is 'the mediator of a new covenant'. When Hebrews was likely to have been composed, the dynamics between Jewish and Gentile Christians were complex. Nonetheless, two thousand years on, in the light of millennia of anti-semitism, stoked and often facilitated by bad readings of the Christian scriptures, there are fresh challenges when we speak of a new covenant.

This is not the place to attempt a deep dive into Hebrews' place in anti-semitic discourse. It is possible, however, to claim a rich understanding of Jesus as the mediator of a new covenant without trashing the old. We read that Jesus 'has appeared once for all at the end of the age to remove sin by the sacrifice of himself'. Christ's self-sacrifice is an invitation for us to encounter God's redemptive love poured out for all. Nonetheless, I have long believed that, in Christ, non-Jews are grafted into an older Jewish story of God's love and salvation. Old and new Covenant are not in competition, but reveal the abiding desire of God for all to be in deep reconciled relationship with him and one another.

Merciful Lord,
you know our struggle to serve you:
when sin spoils our lives
and overshadows our hearts,
come to our aid
and turn us back to you again;
through Jesus Christ our Lord.

COLLECT

Wednesday 13 March

Hebrews 10.1-18

'... every priest stands day after day at his service' (v.11)

Hebrews is rich with the language of priesthood. While its writer is at pains to emphasise the cosmic power of Christ's priesthood at the expense of Old Testament priesthood, the Letter is, nonetheless, an invitation to reflect deeply on the meaning of priestly vocation.

For many of us, whether ordained or not, reflecting on priesthood and vocation too readily resolves into what it means to be a 'dog-collar wearer' or not. However, it is worth reminding ourselves that we are all – through baptism – part of what St Peter calls the priesthood of all believers. This royal priesthood, formed in Jesus Christ, is shaped by service and love. Those who follow Jesus are not called to lord it over others, but to be liberated into service as our Lord serves: 'by a single offering he has perfected for all time those who are sanctified.' This is not the 'holier than thou' perfection of the self-satisfied, but the humility of those who have been liberated to become their true selves.

As one of the 'dog-collar' variety of priests, I am only too conscious that being a priest is one of the ways Christ has called me into loving service. It is Christ who really matters, though. Ultimately, priesthood is the way God holds me and calls me into life. The royal priesthood of all believers flows from Jesus Christ, the priest of all creation.

COLLECT | Merciful Lord,
absolve your people from their offences,
that through your bountiful goodness
we may all be delivered from the chains of those sins
which by our frailty we have committed;
grant this, heavenly Father,
for Jesus Christ's sake, our blessed Lord and Saviour,
who is alive and reigns with you,
in the unity of the Holy Spirit,
one God, now and for ever.

| *Reflection by* **Rachel Mann**

Thursday 14 March

Hebrews 10.19-25

*'... let us consider how to provoke one another to love
and good deeds' (v.24)*

Provocation is not a word one hears very often in church. More often than not we talk of relationship, peace, love, and forgiveness. Provocation appears aggressive; being provocative is something many Christians avoid.

There is something arresting, then, about how the Letter to the Hebrews dares to suggest that there is a place for it. The Letter's first audience is exhorted not only to persevere in its devotion without wavering and to come into God's fellowship with a 'true heart in full assurance of faith', but to find a place for provocation.

'And let us consider how to provoke one another to love and good deeds...' Provocation here might also mean to stimulate or stir-up. However, I like the intensity of the word provocation. It has implications of 'incite' and 'call forth'. I suspect many of us hear such words in connection with acts of violence, or calling forth anger or division. In Hebrews the people of God are invited to incite and call one another to love and good deeds.

We live in challenging times, in both the Church and the wider world. We are exhausted and the world is weary too. We, like the Letter's original audience, might be tempted to neglect 'to meet together' and connect as we ought. Perhaps it's time we were all a bit more provocative. Certainly, the world could do with more love and good deeds.

Merciful Lord,
you know our struggle to serve you:
when sin spoils our lives
and overshadows our hearts,
come to our aid
and turn us back to you again;
through Jesus Christ our Lord.

COLLECT

Reflection by **Rachel Mann**

Friday 15 March

Psalm **102** *or* **139**
Exodus 6.2-13
Hebrews 10.26-end

Hebrews 10.26-end

'It is a fearful thing to fall into the hands of the living God' (v.31)

'Where will you spend eternity? Heaven or hell?' When I was a curate I walked past those lines, printed on a poster in an underpass, every day on my way to church. Though memorable, the questions did not encourage me in my faith. I think the Christian Fellowship that had posted it thought it would motivate readers to follow Jesus. It was a 'gotcha'. While I too want people to come to faith in Jesus, to me the poster read as a cheap threat.

Threats can motivate, but typically only by generating fear of consequences. Today's passage certainly holds its share of threat. It suggests that those in the Christian community who spurn Jesus will deserve a punishment so harsh it will make the death meted out to those who spurned Moses pale into insignificance.

Fear, of course, has multiple meanings. Today's passage says, 'it is a fearful thing to fall into the hands of the living God.' For me, the fearful reality of God generates awe rather than anxiety. The living God is genuinely awesome. If threat is implied, the threat of the living God applies to our craven schemes and desires. The living God 'threatens' us with the fullness of life and love; he offers an opportunity to walk into the fullness of life. Will we have the courage to take that path?

COLLECT

Merciful Lord,
absolve your people from their offences,
that through your bountiful goodness
we may all be delivered from the chains of those sins
which by our frailty we have committed;
grant this, heavenly Father,
for Jesus Christ's sake, our blessed Lord and Saviour,
who is alive and reigns with you,
in the unity of the Holy Spirit,
one God, now and for ever.

Reflection by **Rachel Mann**

Psalms **32** *or* 120, **121**, 122
Exodus 7.8-end
Hebrews 11.1-16

Saturday 16 March

Hebrews 11.1-16

'Faith is the assurance of things hoped for, the conviction of things not seen' (v.1)

In recent years there has been a huge upsurge of interest in tracing one's family tree. The 'ancestry industry' has become vast; searching for family history has never been easier. Perhaps, in these uncertain times and the ongoing societal retreat from organised religion, searching for one's family tree can offer a form of reassurance. A family tree can make one feel as if one has a history and a story to which one / we belong(s).

Scripture, too, has more than its fair share of genealogies, including the genealogy of Jesus in Matthew's Gospel. The Bible doesn't shy away from ancestors and today's reading invites us to meditate on the witness of our forebears in faith.

However, Abraham, Sarah *et al.* are not presented as causes of hope simply because they are ancestors. They matter because of what they reveal about faith. They show that faith involves living by promises and walking into hope. This is a costly way, for, as our forebears in faith reveal, we shall not, in this life, all reach the promised land. Still, we are invited to persist, for faith is 'the assurance of things hoped for'.

Faith is, I think, like planting a tree: one may not live to see it grow to full maturity, but still we plant it, in promise and hope. Faith requires trust: trust that, no matter what, God will bring the tree of goodness to its full flowering.

Merciful Lord,
you know our struggle to serve you:
when sin spoils our lives
and overshadows our hearts,
come to our aid
and turn us back to you again;
through Jesus Christ our Lord.

COLLECT

Reflection by **Rachel Mann**   99

Monday 18 March   Psalms **73**, 121 *or* 123, 124, 125, **126**
Exodus 8.1-19
Hebrews 11.17-31

Hebrews 11.17-31

'...he persevered as though he saw him who is invisible' (v.27b)

Over the past decade, I've had the privilege of working on various projects with theatre creatives. One of the things I've learned is how much the 'end product' – the performance – depends on the preparation. Rehearsal time is crucial; through repetition and reflection, a theatre company not only tests what can be wrung out from the script, but what that script looks like when it is 'put it on its feet', as they say, in real time. Rehearsal can be inspiring, tedious, tense, and hilarious. Theatre creatives want to offer a great end-product, but that simply won't happen without rehearsal.

Today's reading presents a form of rehearsal. The story of God's people is repeated over and over; as the motif 'by faith' is repeated, the hearer is invited deeper into the story. We are invited into the unfolding history of faith, discerning fresh nuance in its rehearsal.

The writer's use of a repeated motif is an example of the classic rhetorical device, *anaphora*. It's a technique used by poets, playwrights and, indeed, politicians, to aid memorability and underline what matters. While such a technique can be used – especially in the hands of a skilled public speaker – to whip up a crowd or bypass independent thought, when it is used to rehearse the story of God's pilgrim people we draw closer to God. We find our place more fully in God's definitive story.

COLLECT

Most merciful God,
who by the death and resurrection of your Son Jesus Christ
delivered and saved the world:
grant that by faith in him who suffered on the cross
we may triumph in the power of his victory;
through Jesus Christ your Son our Lord,
who is alive and reigns with you,
in the unity of the Holy Spirit,
one God, now and for ever.

Reflection by **Rachel Mann**

Psalms 25, 147.1-12
Isaiah 11.1-10
Matthew 13.54-end

Tuesday 19 March
Joseph of Nazareth

Matthew 13.54-end

'Is not this the carpenter's son?' (v.55a)

Joseph of Nazareth is a beautifully ambiguous saint. As Jesus' adoptive father, he is clearly a key figure in Christ's story, yet he is also a marginal one. His role is overshadowed, not least, by that of the Blessed Virgin Mary. Joseph operates both in the margins and in the main text of the Jesus story.

When the villagers ask, 'Is not this the carpenter's son?', I hear something of both shock and put-down. They imply not only that Jesus' true identity is bound up with and limited by his earthly father's, but also that Jesus' authority is no more than that of a carpenter's son.

However, Joseph's adoptive parenthood reconfigures familial authority and relationship in fresh and hopeful ways. He *is* Jesus' father; however, this is parenthood which holds space for Jesus to inhabit his full divine identity, not restricted by traditional social convention.

As we grow into the likeness of Christ, we too are invited to dwell ever more fully in the household of God. While many of us do have rich and nourishing experiences of family, it is by no means so for all. Perhaps part of what makes God's richer conception of family so potent is that there is always space at its heart for those of us, like Joseph, who seemingly have walk-on parts in the kingdom of heaven.

COLLECT

God our Father,
who from the family of your servant David
raised up Joseph the carpenter
to be the guardian of your incarnate Son
and husband of the Blessed Virgin Mary:
give us grace to follow him
in faithful obedience to your commands;
through Jesus Christ your Son our Lord,
who is alive and reigns with you,
in the unity of the Holy Spirit,
one God, now and for ever.

Reflection by **Rachel Mann**

Wednesday 20 March　　　Psalms **55**, 124 *or* **119.153-end**
Exodus 9.1-12
Hebrews 12.3-13

Hebrews 12.3-13

'Endure trials for the sake of discipline' (v.7)

I am just about old enough to remember the use of corporal punishment in schools. One image in particular is seared in my memory: the trembling distress and shame of an eleven-year-old boy in my class after he was slippered in front of us by the teacher. When I read of God disciplining or punishing his people like children, I instinctively balk at the idea. I associate discipline with violence and injustice. I go back to that scene in the classroom.

Perhaps a healthier way of seeing discipline is in terms of the call to discipleship. To grow as a disciple requires a willingness to adapt and shift. I've only met one person on my Christian journey who is the finished article and that's Jesus. When Hebrews says, 'God is treating you as children; for what child is there whom a parent does not discipline?', that question does not necessarily contain a suggestion of violence. The fact is that no child can hope to find her way in this world if she is totally feral; parents know that a child needs guidance.

I'm unconvinced that God deliberately sends trials to test and form us. However, in the company of that most loving parent, God, we have a faithful companion. In the midst of life's inevitable trials, he is present; not to diminish or hurt, but to show us the way to grow through them into the likeness of Christ.

C O L L E C T　Most merciful God,
who by the death and resurrection of your Son Jesus Christ
delivered and saved the world:
grant that by faith in him who suffered on the cross
we may triumph in the power of his victory;
through Jesus Christ your Son our Lord,
who is alive and reigns with you,
in the unity of the Holy Spirit,
one God, now and for ever.

| *Reflection by* **Rachel Mann**

Psalms **40**, 125 *or* **143**, 146   **Thursday 21 March**
Exodus 9.13-end
Hebrews 12.14-end

Hebrews 12.14-end

'See to it that no one fails to obtain the grace of God...' (v.15)

When I was a callow curate, my training incumbent said something which has stayed with me, 'The Church attracts the best and the worst.' I think I said in response, 'And sometimes the best and worst is contained in the same person.' My colleague's simple statement reminds us that we shouldn't be surprised if disagreements and bitter division break out in church: it reflects human life in all its pettiness, poverty, and, sometimes, its promise. Community includes saints and sinners.

The Letter to the Hebrews warns its readers to guard against the growth of bitterness among the community of God. That warning surely applies as much to the Church today. Given the messiness of human nature, and our capacity for division, it's difficult, especially if one feels hard done by, for some to resist the temptation to bitterness. I've certainly been tempted when I've felt the Church has been unjust in its treatment of LGBT+ people like me.

Nonetheless, as people of faith we are invited to live out an extraordinary challenge: 'See to it that no one fails to obtain the grace of God.' It is a command to leave no one behind. In particular, for those of us who exercise leadership in the Church, it is a command which should give us pause, for there is no appropriate collateral damage and no acceptable wastage in the kingdom of God.

Gracious Father,
you gave up your Son
out of love for the world:
lead us to ponder the mysteries of his passion,
that we may know eternal peace
through the shedding of our Saviour's blood,
Jesus Christ our Lord.

COLLECT

Reflection by **Rachel Mann**   103

Friday 22 March

Psalms **22**, 126 *or* 142, **144**
Exodus 10
Hebrews 13.1-16

Hebrews 13.1-16

'Do not neglect to show hospitality to strangers...' (v.2)

'Do not neglect to show hospitality to strangers, for by doing that some have entertained angels without knowing it.' Rightly, this is one of the Bible's most famous lines. It invites its readers to be rich in hospitality. Here, in the depths of the New Testament, is a call-back to that extraordinary encounter between Abraham and the three visitors at Mamre in Genesis 18. In that encounter Abraham and Sarah meet, in the three strangers, the very presence of God. When we are gracious to strangers, we can meet the living God.

This all sounds wonderful in principle. The Greek word used for stranger in this passage can mean foreigner or alien. However, it is increasingly clear that in many nations today there is, either consciously or unconsciously, often a distinction between good and bad foreigners. Some, such as those who have fled Ukraine, are seen as good; others as bad. Politicians and nations may or may not have sound criteria for discerning between those who are welcome to enter its community. However, the Bible is much more challenging. It asks people of faith to centre their lives on grace. Crucially, we are called to commit to forms of hospitality focussed on those outside or on the edge of the community. When we follow that path, we might entertain angels unawares.

COLLECT

Most merciful God,
who by the death and resurrection of your Son Jesus Christ
delivered and saved the world:
grant that by faith in him who suffered on the cross
we may triumph in the power of his victory;
through Jesus Christ your Son our Lord,
who is alive and reigns with you,
in the unity of the Holy Spirit,
one God, now and for ever.

| *Reflection by* **Rachel Mann**

Psalms **23**, 127 *or* **147**　　　　　　　**Saturday 23 March**
Exodus 11
Hebrews 13.17-end

Hebrews 13.17-end

'May the God of peace... make you complete in everything good'
(vv.20-21a)

In the light of Church abuse scandals – scandals centred on how those who hold power exploit the vulnerable – I blanch when I read 'Obey your leaders and submit to them, for they are keeping watch over your souls and will give an account.' Certainly, Hebrews was written in a context different to our own, with its own disciplinary challenges, but still we must read it in the context of our own Church.

Ultimately, however, it is the conclusion of Hebrews which brings us back to heart of the matter: we are called to be centred on the living God who is the God of peace. The crucial closing words of the letter constitute a benediction which invites God – the one who brought back from the dead our Lord Jesus, the great shepherd of the sheep – to make us complete in everything good.

Benediction means nothing more or less than 'speaking good'. I wish we, in the Church today, were more committed to blessing and speaking good of one another. Not because we are naïve about our power problems or are determined to let off a proper accountability those who've done wicked things, but because ultimately, we shall find our final, definitive identity in Jesus Christ. Ultimately, we shall stand before him. In this life, a little more benediction may help us do his will, that we may work among us all that is pleasing in his sight.

Gracious Father,
you gave up your Son
out of love for the world:
lead us to ponder the mysteries of his passion,
that we may know eternal peace
through the shedding of our Saviour's blood,
Jesus Christ our Lord.

COLLECT

Reflection by **Rachel Mann**　　105

Monday 25 March
Monday of Holy Week

Lamentations 1.1-12*a*

'O Lord, look at my affliction, for the enemy has triumphed!' (v.9)

As we walk towards the cross this week, we are summoned to stand there and see the depth and cost of God's love for us in Christ.

Probably written by the prophet Jeremiah who witnessed the fall of Jerusalem in 586 BC, the poems of sorrow, despair and devastation which make up the book of Lamentations have an always been used by the Church to help tell the story of Christ's death. Verses from Lamentations are sung on Good Friday; and particularly this verse, 'Is it nothing to you, all you who pass by? Look and see if there is any sorrow like my sorrow' (v.12), invites us to get inside the story of Christ's passion and the sorrow he carries.

Just as Jerusalem is described as being like a widow weeping, so the Church stands at the cross and weeps for the death of Christ. And even though we know this is not the end of the story, we have to get inside the reality of Christ's death and the meaning of his passion in order to fully receive and understand the resurrection. Therefore, we need to be brought to a place of weeping. And often it is the poems, the music and the drama of our liturgy that helps us to do this.

Jeremiah himself is sometimes called the weeping prophet. This week we are called to be weeping disciples.

COLLECT

Almighty and everlasting God,
who in your tender love towards the human race
    sent your Son our Saviour Jesus Christ
to take upon him our flesh
and to suffer death upon the cross:
grant that we may follow the example of his patience and humility,
and also be made partakers of his resurrection;
through Jesus Christ your Son our Lord,
who is alive and reigns with you,
in the unity of the Holy Spirit,
one God, now and for ever.

| *Reflection by* **Stephen Cottrell**

Psalm 27
Lamentations 3.1-18
Luke 22. [24-38] 39-53

Tuesday 26 March
Tuesday of Holy Week

Lamentations 3.1-18

'I have become the laughing-stock of all my people' (v.14)

Sometimes we read these Old Testament passages and it seems as if they describe the passion of Jesus. Other examples would be Psalm 22 or Isaiah 53. In this case it is almost as if Jesus is speaking to us himself from the cross: 'my flesh and my skin waste away...' (v.4); 'I have become a laughing stock...' (v.14); 'my soul is bereft of peace...' (v.17). But what is particularly disturbing here is that it is *God* who has brought about these travails. '*He* has filled me with bitterness' (v.15) says the writer of Lamentations.

In the context of the fall of Jerusalem, it is clear that this desolation and exile has been brought upon God's people because of their disobedience and faithlessness. But we can't say this of Jesus, the one who is obedient to God in all things.

No, Jesus *chooses* the way of faithful obedience, even to suffering and death. He plumbs the depths of what it is to be human. He carries our sorrows and failings. He even experiences abandonment from God as he cries out in Mark's Gospel, 'Why have you forsaken me?' (Mark 15.34). He experiences the terrible consequences of sin and death, but is without sin himself. He does this for us.

True and humble king,
hailed by the crowd as Messiah:
grant us the faith to know you and love you,
that we may be found beside you
on the way of the cross,
which is the path of glory.

COLLECT

Reflection by **Stephen Cottrell** | 107

Wednesday 27 March

Wednesday of Holy Week

Psalm 102 [*or* 102.1-18]
Wisdom 1.16 – 2.1; 2.12-22
or Jeremiah 11.18-20
Luke 22.54-end

Jeremiah 11.18-20

'I was like a gentle lamb led to the slaughter' (v.19)

The first Christians came to believe that Jesus suffered, died and rose again *in accordance with* the scriptures – a phrase that pops up in scripture itself and in the Nicene Creed which many of us say each week. So when Paul tells the story of his conversion, he insists that he is 'saying nothing but what the prophets and Moses said would come to pass: that the Christ must suffer and... rise from the dead' (Acts 26.22,23). Therefore, they looked at the Old Testament passages that spoke of a suffering servant, or in today's case, 'a gentle lamb led to the slaughter' (v.19), and saw in them a foreshadowing of what God had done for us in Jesus. They then tell the story with reference to these passages.

John's Gospel, for instance, begins with John the Baptist saying, 'Look, there is the Lamb of God' (John 1.29). You could argue that the whole Gospel is then told to help us discover what that means; that what happened to Jesus was according to God's purposes from the beginning, and that Jesus is the Passover Lamb who takes our sins away.

Jesus does commit his cause to the Lord (v.20). He is vindicated. But it is *through* suffering and death, not around it. In these next few days we find out what that means.

COLLECT

Almighty and everlasting God,
who in your tender love towards the human race
    sent your Son our Saviour Jesus Christ
to take upon him our flesh
and to suffer death upon the cross:
grant that we may follow the example of his patience and humility,
and also be made partakers of his resurrection;
through Jesus Christ your Son our Lord,
who is alive and reigns with you,
in the unity of the Holy Spirit,
one God, now and for ever.

| *Reflection by* **Stephen Cottrell**

Psalms 42, 43
Leviticus 16.2-24
Luke 23.1-25

Thursday 28 March
Maundy Thursday

Leviticus 16.2-24

'Thus he shall make atonement...' (v.16)

The book of Leviticus gives careful and precise instructions for how the priests are to conduct the sacrifices in the Temple that, in the sacrifice of Jesus, are rendered superfluous. But they also help us to understand that sacrifice. In this case Jesus himself is become the 'scapegoat' upon whom other people's sins and transgressions are piled.

How does this work? How can Jesus carry my sins? How can he forgive what other people have done wrong? After all, he isn't the victim?

The answer lies on the cross. And since it is true that only the one who has been wronged has the right to forgive, Jesus, the one person who is without sin, becomes, as it were, the ultimate victim. He carries my sinfulness. And its consequence.

On the night before he dies, breaking bread and sharing wine, Jesus shows his friends how his death will be a sacrifice, an offering of himself, his body broken, his blood shed. It is a kind of 'acted parable'. The disciples didn't understand it at the time. How could they? But days later they remembered – and carried on remembering.

For those of us who follow Jesus, this astonishing good news of God's forgiveness is renewed and its benefits given to us in the sacrifice of the Eucharist. We, too, remember. And as this evening falls, Christian people across the world will gather and make this Eucharist, this remembrance, together.

True and humble king,
hailed by the crowd as Messiah:
grant us the faith to know you and love you,
that we may be found beside you
on the way of the cross,
which is the path of glory.

COLLECT

Reflection by **Stephen Cottrell** | 109

Friday 29 March

Good Friday

Psalm 69
Genesis 22.1-18
Hebrews 10.1-10

Genesis 22.1-18

'On the mount of the Lord it shall be provided' (v.14)

These anxious and uncomprehending words of Isaac to his father Abraham, echo down the centuries, 'The fire and the wood are here, but where is the lamb for a burnt-offering?' And they find their fulfilment in Jesus.

Abraham is being asked to do something unimaginably horrific, to sacrifice his own son. Trusting, but also uncomprehending, Abraham replies, 'God himself will provide the lamb for a burnt-offering, my son' (v.8). He cannot imagine that this will be fulfilled upon the cross. At the terrible moment as he draws the knife, he sees a ram caught in as thicket and presumes this is what God meant. But the real understanding is found in St John's account of the passion of Jesus, the account that is read in most churches across the world at the Good Friday liturgy today. Departing from Matthew, Mark and Luke's chronology where Jesus is crucified on the day after the Passover, in John's Gospel Jesus is crucified on the day of the festival itself; and John times the crucifixion precisely so that it takes place at the same time as the Passover lambs are being sacrificed in the Temple. The point is plain. Jesus is the true Passover lamb. The Lord has provided. And carrying his own cross, Jesus is obedient to death. By his wounds, we are healed.

COLLECT

Almighty Father,
look with mercy on this your family
for which our Lord Jesus Christ was content to be betrayed
    and given up into the hands of sinners
    and to suffer death upon the cross;
who is alive and glorified with you and the Holy Spirit,
one God, now and for ever.

| *Reflection by* **Stephen Cottrell**

Psalm 142
Hosea 6.1-6
John 2.18-22

Saturday 30 March
Easter Eve

Hosea 6.1-6

'Let us press on to know the Lord; his appearing is as sure as the dawn' (v.3)

Holy Saturday. The day after. And the day before. The bleakest, loneliest day of the year. The emptiest day. All our hopes buried.

Jesus is dead. And Jesus is not yet risen.

It's hard for us to get inside this day. We are busy polishing brass and arranging lilies for tomorrow's celebrations. But today is the one day of the year when there is no water in the font. We are called to wait for the Lord.

And even if we can't imaginatively lay aside our knowledge of the resurrection, and even if we are busy, it is good to wait. Even for a few moments. For even if we believe that Christ is risen there will be other doubts and sorrows inside us. And provided we don't keep pressing them down, they will find voice in today's scriptures. For our love for God is often like morning mist that quickly disappears. And we are forever making deals with God – or at least trying to! – when what God wants from us is steadfast love.

He has done away with sacrifices now. And he will come to us like the spring showers that water the earth, he will heal us and bind us up.

All this is waiting for us. And we must wait too.

Come, let us return to the Lord.

Grant, Lord,
that we who are baptized into the death
of your Son our Saviour Jesus Christ
may continually put to death our evil desires
and be buried with him;
and that through the grave and gate of death
we may pass to our joyful resurrection;
through his merits,
who died and was buried and rose again for us,
your Son Jesus Christ our Lord.

COLLECT

Reflection by **Stephen Cottrell** | 111

Monday I April

Monday of Easter Week

Psalms **111**, 117, 146
Exodus 12.1-14
I Corinthians 15.1-11

Exodus 12.1-14

'This day shall be a day of remembrance for you' (v.14)

The great festival of Easter is the Christian Passover. Just as the blood of the sacrificed lambs was a sign on the houses of God's people to prevent the angel of death visiting them and to pass over, so the blood of Jesus saves us.

All this talk of blood and sacrifice is hard for us to comprehend today. To be sure, we still know about suffering and sacrifice since so many people in our world today are having to make so many sacrifices. But it's hard for us to understand a sacrificial system whereby the blood of sheep and goats makes peace with God. But that was the world into which Jesus was born, and the point is this: he came to do away with it, to supersede it, to fulfil it.

We do indeed need to make our peace with God. Each of us faces the reality of death and lives with the consequences of our failings and sinfulness. We have fallen short of what we are called be.

Jesus deals with this by becoming the one who takes all this upon himself and unites us to God. The resurrection is the great sign of his vindication. It is God who raises Jesus to life, and us with him. Hence the powerful symbolism of dying and rising in our baptism. We are saved. Not just *from* sin and death, but *for* life eternal.

COLLECT

Lord of all life and power,
who through the mighty resurrection of your Son
overcame the old order of sin and death
to make all things new in him:
grant that we, being dead to sin
and alive to you in Jesus Christ,
may reign with him in glory;
to whom with you and the Holy Spirit
be praise and honour, glory and might,
now and in all eternity.

| *Reflection by* **Stephen Cottrell**

Psalms 112, 147.1-12
Exodus 12.14-36
1 Corinthians 15.12-19

Tuesday 2 April
Tuesday of Easter Week

Exodus 12.14-36

*'The Lord had given the people favour in the sight of
the Egyptians' (v.36)*

The story of the liberation of the people of God from Egypt is stirring
and powerful. Plague after plague is visited on Egypt. Again and
again, Pharoah's heart is hardened against the Hebrew slave people
and their leader, Moses. Eventually a tenth plague strikes down all
the first born: their children, their livestock, everything. Pharoah's
own son is dead: a sorrowful counterpoint to God sparing Isaac and
vindicating Jesus.

What sense can we make of it? Must Pharoah bear all the
responsibility? And more is to come as he sends his troops after the
escaping Israelites and they lose their lives too. Do we still secretly
fear that this is what God is really like – that he may strike us too?

The people of Israel are freed from crushing slavery, but Egypt is
crushed in return. It is all too familiar in a world still full of despots
and slaves, conflict and liberation.

On the cross Jesus embraces all this horror. He dies for oppressor and
oppressed; for Israelite and Egyptian. At Easter he resets the world in
a different way. His first words to Mary Magdalene are addressed to
us as well: 'Why are you weeping? For whom are you looking?' The
risen Christ reaches out to the sorrow of our hearts. He invites us to
set our compass by him (see John 20.15).

God of glory,
by the raising of your Son
you have broken the chains of death and hell:
fill your Church with faith and hope;
for a new day has dawned
and the way to life stands open
in our Saviour Jesus Christ.

COLLECT

Reflection by **Stephen Cottrell** | 113

Wednesday 3 April

Wednesday of Easter Week

Psalms 113, 147.13-end
Exodus 12.37-end
1 Corinthians 15.20-28

Exodus 12.37-end

*'That very day the Lord brought the Israelites out of the land
of Egypt' (v.51)*

The Passover meal is a meal only the saved can share in. Hence the rules about only those who have been circumcised being allowed to share in the meal, for circumcision is the sign of the covenant between the Jewish people and God. This is also why there is so much discussion in the early Church about whether Gentiles coming for baptism need first to be circumcised (you can read about this in Paul's letters and in the Acts of the Apostles).

This is another issue it is quite hard for us to get our heads around. It seems obvious to us that what God has done in the death and resurrection of Christ has created a new covenant of which baptism is the sign, and that baptism trumps everything else—that water is thicker than blood.

But it wasn't obvious then. Not to those who had striven so faithfully to keep the law of Moses, and who knew what happened to those who didn't. But they changed—changed their own traditions—because of what they had seen and experienced in Jesus.

Now we too have a challenge. Who are we excluding from the table? What are the obvious things we are missing? How can we ensure that the aliens in our midst, the strangers and the excluded are invited to the table of the new Passover?

COLLECT

Lord of all life and power,
who through the mighty resurrection of your Son
overcame the old order of sin and death
to make all things new in him:
grant that we, being dead to sin
and alive to you in Jesus Christ,
may reign with him in glory;
to whom with you and the Holy Spirit
be praise and honour, glory and might,
now and in all eternity.

| *Reflection by* **Stephen Cottrell**

Psalms 114, 148
Exodus 13.1-16
1 Corinthians 15.29-34

Thursday 4 April

Thursday of Easter Week

Exodus 13.1-16

'Moses said to the people, "Remember this day..."' (v.3)

God instructs Moses to tell the people that when they enter the Promised Land they are to remember what has happened to them and how their salvation was achieved. They will do this with festivals and customs. In this way, the remembrance of what God has done will be fixed in their memory, enacted year by year, celebrated and understood.

The Christian Eucharist works in the same way. At its heart is the word 'remembrance' which we can now see doesn't simply mean looking back, but, by ritual and thanksgiving, bringing into the present.

For the Israelites this meant unleavened bread, Passover and sacrifice, the offering of the first born of every animal to God and the redeeming of your own first born. But in the description of the Promised Land that they will enter, do we catch a glimpse of the kingdom that is ushered in by Christ's sacrifice, the sacrifice that does away with sacrifices? For this land is described as one that flows with milk and honey. And milk and honey are just about the only food available where no death is required. They are eucharistic. And the Eucharist is a foretaste of the promised land which is heaven itself. Life feeds on life in a kingdom beyond the corruptibility of everything else we know about life, what scripture calls a new heaven and a new earth.

God of glory,
by the raising of your Son
you have broken the chains of death and hell:
fill your Church with faith and hope;
for a new day has dawned
and the way to life stands open
in our Saviour Jesus Christ.

COLLECT

Friday 5 April
Friday of Easter Week

Psalms **115**, 149
Exodus 13.17 – 14.14
1 Corinthians 15.35-50

Exodus 13.17 – 14.14

'The Lord will fight for you, and you have only to keep still.' (14.14)

Amid all the drama and horrors of the Exodus story, this verse about keeping still and the Lord fighting for you captures something vital about the deeper meaning of the narrative, which is not primarily about military victory, but faithfulness to God. An enslaved people is set free because they chooses obedience to God.

Maybe this also helps us make sense of the troubling verses in the story that keep telling us that the Lord is hardening Pharoah's heart again. 'Hasn't Egypt suffered enough?' we might say at this point. Yes, they had been cruel masters. They had forgotten Joseph. God's people had become enslaved and impoverished. But misery upon misery has been heaped upon Egypt and in those moments when Pharoah seemed to err on the side of mercy (or at least common sense) it is God, we are told, who changes Pharoah's mind. But this too is the deeper meaning of the story. The God of Israel is the God of all the world and all the people and nations of the world, even mighty Pharoah.

Those who wrote down this story saw God's mighty hand and outstretched arm in these events. It took the cross and resurrection to learn that this same outstretched arm would have to be wounded itself for us to learn that keeping still must also mean not fighting back.

COLLECT

Lord of all life and power,
who through the mighty resurrection of your Son
overcame the old order of sin and death
to make all things new in him:
grant that we, being dead to sin
and alive to you in Jesus Christ,
may reign with him in glory;
to whom with you and the Holy Spirit
be praise and honour, glory and might,
now and in all eternity.

116 | *Reflection by* **Stephen Cottrell**

Psalms 116, 150
Exodus 14.15-end
1 Corinthians 15.51-end

Saturday 6 April
Saturday of Easter Week

Exodus 14.15-end

'The Israelites went into the sea on dry ground... The Egyptians pursued, and went into the sea after them, all of Pharaoh's horses, chariots, and chariot drivers.' (vv.22,23)

Picasso's painting, *Guernica*, is probably the most powerful anti-war painting in history, painted after the bombing of the Basque town of Guernica by Nazi German and Fascist Italian bombers. Amid the carnage Picasso portrays, one of the most striking images is of a screaming horse's head. It is as if the full horrific depravity of the situation could not be fully captured by depicting human suffering alone. An animal howls in bewildered agony.

Both horse and rider are drowned as the Red Sea turns, engulfing Pharoah's army. It is a scene of incomprehensible chaos and destruction. Triumph and liberation for Israel, but crushing defeat for Egypt. And since the gloating Song of Miriam is said at Morning Prayer throughout Eastertide, I find that after a few days I just can't help thinking about the Egyptian mothers whose sons won't come home – and the horses drowning.

Christ steps into this world of death and grief and temporary victories. In baptism we die with him. We step into the deep waters and are drowned with him. But we are also raised up. Christ and Christ alone is the one who saves us from the endless cycles of war, conquest, suffering and death. He is there for everyone in his victory over death. It is why our victory song is not about winners and losers. We all lost. We all went wrong. We all drowned.

Christ triumphs. Then takes us with him.

God of glory,
by the raising of your Son
you have broken the chains of death and hell:
fill your Church with faith and hope;
for a new day has dawned
and the way to life stands open
in our Saviour Jesus Christ.

COLLECT

Reflection by **Stephen Cottrell** | 117

Monday 8 April

Annunciation of Our Lord
to the Blessed Virgin Mary

Psalms 111, 113
I Samuel 2.1-10
Romans 5.12-end

1 Samuel 2.1-10

'My heart exults in the Lord; my strength is exalted in my God...'
(v.1)

The last time we heard Hannah praying she does so with deep distress and anguished tears, and is unjustly accused of being drunk (1.10, 14). This time when she prays, she does so with a rejoicing heart and a vigorous testimony and is justly remembered for generations. For she discovers not only that she has been personally 'lifted up' by a special gift from God, but also that she is part of a divine narrative where God passes over the haughty and arrogant to lift up and deliver all those on the margins, in the dust and on the ash heap. Hannah's own personal story embodies the continuous and creative acts of God who overturns weakness, poverty, shame and death. Rather than forgetting about her tears, she lets them energise and give life to her understanding of the Lord who raises up those found even in the grave.

Hannah is rightly audacious in singing that she belongs to God's universal story of radical deliverance. Perhaps today, when we remember the Annunciation of Our Lord, we might compare the song of Hannah with Mary's song, the Magnificat (Luke 1.46-55) in which Mary celebrates God weaving her story into his. Maybe today we could name how our story is woven into the divine plan to lift up and bring life. Where do our tears enliven our hope? Where does our rejoicing point to God's victory? How does the trail of dust or ash behind us tell of God's great deliverance for us?

COLLECT

We beseech you, O Lord,
pour your grace into our hearts,
that as we have known the incarnation of your Son Jesus Christ
    by the message of an angel,
so by his cross and passion
we may be brought to the glory of his resurrection;
through Jesus Christ your Son our Lord,
who is alive and reigns with you,
in the unity of the Holy Spirit,
one God, now and for ever.

118 | *Reflection by* **Emma Parker**

Psalms **8**, 20, 21 *or* **5**, 6 (8) **Tuesday 9 April**
Exodus 15.22 – 16.10
Colossians 1.15-end

Exodus 15.22—16.10

'And the people complained against Moses, saying,
"What shall we drink?"' (v.24)

The Exodus story is full of relentless surprises and contrasts. The people of Israel had watched plague after plague, they had witnessed the most extraordinary events, they had 'seen' God in pillars of fire and cloud, they had heard the haunting wails of grief and had sung great songs of victory. And now, having finally escaped, they are in a desert – without water. Are they going to be defeated at this point because of a lack of something as simple as water?

These people were undoubtedly traumatised. However, despite having seen God's power and how he has worked good for them, to protect and save them, here in the wilderness, in this next chapter of surprises, they seem to have forgotten that God hears, he sees, and he fights for them. Why do they wait three days before complaining about the lack of water?

Sometimes, when we are caught up in an intense time of shock or surprise (surprises can be pleasant and unpleasant), it is easy to be overwhelmed and find ourselves strangely silent before God. And when finally we find our voice, sometimes our cries and complaints are empty of memory that would otherwise fill them with anticipation of God's help. May we carve out time today to remember God's faithfulness; and may our remembering mobilise our cries always to be relentlessly expectant.

Almighty Father,
you have given your only Son to die for our sins
and to rise again for our justification:
grant us so to put away the leaven of malice and wickedness
that we may always serve you
in pureness of living and truth;
through the merits of your Son Jesus Christ our Lord,
who is alive and reigns with you,
in the unity of the Holy Spirit,
one God, now and for ever.

COLLECT

Reflection by **Emma Parker** | 119

Wednesday 10 April

Psalms 16, **30** *or* **119.1-32**
Exodus 16.11-end
Colossians 2.1-15

Exodus 16.11–end

'When the Israelites saw it, they said to one another, "What is it?"'
(v.15)

The Israelites are given the promise that in the morning they will be filled with bread (v.12). However, their mouth-watering, bread-filled dreams fall like the dew as they awake to find frost-like flakes causing them to ask, 'What is it?' They are not certain at all – and this uncertainty marks all their moves in this passage. They are certain neither about the gift nor about the trustworthiness of the instructions, and so some ignore them (vv.19-20, 27).

However, behind this uncertainty is not arrogance but fear rising from painful past experiences. How many times as slaves must they have gone hungry, been dehumanised, lost what little they had, and feared for their loved ones? No wonder these people are uncertain in the wilderness. We too can fail to trust in God when our fear of scarcity, powerlessness, and neglect overwhelms our faith. And so we hoard, we cling to the material, we plan according to the principle of uncertainty, and we miss the blessings, asking, 'What is this?'

When these people finally trust the instructions, the miracle is not only found in God abundantly providing food in a place of scarcity, but also in the people letting go of fear and trusting in God. The greatest miracles of God are sometimes the ones he works inside us. May we choose to leave our uncertainly behind and become part of the miracle too.

COLLECT

Almighty Father,
you have given your only Son to die for our sins
and to rise again for our justification:
grant us so to put away the leaven of malice and wickedness
that we may always serve you
in pureness of living and truth;
through the merits of your Son Jesus Christ our Lord,
who is alive and reigns with you,
in the unity of the Holy Spirit,
one God, now and for ever.

| *Reflection by* **Emma Parker**

Psalms **28**, 29 *or* 14, **15**, 16
Exodus 17
Colossians 2.16 – 3.11

Thursday 11 April

Exodus 17

'And Moses built an altar and called it, The Lord is my banner'
(v.15)

Fear over life and death has once again gripped the hearts of the people as they cry desperately to Moses and revert to their uncertainty about the presence, goodness and power of God in this place (v.3). When the way ahead looks unpromising it is easy for them to go back to old rhythms of anxiety even when their recent memories are filled with God's provision. Moses is increasingly frustrated and perhaps even frightened as he cries to God (v.4) and, although the narrator does not say so, the people must have cried in despair once more as they find themselves attacked.

This episode may leave us with many questions, but an overriding theme of the whole passage is that God never gives up on his people. Despite their failings, their propensity to choose fear rather than trust and hope, their anger at Moses and their silence where there should be thanks and praise, God does not turn away. God still hears, sees, and acts. God still loves these people with a passion and he means to stay with them throughout generations. God is their banner and always signals his deliverance.

During this season of Easter, we are reminded that this is still the overriding theme of the whole of creation: that despite and because of ourselves, God still stays. The Risen Christ raises up the banner that points to God's faithfulness and love for a broken world. Alleluia!

Risen Christ,
for whom no door is locked, no entrance barred:
open the doors of our hearts,
that we may seek the good of others
and walk the joyful road of sacrifice and peace,
to the praise of God the Father.

COLLECT

Reflection by **Emma Parker** | 121

Friday 12 April

Psalms 57, **61** *or* 17, **19**
Exodus 18.1-12
Colossians 3.12 – 4.1

Exodus 18.1–12

'Jethro rejoiced... and said, "Blessed be the Lord"' (vv.9-10)

After Miriam's song of praise, accompanied by tambourines and dancing by 'all the women' (15.20-21), the next time we hear rejoicing and praise is not until now, from the mouth of an outsider, Jethro. He wasn't even there to witness first-hand the goodness of the Lord, but as soon as he heard Moses's testimony, he rejoices, praises God, confesses and worships. Mirroring 'all the women' dancing with Miriam, we read that Aaron brings 'all the elders of Israel' to join in with this worship (v.12). My imagination also pictures 'all the women' gathering outside the tent, babies balanced on hips, girls linking arms with their grandmothers, as they dust off their tambourines and join in too.

It is striking that in the 58 verses from 15.22 to today's passage, where God has provided food, water and victory in the wilderness, there has not been a rumour of rejoicing, a word of worship, a peep of praise in response. The Israelites have really struggled; they have girded themselves with a cloak of pity and panic and haven't found a way to shrug it off. But now, it is the spontaneous praise of an outsider who takes off the grave clothes. It is Jethro, from a different place, a different tribe, a different history, who enables this faith community to learn to worship again. May we thank God today for all the 'outsiders' who have led God's people back to praise.

COLLECT

Almighty Father,
you have given your only Son to die for our sins
and to rise again for our justification:
grant us so to put away the leaven of malice and wickedness
that we may always serve you
in pureness of living and truth;
through the merits of your Son Jesus Christ our Lord,
who is alive and reigns with you,
in the unity of the Holy Spirit,
one God, now and for ever.

| *Reflection by* **Emma Parker**

Psalms 63, **84** *or* 20, 21, **23**   **Saturday 13 April**
Exodus 18.13-end
Colossians 4.2-end

Exodus 18.13–end

'What is this that you are doing for the people?' (v.14)

Jethro has brought not only praise, but also perspective. In a tricky situation, we might hear advice that tells us to 'step back' to see it afresh, but Moses has not had the chance to step back for a break, never mind perspective. He has gone from holding up the staff of God on top of a hill to sitting all day and every day in the middle of a throng of arguing people. Jethro, however, comes into this world that Moses is inhabiting, and brings perspective, suggesting a much better way to help the community quickly unpick their disputes and find peace.

Jethro names what is not good and how to make it good: he is able both to criticise and to encourage. This kind of insight is bold and unflinching in articulating harm (actual or potential) and inefficiency, but also generous and caring in offering guidance and encouragement. It has a transformative power too, but only when it is received with Moses-like humility to listen and the courage to change.

Perhaps we and our faith communities need humbly and courageously to search for, recognise, and listen to our own Jethros today. Where might you need the wisdom and encouragement of a Jethro? Or perhaps God is sending you into a meeting or situation today to be a Jethro: may you boldly and generously weave criticism with encouragement, that all might find peace and flourish.

Risen Christ,
for whom no door is locked, no entrance barred:
open the doors of our hearts,
that we may seek the good of others
and walk the joyful road of sacrifice and peace,
to the praise of God the Father.

COLLECT

Reflection by **Emma Parker**   123

Monday 15 April

Psalms **96**, 97 *or* **30**
Exodus 19
Luke 1.1-25

Luke 1.1-25

*'Meanwhile, the people were waiting for Zechariah,
and wondered at his delay...' (v.21)*

Within the sanctuary we find Zechariah: heart thudding, eyes widening, mouth opening – and closing. In a short space of time, everything has changed for him: physically, for he can no longer speak; spiritually, for he is face to face with an angel and is receiving an amazing promise; relationally, for he is to become a parent. In a matter of moments, the angel has packed this space with a rich tapestry of promise, weaving together Zechariah's personal prayers in the past with God's cosmic salvation plan for all.

Outside the sanctuary however, it is a different story. We find the people waiting for Zechariah: feet-shuffling, heads-turning, mouths-yawning. They start to wonder at his delay (with concern? with frustration?). Waiting is never easy, especially when we don't know the reason or when it might end. Outside the sanctuary, it perhaps feels as though time is being wasted, that the space is meaningless, empty, even.

Dealing with delay is difficult. But perhaps the delay is because somewhere else, on the other side of the door, on the other end of the phone, at the end of the corridor, God is filling the space by weaving past and future into the present. And, like the people outside the sanctuary, when the door is finally opened, perhaps we too will discover that the delay, the unexplained space, will be filled with meaning and rejoicing that reaches to eternity (v.14).

COLLECT

Almighty Father,
who in your great mercy gladdened the disciples
    with the sight of the risen Lord:
give us such knowledge of his presence with us,
that we may be strengthened and sustained by his risen life
and serve you continually in righteousness and truth;
through Jesus Christ your Son our Lord,
who is alive and reigns with you,
in the unity of the Holy Spirit,
one God, now and for ever.

| *Reflection by* **Emma Parker**

Psalms **98**, 99, 100 *or* **36**
Exodus 20.1-21
Luke 1.26-38

Tuesday 16 April

Luke 1.26-38

'How can this be...?' (v.34)

Whereas Zechariah's question, 'How will I know that this is so...?' (v.18) is tinted with disbelief, Mary's question 'How can this be...?' comes from a different place. She believes Gabriel's word but can't understand *how* it will happen. Zechariah asks for proof of the veracity of the word; Mary asks for details on the practicalities, already believing it to be true. Perhaps Zechariah's life-experience has taught him to be more wary; perhaps Mary's youth still drives her curiosity.

Mary could have asked for so much more detail: *how* is her child going to be great, *how* is he going to be given the throne, *how* is he going to reign, *how* will his kingdom never end? Instead, she focuses on what seems most immediate: *how* she is going to become pregnant? I'm not sure Gabriel's answer removed any need for further 'how' questions(!), but Mary's curiosity leads her to a place of confident trust, knowing that God's word never fails (v.37).

In our own discipleship, we can often become transfixed by the details, but our curiosity can lead us to anxiety rather than confidence in God. We can be fearful of taking the next step because we don't fully understand. But being reminded of God's trustworthiness enabled Mary's curiosity to lead her to assurance and trust. May we too be reminded of God's faithfulness in our own vocations and find that our curiosity leads to trust – and to worship.

Risen Christ,
you filled your disciples with boldness and fresh hope:
strengthen us to proclaim your risen life
and fill us with your peace,
to the glory of God the Father.

COLLECT

Wednesday 17 April

Psalm **105** *or* **34**
Exodus 24
Luke 1.39-56

Luke 1.39-56

'Blessed are you...' (v.42)

'Oh! It's lovely to see you... you look well... would you like a cup of tea?' This might be our response when someone knocks at our door. But forget the polite cultural responses and even the cup of tea. When Mary arrives, Elizabeth is immediately filled with the Holy Spirit (v.41) and bursting with joy, she cries out in wonder, *'Blessed are you!'* I picture a scene where she drops everything, pushes the furniture out the way, accidentally knocks over a water jar and embraces Mary with loud exclamations of love and welcome.

'Blessed are you!' It's a cry of great gusto that declares that God has been and is at work, a cry that praises Mary's trust in God's faithfulness (v.45). It must have been such an encouragement. Who knows what has been said to Mary (to her face or behind her back, with whispers or judging tuts)? But here Luke tells us that Elizabeth 'cries out with a loud cry'. The repetition emphasises that this declaration of blessedness was said boldly and passionately. And it was answered by a song no doubt sung with equal gusto, a revolutionary song of prophetic praise, from the lips of Mary.

Let us be filled with God's Spirit so that we can speak words of encouragement to those we meet; let us declare someone's *blessedness* with confidence and faith; and let us hope that this may lead to more revolutionary songs of prophetic praise.

COLLECT

Almighty Father,
who in your great mercy gladdened the disciples
    with the sight of the risen Lord:
give us such knowledge of his presence with us,
that we may be strengthened and sustained by his risen life
and serve you continually in righteousness and truth;
through Jesus Christ your Son our Lord,
who is alive and reigns with you,
in the unity of the Holy Spirit,
one God, now and for ever.

| *Reflection by* **Emma Parker**

Psalm **136** *or* **37***
Exodus 25.1-22
Luke 1.57-end

Thursday 18 April

Luke 1.57-end

'... to give light to those who sit in darkness and in the shadow of death' (v.79)

Here we listen to another song of praise – this time from the mouth of Zechariah, who is also filled with the Holy Spirit. He praises God for what he is about to do both in Jesus and in John; he roots it in the ancient promises of Israel, he tells of God's merciful memory and power, and swings the lens round to the present and the future, for through the ministry of John and Jesus, the people will know and experience God's freedom, forgiveness, salvation and peace.

It is a song about life and light, sung in the wake of the birth of a treasured baby boy. It is music amidst great wonder and expectation. And yet, it is a song that does not forget those in darkness and those who are dying. Those who are sitting in darkness and in the shadow of death are not ignored in this scene of celebration and revelry. This truly is the mark of God, and the mark of true praise. Lament should never be displaced from our doxology. In looking at life and light we should never be numb to the grief, never turn away from the dying. Grief and hope always belong together. Without grief, hope is meaningless. Without hope, grief is despair. Instead, they are part of the same story, part of the same song, part of God's great mercy-plan. Thanks be to God.

No wonder this joyous song is said or sung every day at morning prayer in churches around the world. We cannot hear its good news often enough.

Risen Christ,
you filled your disciples with boldness and fresh hope:
strengthen us to proclaim your risen life
and fill us with your peace,
to the glory of God the Father.

COLLECT

Friday 19 April

Psalm 107 or 31
Exodus 28.1-4a, 29-38
Luke 2.1-20

Luke 2.1-20

*'In that region there were shepherds living in the fields,
keeping watch over their flock by night' (v.8)*

I cannot read this passage without picturing six-year-olds with tea towels draped over their heads, grinning and singing 'While shepherds washed their socks by night...'. This picture might not be too far from the truth, as in some cultures shepherds are young children (like David, see 1 Samuel 17). The Greek for v.8 literally reads that they were 'living outside'. Given their occupation, this is unsurprising, but perhaps Luke also means this metaphorically. These shepherds were outsiders not only geographically but also socially, outside the circles of the rich, the respectable and the powerful – and even the religious as they were barred from the temple.

Jesus, the Lord of lords and King of kings, has just been born. And what does God do first? He sends a host of angels to those who are outside any claim to social, religious or political importance. God's heart for those who are found 'outside' always drives his movements and challenges ours. That God wanted these outsiders, with dirt under their fingernails and moonlight in their hair, to be the first people to see Jesus (the one who will profoundly shake-up our social, religious and political structures), should tell us so much about the unfolding of the gospel, and how we are to embody it.

So great is God's love, that at the turning point in all of history, at the greatest cosmic moment, he should invite outsiders to gaze first upon his face. What might this mean for us today in our own lives, in our churches, in our streets?

COLLECT

Almighty Father,
who in your great mercy gladdened the disciples
    with the sight of the risen Lord:
give us such knowledge of his presence with us,
that we may be strengthened and sustained by his risen life
and serve you continually in righteousness and truth;
through Jesus Christ your Son our Lord,
who is alive and reigns with you,
in the unity of the Holy Spirit,
one God, now and for ever.

| *Reflection by* **Emma Parker**

Luke 2.21-40

'... they returned to Galilee, to their own town of Nazareth' (v.39)

We've had crowds of people, family, strangers, neighbours, shepherds, hosts of angels.

We've had fear, amazement and wonder.

We've had promises made and fulfilled.

We've had singing, naming, blessing and praising.

We've had prophecies, signs and miracles.

We've had proclaiming and treasuring.

And now, Mary, Joseph and Jesus, after all this, simply return home. There is something unexpectedly normal about this. But how do they return home after everything they have heard and experienced? We might sometimes find ourselves asking after an extraordinary experience: how do I just go back to normal now?

But this is the thing about God: God's story here involved 'normal' people who need to return home at the end of the day. And God's story still involves people who return home, and to the tills, the offices, the bedsides, the streets and the classrooms, to work and to play, to look after their little ones or their elderly parents or their pets. God's story involves the normal stuff amidst the extraordinary stuff. But God always weaves the two together so that whilst the 'return' might look 'normal' on the outside, those making this journey do so with hearts full of wonder, ears ringing with divine promises, minds treasuring memories, eyes seeking hope.

Whatever return journeys we might make today, let us do so knowing that although they may seem normal, they are nevertheless sacred, because we have been touched by the extraordinary, merciful, loving ways of God.

Risen Christ,
you filled your disciples with boldness and fresh hope:
strengthen us to proclaim your risen life
and fill us with your peace,
to the glory of God the Father.

COLLECT

Reflection by **Emma Parker**

Monday 22 April

Psalms **103** *or* **44**
Exodus 32.1-14
Luke 2.41-end

Luke 2.41-end

'Did you not know that I must be in my Father's house?' (v.49)

Anyone who has ever been on a Holy Land pilgrimage knows one essential routine. That is to check everyone is back on the coach when it is time to go. People get missed surprisingly easily. A twelve-year old child though? And missing for *two days*? But scripture is not social media. There is no blaming of the parents. Rather, we are glimpsing the enviable securities of shared life in ancient, close-knit communities.

A four-day search ends in the temple where Jesus shows no sensitivity to what his parents have been going through. Where he must be and why is obvious to him. He speaks out of confident knowledge of his divine identity. Where did this come from? Did he wake up one day and realise 'I am the Son of God'? Or had this relationship with his heavenly Father always been as natural as breathing to him? It will not be the last time that Jesus is surprised that others do not understand what is in plain sight to him. What he is beginning to learn is that things so obvious to him were not to those around him.

The story has two outcomes. This does not happen again. Jesus returns to home and is obedient to his earthly parents. But Mary, we are told, 'treasured all these things in her heart'. Hers is the trusting response of, as yet, uncomprehending faith. And we must follow her example.

COLLECT

Almighty God,
whose Son Jesus Christ is the resurrection and the life:
raise us, who trust in him,
from the death of sin to the life of righteousness,
that we may seek those things which are above,
where he reigns with you
in the unity of the Holy Spirit,
one God, now and for ever.

Reflection by **David Runcorn**

Psalms 5, 146
Joshua 1.1-9
Ephesians 6.10-20

Tuesday 23 April

George, martyr,
patron of England

Ephesians 6.10-20

'Put on the whole armour of God, so that you may be able to stand against the wiles of the devil' (v.11)

Armed soldiers were regular company for Paul. So much so that he had time to consider how their equipment symbolised core aspects of his faith. Faith is active service in an often hostile and conflicted world.

A prayer group was taking part in an imagination exercise, putting on each piece of the armour of God. It was a transformative experience for one group member. The moment came as she contemplated the belt. It was vital clothing in that ancient world, gathering everything in and holding it all firmly in place. Paul called it 'the belt of truth'. The member told how she could visualise her only belt as a length of very worn, frayed leather. And this was most often how this person felt about herself – lacking confidence and of little value. But when invited to imagine the buckle she were amazed to find herself seeing a beautiful piece of metalwork. What was it doing on the end of such worthless leather? She had yet to put on the belt. It felt presumptuous to contemplate joining something so shabby to a buckle of such worth. But when she did, it fitted *perfectly*. It was a moment of truth. She knew the buckle was Christ. She was securely joined to him, held firm in the truth of his protecting love for her.

What unlikely symbol for our faith might we find today?

God of hosts,
who so kindled the flame of love
in the heart of your servant George
that he bore witness to the risen Lord
by his life and by his death:
give us the same faith and power of love
that we who rejoice in his triumphs
may come to share with him the fullness of the resurrection;
through Jesus Christ your Son our Lord,
who is alive and reigns with you,
in the unity of the Holy Spirit,
one God, now and for ever.

COLLECT

Reflection by **David Runcorn** | 131

Wednesday 24 April

Luke 3.15-22

*'... and when Jesus also had been baptized and was praying,
the heaven was opened' (v.21)*

After the intensifying mood of wonder and anticipation we meet
Jesus down by the riverside. He has just been baptised and is praying
– something Luke always stresses. Three things now happen: heaven
opens, the Spirit descends on the Son, the Father speaks. Something
of the whole life of God is now revealed on earth as it is in heaven.

Jesus will shortly be driven into the wilderness by the same Spirit.
But before any ministry has begun or work achieved, the Father
declares his love and delight in him. This is what God's love is like. It
is always fore-given. It is gift, not reward. It is gratuitous, not earned.
And this is such good news. For if divine love were payment or
reward, we could be sure we would never merit it. But God's love
needs no reason or cause. God is just being himself. This is what is
revealed in that glimpse of heaven opened.

A conference of counsellors and spiritual directors was asked what
the most common struggle or issue was among those who came to
them. 'To know they are loved' was the reply. There by the riverside,
the Father, the Son and the Spirit – under heaven opened – reveal the
truth of our baptism too. Can you hear the voice? '(*Your name*) – you
are my beloved son/daughter'. All is fore-given.

COLLECT

Almighty God,
whose Son Jesus Christ is the resurrection and the life:
raise us, who trust in him,
from the death of sin to the life of righteousness,
that we may seek those things which are above,
where he reigns with you
in the unity of the Holy Spirit,
one God, now and for ever.

| *Reflection by* **David Runcorn**

Psalms 37.23-end, 148
Isaiah 62.6-10
or Ecclesiasticus 51.13-end
Acts 12.25 – 13.13

Thursday 25 April

Mark the Evangelist

Acts 12.25 – 13.13

'While they were worshipping the Lord and fasting, the Holy Spirit said, "set apart for me Saul and Barnabas…"' (13.2)

Saul and Barnabas are, it seems, only just back from one long missionary journey when they are sent by the Holy Spirit on another one. What their churches felt about this we are not told. No community lightly gives away its two most significant leadership resources to pursue unrevealed strategies elsewhere. Perhaps that is why Luke names a number of other significant ministers in Antioch. The twin focus on teachers and prophets grounds the Church in understanding and in the will and purposes of God.

An uncompromising obedience to the sovereign will of the Holy Spirit runs through the entire chronicles of the Acts of the Apostles. In today's brief passage alone, the Spirit is to be found three times decisively guiding, shaping and empowering the outcomes.

In those early days in the life of the emerging Church its core priorities are simple and clear. Worship, prayer, teaching and prophecy under the empowering initiatives and guidance of Holy Spirit. In truth those whole communities were 'set apart' to the Spirit. They too were on a journey. Here is faith – trusting, obedient and, surely, as vulnerable as it is bold. Here is faith, with little history to build upon, open, adventurous, willing to be set apart for the unknown future of God.

Almighty God,
who enlightened your holy Church
through the inspired witness of your evangelist Saint Mark:
grant that we, being firmly grounded in the truth of the gospel,
may be faithful to its teaching both in word and deed;
through Jesus Christ your Son our Lord,
who is alive and reigns with you,
in the unity of the Holy Spirit,
one God, now and for ever.

COLLECT

Friday 26 April

Psalm **33** *or* **51**, 54
Exodus 35.20 – 36.7
Luke 4.14-30

Luke 4.14-30

'Today this scripture has been fulfilled in your hearing' (v.21)

What kind of sermon so infuriates its hearers that they try to kill the preacher?

Historically, Nazareth and Galilee were where some of the ancient tribes of Israel originally settled. But in Jesus' time it was heavily colonized by occupying powers. God's people endured the routine humiliations of daily life under foreign control, mourning their own lost history. It was hugely resented.

In the synagogue Jesus reads from Isaiah. The core of that prophecy is the promise that God will vindicate his people in the face of their enemies. In first century, enemy-occupied Galilee, God's people lived for that day. Who wouldn't? But Jesus reads very selectively. He omits precisely those verses that promise their exclusive vindication and restoration. Instead, he tells stories of God's favour and blessing to *outsiders* and holds them up as examples. 'A text of judgment was transformed into a message of grace, and his listeners were incensed.'*

So is revealed the shocking, unbordered, inclusiveness of God's love. And if it doesn't unsettle us too perhaps, we have not yet understood it either. The scandal of the gospel is that it is simply not fair! All this blessing, favour, mercy and love keeps falling into the hands of the wrong people! There in Nazareth they either have to kill him or endure a theological meltdown. It is as serious as that.

*Kenneth Bailey, *Jesus through Middle Eastern Eyes,* p.171. SPCK, 2008.

COLLECT

Almighty God,
whose Son Jesus Christ is the resurrection and the life:
raise us, who trust in him,
from the death of sin to the life of righteousness,
that we may seek those things which are above,
where he reigns with you
in the unity of the Holy Spirit,
one God, now and for ever.

| *Reflection by* **David Runcorn**

Psalm **34** *or* **68**
Exodus 40.17-end
Luke 4.31-37

Saturday 27 April

Luke 4.31-37

'I know who you are, the Holy One of God' (v.34)

The first stories of Jesus in the gospels were carefully selected to set the agenda and highlight the core themes of his ministry. One of these is Jesus' victory over evil.

In the middle of a synagogue, the community centre of faith, the presence of Jesus flushes out evil into the open. So it is that, in Luke's gospel, the first unambiguous testimony to Jesus' true identity is by a demon, who plainly knows that this means its end.

The actual substance or source of evil is always a mystery. It is, of itself, wholly useless. It only traps and destroys. Why would anyone choose it? But we do. Or we fall into its grip within a world that, in its folly, keeps giving foothold to it.

Jesus hates what is evil and mourns over what it lays waste to. And in his name, so must we. We are to hate what is evil in this life.

Talk of the devil tends to fall into two extremes. The tendency is to take the devil too seriously, or not seriously enough. 'Deliver us from evil' is what Jesus teaches us to pray. Today's story reminds us of the need for this petition. It is for praying in trust and faith until this victory is at last established in all God has made.

Risen Christ,
faithful shepherd of your Father's sheep:
teach us to hear your voice
and to follow your command,
that all your people may be gathered into one flock,
to the glory of God the Father.

COLLECT

Reflection by **David Runcorn** | 135

Monday 29 April

Psalm 145 *or* 71
Numbers 9.15-end; 10.33-end
Luke 4.38-end

Luke 4.38-end

*'At daybreak he departed and went into a deserted place.
And the crowds were looking for him' (v.42)*

Wildernesses and deserts are important places in the Bible. The call to John the Baptist comes in the wilderness. It is to the desert he calls people to be baptised and to 'prepare the way of the Lord'. After his own baptism Jesus was led (or driven, as Mark's gospel says) into the wilderness by the Spirit and he returned to those rugged, silent wastes throughout his ministry.

'The crowds' represent undiscerning activism. 'What are you doing out here?', they demand, 'There is work to be done!' Since deserts are dry, inhospitable places we can easily think that to find ourselves there is a failure of faith. Surely 'real' faith is full of life and fruitfulness? But there are few people and communities in the Bible whose faith was not significantly formed by times there. This is the wilderness that is a gift of the Spirit's ministering presence, not an absence.

I have a check list used by an unnamed priest when he was needing to discern a call to a new church or ministry. Among the questions he asked of the community were these: 'Is its wilderness wild enough? Is its desert dry enough?'

Where is your desert? Where are those quiet places for waiting, for unproductive listening and for the forming, testing work of Spirit? We will find Jesus there too.

COLLECT

Almighty God,
who through your only-begotten Son Jesus Christ
have overcome death and opened to us the gate of everlasting life:
grant that, as by your grace going before us
   you put into our minds good desires,
so by your continual help
we may bring them to good effect;
through Jesus Christ our risen Lord,
who is alive and reigns with you,
in the unity of the Holy Spirit,
one God, now and for ever.

| *Reflection by* **David Runcorn**

Psalms **19**, 147.1-12 *or* **73**　　　　**Tuesday 30 April**
Numbers 11.1-33
Luke 5.1-11

Luke 5.1-11

'Put out into the deep water' (v.4)

Boats and sea crossings feature regularly in the early ministry of Jesus, which was centred in the region of Galilee. It is interesting how often the destination is almost irrelevant. What happens on the journey itself is the point of the story. Out there on the deep, even professional sailors are reduced to terror and fear for their lives by the winds, storms, and waves. But threat, powerlessness and danger became places of encounter, recognition, and discovery. In the presence of Jesus, those times became moments of revelation, a call to faith and trust, and a deepening wonder and recognition of who he really is.

But that is to anticipate the stories to come. Until now Jesus has been working alone. Here he is beginning to gather his first significant followers. The sermon over, he asks them to 'put out into the deep water'. A world so familiar to those fishermen is about to move vastly beyond their understanding and control. They will be out of their depth in more ways than one. Luke's focus is not so much the huge catch of fish in previously empty nets. It is the awe and wonder at who is in their midst. In the first instance they simply cannot cope. 'Depart from me', pleads Peter. But the call to follow proves more compelling still. And out into the deep they go, leaving everything they know.

Risen Christ,
your wounds declare your love for the world
and the wonder of your risen life:
give us compassion and courage
to risk ourselves for those we serve,
to the glory of God the Father.

COLLECT

Reflection by **David Runcorn**　　│　137

Wednesday 1 May

Philip and James, Apostles

Psalms 139, 146
Proverbs 4.10-18
James 1.1-12

James 1.1-12

'Whenever you face trials of any kind, consider it nothing but joy' (v.2)

The call to rejoice through struggles, difficulties and in all circumstances is one of the refrains in the New Testament. The reasons vary. Rejoice 'because great is your reward in heaven', said Jesus (Matthew 5.12). Rejoice because 'the Lord is near', says Paul (Philippians 4.5). James is writing to Christians being persecuted for following Jesus. Rejoice! He says, for these trials build Christian character. 'You know that under pressure, your faith-life is forced into the open and shows its true colors. So don't try to get out of anything prematurely. Let it do its work...' (James 1.3-5 in *The Message*)

Christian rejoicing is a work of faith-full resistance. It subverts the scripts that dominate our culture and mocks their claims. This joy insists on the celebration of a different story, yet to be revealed. It radically re-focuses the world and our experience in it, breaks though our narrow preoccupations and widens our vision.

Pastor Richard Wurmbrand was imprisoned and tortured for many years in communist Romania. Though enduring appalling suffering and broken health, he tells how he learned to rejoice in his cold, dark cell, leaving his guards bewildered by what they saw. 'I found that joy can be acquired like a habit. I learned to rejoice in the worst conditions.'* This joy is nothing less than the presence of Jesus. It is therefore faith in action. It takes practice.

*Richard Wurmbrand. *In God's underground*. Kindle 720–1

COLLECT

Almighty Father,
whom truly to know is eternal life:
teach us to know your Son Jesus Christ
as the way, the truth, and the life;
that we may follow the steps of your holy apostles
     Philip and James,
and walk steadfastly in the way that leads to your glory;
through Jesus Christ your Son our Lord,
who is alive and reigns with you,
in the unity of the Holy Spirit,
one God, now and for ever.

| *Reflection by* **David Runcorn**

Psalms **57**, 148 *or* **78.1-39***
Numbers 13.1-3, 17-end
Luke 5.27-end

Thursday 2 May

Luke 5.27-end

'Levi gave a great banquet for him in his house' (v.29)

How often, in Luke's Gospel, Jesus is found going to, or coming from, a meal somewhere. References and allusions to food are everywhere. The message is clear. If you want to follow Jesus, be prepared to do a lot of travelling and eat a lot of meals. But expect to be very challenged by who else you find at table with you.

In fact, Luke's narrative is centred on eight meals with Jesus. And those meals are always teaching occasions. Themes of evangelism, justice and the life of the kingdom are expounded. The social and religious world of his day, with its hierarchies, prejudices and presumptions, is exposed and judged.

At those meals Jesus is not only teaching the life of the kingdom, but he is also living it out. A new community of radical welcome and inclusion is revealed. Here is the gospel in action. The offer of hospitality and meals in that culture was not made lightly. It was a significant and very visible statement of belonging, honouring, status and acceptance. Wherever Jesus ate, those times invariably became, for some, occasions of scandal, conflict and confrontation. For others, they were encounters with astonishing love, acceptance and unexpected homecoming from far-away places. So, they were always places of gift and danger. One writer puts it very succinctly. 'Jesus got himself crucified by the way he ate.'*

*Quoted in *The Ongoing Feast*, Arthur Just Jr. (128)

Almighty God,
who through your only-begotten Son Jesus Christ
have overcome death and opened to us the gate of everlasting life:
grant that, as by your grace going before us
you put into our minds good desires,
so by your continual help
we may bring them to good effect;
through Jesus Christ our risen Lord,
who is alive and reigns with you,
in the unity of the Holy Spirit,
one God, now and for ever.

COLLECT

Reflection by **David Runcorn** | 139

Friday 3 May

Psalms **138**, 149 *or* **55**
Numbers 14.1-25
Luke 6.1-11

Luke 6.1-11

'After looking around at all of them, he said to him, "Stretch out your hand" ' (v.10)

The healing miracles in the gospels have symbolic meaning as well as practical gift. Who and what is healed – and where – is important. The context here is familiar. Jesus is in the synagogue teaching on the sabbath. The audience is also familiar. His hostile religious opponents are there at the back, looking to catch him out. Present too is vulnerable, lost humanity – represented by a man with a withered right hand. (The right hand in that culture is the 'public', functioning hand). There is something very familiar about humanity found, on the one hand, clustering in faceless, intimidating pressure groups or sitting in paralysed isolation on the other. Both are disabling places to be. Both need freeing. Jesus stands between them as the one who calls out life.

He questions the legalistic, inhumanity of herd religion. Does the law forbid saving life? He does not wait for their reply. He gives them a visual aid of what he means. The Lord of the Sabbath turns and calls out the man to the front. (Notice it is not just his hand that is withered. So is his voice and will in the face of his own deepest needs). At the invitation of Jesus, he stretches out his hand and life is restored. But his opponents retreat further into paralysing hatred and bitterness.

COLLECT

Almighty God,
who through your only-begotten Son Jesus Christ
have overcome death and opened to us the gate of everlasting life:
grant that, as by your grace going before us
   you put into our minds good desires,
so by your continual help
we may bring them to good effect;
through Jesus Christ our risen Lord,
who is alive and reigns with you,
in the unity of the Holy Spirit,
one God, now and for ever.

| *Reflection by* **David Runcorn**

Psalms **146**, 150 *or* **76**, 79
Numbers 14.26-end
Luke 6.12-26

Saturday 4 May

Luke 6.12-26

*'But woe to you who are rich, for you have received
your consolation' (v.24)*

Like all the rabbis, Jesus liked to make his point by using extreme opposites or by making contradictory assertions. The purpose was to shock and jolt out of familiar assumptions. The poor, hungry and grief-stricken are not usually thought of as 'happy'. But if God's blessing is very particularly declared where it is normally experienced as painfully absent, then something new is surely going on. And if God's blessing is for finding in the most harrowed corners of human experience, then surely no one and nowhere is beyond its reach.

Alongside the blessings upon the poor, Luke records a series of woes to those who have plenty. They are not being condemned here for being wealthy and happy, nor for depriving others in need – though that is serious, and strongly judged elsewhere. Rather, their woe, whether they yet know it, is a matter of practical consequence. What is stressed is that have it all already. There is nothing more for them. They have chosen a way of blessing that will leave them empty. Wealth, with its accompanying lifestyle, is so easily built upon presumptions of importance and deserving – of entitlement. Their woe lies in the utter folly of this belief. They are on the edge of complete moral, spiritual, vocational bankruptcy, as the blessed poor enter the Kingdom ahead of them and are filled.

Risen Christ,
your wounds declare your love for the world
and the wonder of your risen life:
give us compassion and courage
to risk ourselves for those we serve,
to the glory of God the Father.

COLLECT

Reflection by **David Runcorn** | 141

Monday 6 May

Luke 6.27-38

'... for the measure you give will be the measure you get back' (v.38)

No one would quibble with the instruction that we should 'do to others as you would have them do to you'. Primary schools of all faiths and none promote this value. But while we might need to check the automatic urge to retaliate, these sayings are problematic in situations of systematic abuse. They may give comfort to the abuser and disempower the victim.

The right to self-defence is intrinsic to every person's God-given dignity. How many of us would watch our loved ones being slaughtered rather than resist in kind? On the other hand, non-violent resistance to injustice has a moral authority that often changes hearts and minds.

Taken together, these verses cover too much ground to provide a detailed ethic for responding to violence. But they do reveal the self-interest that often lurks behind respectable, apparently moral behaviour.

Many of us struggle with two limitations identified here: a complacent sense of our own goodness, and judgementalism. This passage underlines the stark distinction between the self-satisfied moralism of an in-group, and self-giving love. Yet it takes enormous courage and trust to venture into the radical freedom of the gospel.

God knows how difficult this is and is kind to us and to all the 'ungrateful and wicked'. Day by day, we must learn how to develop a way of life that is rooted in mercy and generosity. Only then will we be able to receive the overflowing abundance Jesus promises.

COLLECT

God our redeemer,
you have delivered us from the power of darkness
and brought us into the kingdom of your Son:
grant, that as by his death he has recalled us to life,
so by his continual presence in us he may raise us
    to eternal joy;
through Jesus Christ your Son our Lord,
who is alive and reigns with you,
in the unity of the Holy Spirit,
one God, now and for ever.

| *Reflection by* **Alan Everett**

Psalms 124, 125, **126**, 127 *or* 87, **89.1-18**　　**Tuesday 7 May**
Numbers 16.36-end
Luke 6.39-end

Luke 6.39-end

'... and great was the ruin of that house' (v.49)

The phrase 'the blind leading the blind' has become a shorthand way of commenting on poor leadership. But the proverb drives the point home, with a cruel twist, 'Will not both fall into a pit?' Each illustration touches a raw nerve. A speck of dust in the eye is painful enough; imagine if it were a log! The images that follow – figs from thorns and grapes from a bramble bush – are surreal and disturbing.

The final image of a falling house is the most violent of all and would have struck a chord with Jesus's hearers. The collapse of buildings still results in a disastrous loss of life in many parts of the world. But cost-cutting shortcuts can put people's lives at risk everywhere; this dramatic picture speaks to everyone.

Moving from metaphor to practice: what shortcuts do we take, in our prayer life or ethical choices? The impact of these sayings is cumulative, forcefully reminding us that spiritual ruin is a real possibility.

The gospels never offer an escape from rising floods but remind us unequivocally that we confront them by digging deep. Embedding ourselves in God may seem arduous at times, but the rockiness of the terrain is what saves us.

God's love is challenging, honest, testing, and unsentimental. It purges self-defeating illusions, enabling us to sing, with hard-won and joyful conviction: 'The Church's one foundation / Is Jesus Christ, her Lord.'

Risen Christ,
by the lakeside you renewed your call to your disciples:
help your Church to obey your command
and draw the nations to the fire of your love,
to the glory of God the Father.

COLLECT

Wednesday 8 May

Psalms **132**, 133 *or* **119.105-128**
Numbers 17.1-11
Luke 7.1-10

Luke 7.1-10

'I tell you, not even in Israel have I found such faith' (v.9)

The New Testament invites questions about social structures during the occupation of Israel. It seems that the middle ranks of the military sometimes had humanising interactions with those they ruled, including their own slaves. Was this partly because they were in a bit of a backwater, far from Rome?

Matthew also recounts this event (8.5–13), but without Luke's enlivening detail that the centurion concerned had built a synagogue. Centurions feature elsewhere. In Acts, the centurion Cornelius helps persuade Peter that the Holy Spirit has been poured out on Gentiles (10.1–11.18). Gentiles can be believers too – sometimes even more so.

A centurion witnesses Jesus' death in all three synoptic gospels. In Mark and Matthew, he declares him to be God's Son. Luke's centurion asserts that Jesus was innocent (23.47), just four verses after the conversion of the penitent thief, unique to this Gospel. Luke's perspective is distinctively inclusive, and political.

This context of today's scene is the exercise of authority. When we speak of 'unconscious bias' against 'the other', we rightly focus on the vulnerability of those we exclude. But we may also fail to recognise the image of God in those who exercise power – especially if their policies are ones we oppose. While the biblical condemnation of injustice is uncompromising, there can be people of goodness and spiritual depth even within oppressive systems. We fail to represent 'the wideness of God's mercy' if we overlook this.

COLLECT

God our redeemer,
you have delivered us from the power of darkness
and brought us into the kingdom of your Son:
grant, that as by his death he has recalled us to life,
so by his continual presence in us he may raise us
    to eternal joy;
through Jesus Christ your Son our Lord,
who is alive and reigns with you,
in the unity of the Holy Spirit,
one God, now and for ever.

| *Reflection by* **Alan Everett**

Psalms 110, 150
Isaiah 52.7-end
Hebrews 7. [11-25] 26-end

Thursday 9 May
Ascension Day

Hebrews 7. [11-25] 26-end

'... a priest for ever, according to the order of Melchizedek' (v.17)

The Letter to the Hebrews is a complex reflection on Christ's self-offering. Christ eliminates the repetitive cycle of temple sacrifice through the unified action of his human and divine natures. As a man he suffers and dies; as God he raises humanity to eternal life. He is both victim and priest; priest and king. Consequently, Christ's prototype is the righteous king Melchizedek, who appears fleetingly to bless Abram (Genesis 14.18–20).

In contrast with some later atonement theories, Hebrews speaks not of 'satisfaction' so much as 'intercession'. While Christ's sacrifice was 'once and for all', his intercession continues. This eternal and merciful action is affirmed in the glorious Ascension Day hymn, 'Hail the day that sees him rise': 'Still for us he intercedes... His prevailing death he pleads...'

The themes of Hebrews are further enlarged by contemporary reflections on priesthood. In the sacraments, ordained priests represent the continuing actions of divine forgiveness, adoption, and sanctification. But the whole people of God embody Christ's priesthood, ministering in the world and for the world. Ascension Day turns our thoughts to what this means:

> See! he lifts his hands above: Alleluya!
> See! he shows his prints of love: Alleluya!
> Hark! his gracious lips bestow: Alleluya!
> Blessings on his Church below: Alleluya!

As the body of Christ, we are called to make Christ's 'prints of love' visible, and to share the blessings he bestows. Alleluya!

COLLECT

Grant, we pray, almighty God,
that as we believe your only-begotten Son
our Lord Jesus Christ
to have ascended into the heavens,
so we in heart and mind may also ascend
and with him continually dwell;
who is alive and reigns with you,
in the unity of the Holy Spirit,
one God, now and for ever.

Reflection by **Alan Everett** | 145

Friday 10 May

Psalms 20, **81** *or* **88** (95)
Exodus 35.30 – 36.1
Galatians 5.13-end

Exodus 35.30 – 36.1

'He has filled them with skill . . .' (35.35)

A delight in craft sings through this passage, recalling the much-loved hymn 'Angel-voices ever singing', in which its author Francis Pott astutely observes, 'Craftsman's art and music's measure / For thy pleasure / All combine' – these give pleasure not only to us, but also to God.

Historically, Christians have had an uneasy relationship with pleasure, and this has sometimes led to the repression of vital gifts. But the arts of worship are a form of sanctified delight, shared with one another and with God. At its best, this holy pleasure creates a celebratory culture that is immensely attractive to newcomers.

God is not a dour puritan but enjoys diverse expressions of creativity – across culture, age, and church tradition. And the experience of sanctified pleasure has an impact outside worship. How many of us have left church and seen others with new eyes, as a precious sacramental gift?

In this passage, the writer lingers appreciatively over both raw materials and their transformation. The 'skill and understanding' of the work of the sanctuary call forth further expressions of delight. Design, craft, and linguistic celebration weave a tapestry of praise.

The arts give glory to God in a way that far exceeds any individual contribution. But some distrust creativity in worship and elsewhere. Why is that?

COLLECT

Grant, we pray, almighty God,
that as we believe your only-begotten Son
    our Lord Jesus Christ
to have ascended into the heavens,
so we in heart and mind may also ascend
and with him continually dwell;
who is alive and reigns with you,
in the unity of the Holy Spirit,
one God, now and for ever.

| *Reflection by* **Alan Everett**

Psalms 21, **47** *or* 96, **97**, 100   **Saturday 11 May**
Numbers 11.16-17, 24-29
1 Corinthians 2

Numbers 11.16-17, 24-29

'Would that all the Lord's people were prophets, and that the Lord would put his spirit on them!' (v.29)

The appointment of seventy elders may relate to the advice given to Moses by his father-in-law that he should share his duties with others to ease the burden of leadership (Exodus 18.13-26). Those chosen may have been key figures such as tribal chiefs who had already been in a position to provide support.

They experienced a direct encounter with Yahweh, alongside Moses, and the gift of prophecy. Was this an ecstatic utterance anticipating the 'tongues' experienced in the Church in Corinth (1 Corinthians 14)? Quite possibly. But the gift was temporary, either because it was a form of initiation, or because of the risk of unexpected consequences.

This may account for Joshua's alarm at discovering Eldad and Medad prophesying in the camp. Was he afraid their actions might be contagious? But Moses calmed Joshua's fears. He did not worry about the subversion of his authority but rejoiced in sharing of Yahweh's spirit.

Moses is a useful model for today's spiritual leaders. It is not always easy to discern when to celebrate new expressions of faith and when to proceed more cautiously. What may enlarge mission and ministry in one context may undermine it in another. No 'one size' fits all. Emotional maturity, theological wisdom, and a willingness to work humbly with others are needed to govern, and to harness creative energy.

Risen Christ,
you have raised our human nature to the throne of heaven:
help us to seek and serve you,
that we may join you at the Father's side,
where you reign with the Spirit in glory,
now and for ever.

COLLECT

Reflection by **Alan Everett**   147

Monday 13 May

Psalms **93**, 96, 97 *or* **98**, 99, 101
Numbers 27.15-end
1 Corinthians 3

Numbers 27.15-end

'So Moses did as the Lord commanded him' (v.22)

The commissioning of Joshua, occurring before the end of Numbers, involved the partial transfer of Moses's authority. Unlike Moses, Joshua would never see God face to face; Moses was a prophet unlike all others. Even so, it was Joshua who would take the Israelites into the promised land. Moses died in Moab (Jordan). Deuteronomy notes that 'no one knows his burial place to this day' (34.1-6).

Our public spaces and churches are populated by monuments to the great and sometimes not-so-good. We assiduously preserve them, even if those we commemorate participated in acts of oppression and exploitation, such as slavery, though this is beginning to change. In contrast, Moses' bones lie in a forgotten piece of ground – disintegrating, even 'to this day'.

Numbers continues for another nine chapters, covering various laws and a war with Midianites. Like Leviticus, it concludes by affirming that these were commandments given to the Israelites through Moses. The commandments were even more important than Moses.

Moses, a founder of the ancient Israelite civilisation, performed the task given to him to God and was buried in obscurity. He shaped essential laws and equipped a leader to succeed him. The Book of Joshua opens with Joshua's decisive conquest of the land beyond the river Jordan. The contrast between Moses's leadership and our valorisation of those who shape and govern nations today could hardly be greater. No taint of the cult of personality lingers around either Moses or Joshua.

COLLECT

O God the King of glory,
you have exalted your only Son Jesus Christ
with great triumph to your kingdom in heaven:
we beseech you, leave us not comfortless,
but send your Holy Spirit to strengthen us
and exalt us to the place where our Saviour Christ is gone before,
who is alive and reigns with you,
in the unity of the Holy Spirit,
one God, now and for ever.

Reflection by **Alan Everett**

Psalms 16, 147.1-12
1 Samuel 2.27-35
Acts 2.37-end

Tuesday 14 May

Matthias the Apostle

1 Samuel 2.27-35

'I will raise up for myself a faithful priest...' (v.27)

Eli is elderly and living in spiritually enervated times: 'The word of the Lord was rare in those days: visions were not widespread' (3.1). We learn that Eli's own eyesight has grown dim (3.2). The absence of visions and his failing eyesight are connected.

When Samuel's mother Hannah, distressed and weeping, prays at the temple, Eli thinks she is drunk because her mouth moves silently (1.12-13). This speaks of a lack of spiritual insight. Later, the Lord explicitly tells Samuel that Eli will be punished because he did not restrain his sons from their blasphemy (3.13).

In today's passage, at the centre of the narrative, a man of God passes judgement on Eli. He has been complicit in his sons' abuse of their priestly role, looking with 'greedy eyes' on the choicest parts of the people's offerings. Eli's greedy (but now dimming) eyesight is in counterpoint to Samuel's experience of visions he does not yet understand. Samuel does as any young person would: he runs to his sleeping mentor Eli, mistaking their origin. The intimacy this implies is touching.

But whatever sympathy we may feel for Eli, the message is unequivocal. Those with spiritual responsibilities will be superseded if they fail in their calling. The privilege of serving God should never be taken for granted or exploited. On the contrary, it raises the bar for ethical behaviour.

On this feast day of St Matthias, who replaced Judas, we take note.

Almighty God,
who in the place of the traitor Judas
chose your faithful servant Matthias
to be of the number of the Twelve:
preserve your Church from false apostles
and, by the ministry of faithful pastors and teachers,
keep us steadfast in your truth;
through Jesus Christ your Son our Lord,
who is alive and reigns with you,
in the unity of the Holy Spirit,
one God, now and for ever.

COLLECT

Reflection by **Alan Everett**

Wednesday 15 May

1 Kings 19.1-18

'He asked that he might die' (v.4)

Elijah's confrontation with Ahab and Jezebel has cost him everything. The scale of his collapse is apparent from his prayer for death, 'for I am no better than my ancestors'.

There is an incomparable quality of stillness in the subsequent narrative of healing. Sleep beneath a broom tree, an angel touching his shoulder, a cake baked on hot stones, a jar of water, more sleep, further sustenance. And then onward, for a gruelling forty days to the sacred mountain of Horeb, to spend the night in a cave.

The final verse of the hymn 'Dear Lord of Father of mankind' references Elijah's subsequent encounter with God:

Breathe through the heats of our desire
Thy coolness and thy balm;
Let sense be dumb, let flesh retire;
Speak through the earthquake, wind, and fire,
O still, small voice of calm!

But wonderful as this hymn may be, Elijah is combatting far more than the 'heats of desire'. Momentary rest and quietness are the minimum he needs for survival as he combats corrupt and savage rulers. Immediately after the revelation of God in the 'sound of sheer silence', he returns to the fray. Two kings and the prophet Elisha will continue his work, this time by the sword.

Extraordinary resilience is demanded of God's prophets. This riveting account of traumatised faith strips away conventional pieties and interrogates us. How much do we risk for truth and justice?

COLLECT

O God the King of glory,
you have exalted your only Son Jesus Christ
with great triumph to your kingdom in heaven:
we beseech you, leave us not comfortless,
but send your Holy Spirit to strengthen us
and exalt us to the place where our Saviour Christ is gone before,
who is alive and reigns with you,
in the unity of the Holy Spirit,
one God, now and for ever.

| *Reflection by* **Alan Everett**

Psalms **24**, 72 *or* 113, **115**   **Thursday 16 May**
Ezekiel 11.14-20
Matthew 9.35 – 10.20

Ezekiel 11.14-20

'I will remove the heart of stone from their flesh and give them a heart of flesh' (v.19)

Exile, fragmentation, hard-heartedness, and spiritual death fuse in the white heat of Ezekiel's imagination. The promise of a new heart speaks to the experience of failure and loss. We may already be conscious of a lack of connection – with others, with our faith. Alternatively, this imagery may give us an unwelcome glimpse of our shallowness and inauthenticity. But for Ezekiel, as for us, judgement precedes renewal. We must first acknowledge that the heart has stopped for it to beat again.

At the end of a period of spiritual dryness, the whole person is refreshed. We feel less fragmented – as if we have come back to God, and to others. But how do we understand the communal call to wholeness?

For many it is as if we live in a condition of religious, social, and cultural exile – as if we have lost our bearings. The danger at this time of instability, when together we face massive global challenges, is twofold. First, that we may romanticise the past—as if there ever was a golden era of peace and unity, and second, that we may lose hope.

But we can take heart. Ezekiel speaks directly to our longing. This passage is a call to honest and searching prayer: to place before God our profound disorientation. The appeal for God's healing, liberating love only carries weight and conviction when we acknowledge the extent of our need.

Risen, ascended Lord,
as we rejoice at your triumph,
fill your Church on earth with power and compassion,
that all who are estranged by sin
may find forgiveness and know your peace,
to the glory of God the Father.

COLLECT

Reflection by **Alan Everett**   151

Friday 17 May

Ezekiel 36.22-28

'I will put my spirit within you' (v.27)

Ezekiel conveys Yahweh's promise of a heart of flesh (reiterating yesterday's reading), and an end to exile. After cleansing by sprinkled 'water', Yahweh's spirit will enter the Israelites, and they will live in peace on their own land.

While our language of baptismal adoption reflects Ezekiel, we do not envisage a return to an ancestral kingdom. Christ's kingdom is not tied to a single state but will renew all nations.

The Christian presence in the Middle East has dramatically declined. At the high point of the reign of Justinian I (527–565), the Church was governed by the patriarchs of Rome, Constantinople, Alexandria, Antioch, and Jerusalem. But this ancient order no longer prevails.

Population movement and missionary activity – Christian and Muslim – have transformed the Church. Of these five patriarchates, only Rome and Constantinople still have a major role – and the Ecumenical Patriarch's position in Istanbul is precarious.

In the West, many churches struggle for significance, reflecting a shift of energy to the Global South. The worldwide Christian community is volatile, dispersed and at times divided. Unsettled by rapid change, the loss of certainties and radical social instability we may be tempted to turn inward: to see the Church as a gathering of like-minded individuals, from a similar socio-economic background to our own; to abandon hope in God's mission to renew the whole world.

Ezekiel encourages us to commit ourselves to the deepest and widest promises of our faith. Can we do this?

COLLECT

O God the King of glory,
you have exalted your only Son Jesus Christ
with great triumph to your kingdom in heaven:
we beseech you, leave us not comfortless,
but send your Holy Spirit to strengthen us
and exalt us to the place where our Saviour Christ is gone before,
who is alive and reigns with you,
in the unity of the Holy Spirit,
one God, now and for ever.

Reflection by **Alan Everett**

Psalms 42, **43** *or* 120, **121**, 122
Micah 3.1-8
Ephesians 6.10-20

Saturday 18 May

Micah 3.1-8

'Should you not know justice?' (v.1)

In recent years, a loss of trust in politicians and other authority figures has contributed to the rise of dark populism. Verbal and physical attacks are increasingly experienced by those in public life. Social media 'trolling' has become all-too common, and its mental health effects are often catastrophic.

Even so, those who govern need to uphold the highest standards of integrity and honesty. Sadly, news agencies often now have no option but to fact-check claims by leading politicians. We seem at times to be living an echo-chamber of lies and half-truths, a disorientating world that makes us uncertain of the present and fear for the future.

Although we may dislike extreme language, we can see the value of Micah's graphic portrayal of Judah's privileged elite as cannibals. His prophecy speaks a much-needed truth about exploitation, even if we would recoil from hearing it in a public forum today.

The passage of time has created a buffer, enabling us to appreciate the literary and moral qualities of this outstanding piece of rhetoric. But Micah doesn't need our admiration. He needs us to listen.

Sennacherib's invasion of Judah in 701 BC drove home the consequences of corruption and greed. A society where the rich prey on the poor has lost its vision and purpose. Without a clear set of values, without mutual flourishing, our common life becomes degraded.

Whether we like it or not, the biblical opposition to injustice propels the Church into the public square.

Risen, ascended Lord,
as we rejoice at your triumph,
fill your Church on earth with power and compassion,
that all who are estranged by sin
may find forgiveness and know your peace,
to the glory of God the Father.

COLLECT

Reflection by **Alan Everett** | 153

Monday 20 May
Psalms 123, 124, 125, **126**
Joshua 1
Luke 9.18-27

Luke 9.18-27

'While he was praying privately...' (v.18)

For all the busyness and action of the three years of Jesus' public ministry, and there is a lot of both, there are also very significant moments where he disappears from view, either goes up a mountain or somewhere else out of sight, and withdraws into prayer. It's striking though that in Luke's account of this conversation, he has spent time alone, and the first question he asks when he comes out of this time is 'What are the crowds saying about me?'

This captures one of the key features of Jesus's life, which is lived both intensely publicly and resolutely privately. In order to face the vocation that he mentions here – to take up the cross – perhaps the most public and humiliating way of dying ever invented – he needs to know who he is, what he's about, and to whom he belongs.

It's no different for us. Prayer is life, and life is prayer. And our prayer encompasses all our experiences, including the shame and loss that Jesus speaks about. But in order for us to be able to live as Christ's disciples in the world, whatever our personality or preferences for company, if Jesus needed time to withdraw alone, so do we.

COLLECT

O Lord, from whom all good things come:
grant to us your humble servants,
that by your holy inspiration
we may think those things that are good,
and by your merciful guiding may perform the same;
through our Lord Jesus Christ,
who is alive and reigns with you,
in the unity of the Holy Spirit,
one God, now and for ever.

| *Reflection by* **Lucy Winkett**

Psalms **132**, 133
Joshua 2
Luke 9.28-36

Tuesday 21 May

Luke 9.28-36

'While he was praying, the appearance of his face changed' (v.29)

This mysterious moment on top of Mount Tabor shimmers as one of the 'theophanies', that is, manifestations of the divine in the world, that are evident throughout the gospels. But it's important not to misunderstand the nature of these sorts of stories. They're not magic tricks, but as the gospels use them, signs that point beyond themselves. Conversations, realisations, actions that reveal that there is more to life than what is discernible through five senses, and therefore an indication that God is present and active in the world around us.

It's easy when reading this sort of theophany story, to start thinking – well I've never had that kind of God revelation so I must not be doing it properly or I'm not good enough. It's a natural reaction, but one that must be resisted! Peter has the most natural reaction, feeling that this moment of clear sightedness, when he can really see what it's all about, what life is for, should last for ever. It's a recognisable aspect of human living, that sometimes, we do get the sense that in an ordinary day, things become a lot clearer, we're suddenly aware of our connectedness with all that lives, or we feel a sort of overwhelming compassion for strangers on the bus. God in Christ is present all day every day, and those sorts of mountaintop experiences, wherever they occur and however rare they are, help to cultivate the courage we need to endure the valleys below.

O Lord, from whom all good things come:
grant to us your humble servants,
that by your holy inspiration
we may think those things that are good,
and by your merciful guiding may perform the same;
through our Lord Jesus Christ,
who is alive and reigns with you,
in the unity of the Holy Spirit,
one God, now and for ever.

COLLECT

Reflection by **Lucy Winkett** | 155

Wednesday 22 May

Luke 9.37-50

'Everyone was amazed at all that he was doing...' (v.43)

Jesus is often frank, bordering on rude, to the people closest to him. He is brusque with his mother at the wedding in Cana, and here his pretty excoriating 'You faithless and perverse generation' is directed at his disciples, the ones who have given up everything to be with him. This isn't Jesus meek and mild at all. This is the urgent, disciplined voice of one who knows there is never much time and that so much is wrong in the world. At moments like this, the personality of Jesus of Nazareth becomes evident, alongside the more gentle exchanges with the people he encounters.

But there's more than this too, given the theological reflections necessary for understanding the full meaning of the life of Christ, facing crucifixion and anticipating resurrection too. This urgency and truth-telling reveals not only the earthly life of the prophetic nomadic healer Jesus, but also reveals the nature of God in the world when the reality of the fracturedness of life becomes real in the life of a human being, like this person, clearly suffering and disturbed by a condition unnamed and unknown.

The dual meaning of this urgent and forthright intervention is captured by verses 43 and 44. 'All were astounded at the greatness of God' and 'amazed' by Jesus. They are, in this incident, as in the whole Christ-event, the same thing.

COLLECT

O Lord, from whom all good things come:
grant to us your humble servants,
that by your holy inspiration
we may think those things that are good,
and by your merciful guiding may perform the same;
through our Lord Jesus Christ,
who is alive and reigns with you,
in the unity of the Holy Spirit,
one God, now and for ever.

| *Reflection by* **Lucy Winkett**

Psalms **143**, 146
Joshua 4.1 – 5.1
Luke 9.51-end

Thursday 23 May

Luke 9.51-end
'He set his face to go towards Jerusalem' (v.51)

One of the foremost New Testament scholars of the twentieth century, Geza Vermes, compiled what he assessed to be the most likely verbatim phrases from Jesus of Nazareth. Given the Greek translation of Aramaic phrases, he took the words quoted by the evangelists and analysed them to find behind them the rhythms and cadences of Jesus's mother tongue. One of the phrases that he assessed to be perhaps one of the most authentic verbatim sayings from the mouth of Jesus was in this passage, 'Foxes have holes and birds of the air have their nests, but the Son of Man has nowhere to lay his head.' If this is right, then we have a beautiful insight into the mind, spirit and heart of Jesus. He says it in response to a perhaps rather passionate comment from a bystander 'along the road' who says they will follow him wherever he goes. Jesus's reply is by way of warning perhaps, that it won't be easy, but it is, in the fundamental challenge that it represents, a poetic, evocative invitation to life lived interdependently with all that lives on the earth.

Jesus's invitation emphasises that human beings are somehow in the same society, if you like, as feral animals and flighted birds. The 'Son of Man' can be translated as a particular person, Jesus, alone, or equally as an exemplar of all human beings: the phrase has long been debated and isn't clear. As ever, in his nature, Jesus shows his disciples and now us, what God is like, but maybe more challengingly, shows us what it could be like to be human.

O Lord, from whom all good things come:
grant to us your humble servants,
that by your holy inspiration
we may think those things that are good,
and by your merciful guiding may perform the same;
through our Lord Jesus Christ,
who is alive and reigns with you,
in the unity of the Holy Spirit,
one God, now and for ever.

COLLECT

Friday 24 May

Psalms 142, **144**
Joshua 5.2-end
Luke 10.1-16

Luke 10.1-16

'I am sending you out like lambs into the midst of wolves' (v.3)

The collection of sayings of Jesus that we have been reading over the past few days now are applied not only to him and his vocation, but now to his closest friends and followers. The link was in the final verse of yesterday's reading: that disciples of Christ are asked not to look back, but to keep moving forward. This means that whatever possessions they have, whatever relationships they maintain, whatever place they might call theirs, is ultimately a gift from God, and therefore should be held lightly, with unclenched hands, knowing that all belongs to God in the end anyway.

What can sound like somewhat harsh teaching by Jesus, urging his friends to, in the old phrase, 'shake the dust from your feet' if a town is unwelcoming, is more helpfully understood as a teaching to tread lightly on the earth. Take each day as it comes, says Jesus, heal the person in front of you, eat what you're given, let your first words to anyone be of peace. And, because everyone has the freedom to say no, don't let your words of peace turn into an attitude of coercion. Leave people alone if they are not open to your presence there. And although Jesus proclaims a woe towards the ones who will reject this message of peace, he is adamant that the disciples simply proclaim the kingdom of God anyway.

It is a way of life that is resolute, respectful and authentic, proclaiming peace, whether or not that proclamation is heard and accepted.

COLLECT

O Lord, from whom all good things come:
grant to us your humble servants,
that by your holy inspiration
we may think those things that are good,
and by your merciful guiding may perform the same;
through our Lord Jesus Christ,
who is alive and reigns with you,
in the unity of the Holy Spirit,
one God, now and for ever.

| *Reflection by* **Lucy Winkett**

Saturday 25 May

Luke 10.17-24

'You have hidden these things from the wise and intelligent and revealed them to infants' (v.21)

Jesus at his most poetic and vivid continues his teaching in these verses regarding the fate of all those who live in the way that he is urging them to live. The seventy come and tell him, perhaps rather boastfully, that they're finding they are masters of all they survey. He doesn't let them get away with this, but reminds them of the perspective they must maintain, that is, the perspective of eternity, not earthly achievement.

One of Luke's favourite themes is emphasised here, that God's 'gracious will' or pleasure as the Greek might also be translated (v.21) is when the poorest, the least, the simplest, grasp the nature of the message before the wise, rich or intelligent. In verse 23, there is a beautiful detail often used by Luke, which is that Jesus 'turns to' his disciples. This can remind us of the baptism promises we make, that we turn to Christ ourselves. When we turn to Christ, we find him turning back to address us. And the words we hear are those of the disciples here: that our discernment in seeing the miracle of the presence of God in the world brings with it blessing and the fulfilment of our desire to be fully, abundantly alive.

O Lord, from whom all good things come:
grant to us your humble servants,
that by your holy inspiration
we may think those things that are good,
and by your merciful guiding may perform the same;
through our Lord Jesus Christ,
who is alive and reigns with you,
in the unity of the Holy Spirit,
one God, now and for ever.

COLLECT

Reflection by **Lucy Winkett** | 159

Monday 27 May

Luke 10.25-37

'Go and do likewise' (v.37)

One of Jesus' favourite teaching techniques is not to answer a straight question with a closed 'yes' or 'no' but to tell a story, nuanced, imaginative, designed to make the hearers think harder, giving them more chance to live differently. Here the lawyer wants to justify himself so asks what might seem to be a straightforward question: who is my neighbour?

There are any number of ways to define this if Jesus wanted to answer a point of law to the lawyer, but as ever, his story opens up whole new vistas of understanding of what it means to be human in the world. The genius of Jesus the playwright is that at any given time, any of us are all of these characters. The thumbnail sketches by turns convict and comfort all of us: sometimes we're too busy to stop, sometimes we feel as if we're bleeding out, sometimes we're OK to take someone in and look after them, sometimes we're cruel, even verbally violent like the gang, and sometimes we find we have the capacity to stop what we're doing, and tend to the wounds of the person in front of us.

Dr Martin Luther King Jr put it best when he commented on this parable that most of us think 'What will happen to me if I stop?', but the more Christ-like question is 'What will happen to him if I don't?'

COLLECT

Almighty and everlasting God,
you have given us your servants grace,
by the confession of a true faith,
to acknowledge the glory of the eternal Trinity
and in the power of the divine majesty to worship the Unity:
keep us steadfast in this faith,
that we may evermore be defended from all adversities;
through Jesus Christ your Son our Lord,
who is alive and reigns with you,
in the unity of the Holy Spirit,
one God, now and for ever.

| *Reflection by* **Lucy Winkett**

Tuesday 28 May

Luke 10.38-end

'A woman named Martha welcomed him into her home' (v.38)

The little family of Martha, Mary and Lazarus were obviously important to Jesus, as he seems to have visited them often and eaten with them more than once. Martha is captured in this particular story as one who is too busy for the contemplative attitude that her sister shows towards Jesus, and is therefore criticised for it.

Women in churches down the centuries have inhabited this 'Martha' identity, and have either been criticised for it by others or have felt guilty themselves. But Martha is a rounded character, not only to be characterised by the cleaning and washing up. In John's Gospel she is the faithful theologian, confessing Jesus as the Messiah; she is brave when in front of the crowd at her brother's grave she challenges Jesus, calling out the fact that the body will be 'stinking'. She is honest and forthright, just the qualities Jesus has been looking for in a disciple. But here, yes, her exchange with Jesus is evidence that our own worries and distractions can lead us to lose perspective.

As we've seen, Jesus needed time and space to stop, pray, be alone, withdraw. While it's important not to let Martha be locked up in this persona, in contrast to her more contemplative sister, it is a theme of these past few chapters, that however hectic or worrisome life gets, and it really does get too much for many of us at times, the perspective of eternal love, indiscriminate blessing, and focus on what is most important, is the gift that Martha's question to Jesus elicits for us as modern readers.

Holy God,
faithful and unchanging:
enlarge our minds with the knowledge of your truth,
and draw us more deeply into the mystery of your love,
that we may truly worship you,
Father, Son and Holy Spirit,
one God, now and for ever.

COLLECT

Wednesday 29 May

Psalm 119.1-32
Joshua 8.1-29
Luke 11.1-13

Luke 11.1-13

'So I say, "search and you will find"' (v.9)

It's a question still asked by many today: what is prayer? How can I, how should I pray? What's the best way to do it? The disciples' question to Jesus is a common one, responding to an innate sense that there is more to life than what we can see, and we yearn sometimes to connect with God in conversation. Mother Theresa was asked once by a journalist what prayer was. She answered that it was listening to God. The journalist was intrigued and asked a follow up question, wanting to know that if she was listening, what was God saying? Mother Theresa said rather cryptically that she didn't know, because God wasn't saying anything, God was listening to her.

In the repetition of the prayer that Jesus teaches his disciples in this passage, there is a spaciousness that makes sense of that mutual listening. The prayer is famously direct, no flowery language but straightforwardly addressed to God, with a focus on mutual forgiveness, and a future-orientated hope for the kingdom to come when all are fed each day, where the time of trial is endured safely or avoided altogether. The key for this is that it's not prayed once and then it's either 'worked' or not, but this prayer becomes the element in which we live and move and have our being.

Perseverance, like the person who bangs on the door at midnight, persistence, the every-day-ness of praying means that we can get close to the promise that Jesus makes, that somewhere, somehow, sometime, the door will be opened and we can move through.

COLLECT

Almighty and everlasting God,
you have given us your servants grace,
by the confession of a true faith,
to acknowledge the glory of the eternal Trinity
and in the power of the divine majesty to worship the Unity:
keep us steadfast in this faith,
that we may evermore be defended from all adversities;
through Jesus Christ your Son our Lord,
who is alive and reigns with you,
in the unity of the Holy Spirit,
one God, now and for ever.

| *Reflection by* **Lucy Winkett**

Psalm 147
Deuteronomy 8.2-16
1 Corinthians 10.1-17

Thursday 30 May

Day of Thanksgiving for the
Institution of Holy Communion
(Corpus Christi)

1 Corinthians 10.1-17

'We who are many are one body' (v.17)

The feast of Corpus Christi, celebrated around the world today, is around a thousand years old being founded in 1264. It's a day to focus on the holy meal shared by Christians in all denominations, variously called the Lord's Supper, Holy Communion, Eucharist, the Mass. Paul's letter to the Corinthians sets out the philosophy of sharing bread together, a practice shared by many religious traditions, from the Christian perspective.

There is some deep thinking going on in this passage, which essentially can be expressed in the traditional teaching of what a sacrament is: an outward and visible sign of an inward and spiritual grace. Paul is urging against idolatry, which would focus on the bread itself, testing Christ as Christ was himself tested by being urged to turn stones into bread in the wilderness. Instead, he says, remember the meaning of this sharing, which is that we express the truth that we are all one body because we share in this one bread.

Paul urges his readers not to lose perspective, not to distract ourselves by complaining or becoming too boastful (the lovely picture he offers of us thinking we are standing proud when in fact all that means is that we are more likely to fall). Instead, lean on the nourishment and life-giving presence of Christ in the Eucharistic bread and wine. Whatever the theologies that have grown up around this sharing, the deepest possible connection is made between God and humanity by knowing we are one by sharing this meal whenever we gather to do so.

COLLECT

Lord Jesus Christ,
we thank you that in this wonderful sacrament
you have given us the memorial of your passion:
grant us so to reverence the sacred mysteries
of your body and blood
that we may know within ourselves
and show forth in our lives
the fruits of your redemption;
for you are alive and reign with the Father
in the unity of the Holy Spirit,
one God, now and for ever.

Reflection by **Lucy Winkett**   163

Friday 31 May

Visit of the Blessed Virgin Mary
to Elizabeth

Psalms 85, 150
I Samuel 2.1-10
Mark 3.31-end

Mark 3.31-end

'Whoever does the will of God is my brother and sister and mother'
(v.35)

Today the Church celebrates the visit of Mary, the mother of Jesus, to her cousin Elizabeth, who was also pregnant at the time with her son, John, later known as John the Baptist. The two women meet and no doubt support each other in their pregnancies, and it's from Luke's account of the meeting, that the great song of Mary, the Magnificat, comes.

Here we see Jesus bringing together his birth family and his chosen family in a remark that could sound a little harsh, if his mother has been waiting for him a long time as it seems. But the point that Jesus makes is one of more, not less connection and an extension of family rather than a rejection of blood relatives. Mary is a constant and strong presence in the gospels, right up until the end, when the witnessing of the torture and execution of her son must be more than a mother can bear. She has learned to share Jesus with everyone else, a painful and no doubt disorientating vocation for any mother. But Mary is a figure for the rest of us to find inspiration in, as she bears God into the world, and carries the presence of Christ as the first evangelist in a waiting world.

COLLECT

Mighty God,
by whose grace Elizabeth rejoiced with Mary
and greeted her as the mother of the Lord:
look with favour on your lowly servants
that, with Mary, we may magnify your holy name
and rejoice to acclaim her Son our Saviour,
who is alive and reigns with you,
in the unity of the Holy Spirit,
one God, now and for ever.

| *Reflection by* **Lucy Winkett**

Psalms 20, 21, **23**
Joshua 10.1-15
Luke 11.37-end

Luke 11.37-end

'You tithe mint and rue and herbs... and neglect justice' (v.42)

As often happens in Luke's Gospel, we are teleported here into a domestic scene where Jesus is out for dinner. It's a normal and usual evening meal that gives occasion to some fierce reflections from the prophetic and urgent Christ. He really is speaking truth to power here, surrounded as he is by what seems to be rather a smart dinner party set of religious teachers, lawyers and leaders of society.

His main point is made to anyone who reads the gospel and has ears to hear. It is simply no good, he says, going through the motions of religious or legal observance, what might be called the letter of the law, without the meaning and impact of the spirit of the law being taken into consideration. The link between intention and action matters. And his fiercest criticism, echoing his teaching earlier in the previous chapter, is reserved for those who not only act hypocritically themselves, but, worse, hinder other people's progression in life and faith. His excoriating remarks are reserved for those who abuse their power, rest on their superior knowledge and use this influence to prevent the flourishing of others.

The seeds of this behaviour are to be found in every human heart, vulnerable as we are to the need to be acknowledged, competitive as we are when we feel our position is under attack or being undermined. The hostility Jesus provokes at the end of this chapter is recognisable to any of us who have read his teaching on justice and love, and thought 'Well he can't really mean that, it's impossible.'

COLLECT

Almighty and everlasting God,
you have given us your servants grace,
by the confession of a true faith,
to acknowledge the glory of the eternal Trinity
and in the power of the divine majesty to worship the Unity:
keep us steadfast in this faith,
that we may evermore be defended from all adversities;
through Jesus Christ your Son our Lord,
who is alive and reigns with you,
in the unity of the Holy Spirit,
one God, now and for ever.

Reflection by **Lucy Winkett**   165

Monday 3 June

Psalms 27, **30**
Joshua 14
Luke 12.1-12

Luke 12.1-12

'Whatever you have said in the dark will be heard in the light ...'
(v.3)

In this passage, we read stern words from Jesus to his disciples. The scene begins with a large crowd gathered in their thousands, with so many there that people are trampling on one another. This extra detail perhaps shows the writer emphasising just how much people wanted to see and hear Jesus. This throws into prominence Jesus' decision to address his followers first. In this moment, surrounded by those eager to hear from him, Jesus turns first to the disciples. Clearly what he has to say is so important that he cannot wait till later, when they are alone. In front of the crowd, he warns them against hypocrisy.

I wonder what had prompted him to do so right at that point. What had happened in the moments before? Had he perhaps heard one of his disciples saying something about his own personal piety that Jesus knew was not true? Had he heard a group of his followers speaking ill about someone behind their back yet being friendly to their face? Jesus is clear that hypocrisy is not only wrong, but futile, because it will always be found out. What is said in the darkness will be heard in the light. It is a reminder to us today to be authentic and truthful, to encounter people with grace, to treat others as we would like to be treated.

COLLECT

O God,
the strength of all those who put their trust in you,
mercifully accept our prayers
and, because through the weakness of our mortal nature
we can do no good thing without you,
grant us the help of your grace,
that in the keeping of your commandments
we may please you both in will and deed;
through Jesus Christ your Son our Lord,
who is alive and reigns with you,
in the unity of the Holy Spirit,
one God, now and for ever.

| *Reflection by* **Chine McDonald**

Tuesday 4 June

Luke 12.13-21

'So it is with those who store up treasures for themselves but are not rich toward God ...' (v.21)

While at the christening of a dear friend's child recently, I was struck by the words of the familiar hymn 'Be thou my vision' and in particular the lines:

'Riches I heed not, nor man's empty praise.
Thou mine inheritance, now and always.'

We live in a world of extreme wealth inequality, where some have nothing and are struggling to meet the costs of daily living, while others have more wealth and possessions than they can possibly spend in a lifetime. It is an understandable human desire to want to hold onto what we have: to accumulate wealth and possessions and to ensure we secure our inheritance. For the person in the crowd in today's passage who asks Jesus to make his brother share his inheritance with him, this is the foremost issue he wants to bring to the Messiah. Jesus, though, responds through a parable with another rebuke, warning against storing up treasures for ourselves rather than being rich towards God. While worrying about what we have and fear of losing it might be entirely human, this cannot be how it is in the kingdom of God.

In this countercultural kingdom, our reliance will and should be on God and not on the things we have. As the hymn reminds us, 'Thou mine inheritance, now and always.'

COLLECT

God of truth,
help us to keep your law of love
and to walk in ways of wisdom,
that we may find true life
in Jesus Christ your Son.

Reflection by **Chine McDonald** | 167

Wednesday 5 June

Psalm **34**
Joshua 22.9-end
Luke 12.22-31

Luke 12.22-31

'And .... do not keep worrying ...' (v.29)

I am a planner. In my family that is most evident in the fact that we do what this passage tells us that we should not do. We literally plan what we will eat and drink, and it is a rare occurrence for us to have to ask the question, 'What shall we have for dinner today?' Part of me envies those who are able to be more spontaneous when it comes to their food choices. But if I'm honest, my approach to food – much like my need to plan things to the last detail – is a symptom of my anxiety and worry. Like many others, setting my heart and busying my mind on planning future things is a way of feeling that I have a sense of control in the midst of what often seems chaotic. But as Jesus says, there really is very little point in worrying about these things when we have a God in heaven who is in control and loves us with an everlasting love.

Sometimes it is good to think ahead, but not because we are so anxious about the future that we lose sight of God's provision and love for us. This is not to say that everything always goes to plan, but that whatever happens, we are loved and cared for. This reminder may help to soothe our anxious souls.

COLLECT

O God,
the strength of all those who put their trust in you,
mercifully accept our prayers
and, because through the weakness of our mortal nature
we can do no good thing without you,
grant us the help of your grace,
that in the keeping of your commandments
we may please you both in will and deed;
through Jesus Christ your Son our Lord,
who is alive and reigns with you,
in the unity of the Holy Spirit,
one God, now and for ever.

| *Reflection by* **Chine McDonald**

Psalm **37***
Joshua 23
Luke 12.32-40

Thursday 6 June

Luke 12.32-40

'For where your treasure is, there your heart will be also ...' (v.34)

Banking apps have developed so much in recent years. As well as being able to cash a cheque with a few taps on your phone, pay bills and transfer money for goods, many banking apps can analyse how we spend our money: revealing what we spend on leisure, entertainment, clothing, mortgages, food, charitable giving – all our spending listed. It's now easier than ever to be able to see quite literally where we place our treasure.

In today's passage, Jesus is making a suggestion about what it is that we might do with our treasure: sell it all and give it to the poor. Jesus is warning hearers of the dangers that come with clinging to possessions and money. It can become the thing upon which we focus and want to hang on to. We may fear being without it because of the consequences of having nothing. But there is power in the reminder that God has already given us everything we need: God has given us the kingdom. Nothing else really matters. With this should come a liberation that means we can hold our treasures and possessions lightly, being generous with them.

This is all easier said than done. What is clear is that we need the Holy Spirit's power in order to be truly liberated from the risk of our possessions possessing us. How might you begin to do that today?

God of truth,
help us to keep your law of love
and to walk in ways of wisdom,
that we may find true life
in Jesus Christ your Son.

COLLECT

Reflection by **Chine McDonald** | 169

Friday 7 June

Psalm 31
Joshua 24.1-28
Luke 12.41-48

Luke 12.41-48

'From everyone to whom much has been given, much will be required' (v.48)

My parents were refugees during the Nigerian Civil War that took place in the late 1960s. My father has talked about his fear of one day seeing himself in the black and white archive footage of scenes from the war that gripped the hearts of the British public during the conflict. Some have suggested that the Biafran war sparked the beginning of the humanitarian movement in the UK, with several Christian aid agencies beginning as a response to it.

Having worked for several years in the development sector, I have become acutely aware of the disparity and inequality that exists between the richest nations and the poorest: the so-called 'developing' ones. The past centuries have seen some countries thrive, becoming rich at the expense of others. But there is now a movement to rectify that. It's almost as though the Global North is waking up to the fact that to whom much is given, much is demanded. As we face the climate crisis, it is the poorest around the world who are on the front line, despite the fact that the richest nations have contributed the most to global warming. It is easier for us to heed Jesus's words in today's passage at a national or even global level, but as individuals, how are we responding to the challenges facing us? How might we as those to whom much has been given, give back?

COLLECT

O God,
the strength of all those who put their trust in you,
mercifully accept our prayers
and, because through the weakness of our mortal nature
we can do no good thing without you,
grant us the help of your grace,
that in the keeping of your commandments
we may please you both in will and deed;
through Jesus Christ your Son our Lord,
who is alive and reigns with you,
in the unity of the Holy Spirit,
one God, now and for ever.

170 | *Reflection by* **Chine McDonald**

Psalms 41, **42**, 43
Joshua 24.29-end
Luke 12.49-end

Saturday 8 June

Luke 12.49-end

'... you not know how to interpret the present time...' (v.56)

A few weeks before the first Covid lockdown in 2020, a friend told me about an article that predicted hundreds of thousands would be killed by the virus. I remember laughing at how ridiculous it sounded. Surely not! But we all know what happened next.

People have built careers around predicting the future. Weather professionals tell us the forecasts for the coming days and help us plan accordingly. Futurologists predict trends across different sectors and provide wisdom for leaders to know how to respond. But who could have predicted the past few years? We have seen pandemics and, with that, unprecedented scientific advancement; we have seen political turbulence at home and away the likes of which we have never known in our lifetimes. We cannot predict the future, nor be certain about what will happen.

This uncertainty is a reminder to put our trust not in earthly things, possessions, wealth or knowledge, but in the One who stands above it all. Although we cannot forecast the future, the Holy Spirit can help us discern what is going on beneath the surface. The Spirit can help give us wisdom to know how to respond and, in whatever may come, draw others towards healing, wholeness and being in right relationship with God. In the busyness of life and the turbulent times, how might we make room to see beyond what is in front of our noses and discern what is really going on underneath?

God of truth,
help us to keep your law of love
and to walk in ways of wisdom,
that we may find true life
in Jesus Christ your Son.

COLLECT

Monday 10 June

Psalm **44**
Judges 2
Luke 13.1-9

Luke 13.1-9

'If it bears fruit next year, well and good; but if not, you can cut it down. (v.9b)

'The only certainty is death,' the French author Guy de Maupassant once wrote. No one knows whether our own demise will take place in the coming seconds or decades from now. As we grow older, death moves from being something that happens to other people to becoming a normal part of life. I've been struck in recent months that with the passing of time comes the passing of the generations above us: grandparents, parents, famous faces we had grown up with – from Pope Benedict XVI to Queen Elizabeth II.

Jesus, in today's passage, is delivering a difficult message to the disciples: for those of us who believe, as it is it with those who do not, death is an inevitability. But there is hope. Repentance of those things we have done wrong, the ways in which we have fallen short of God's ideal, can lead us to the lightness that comes with forgiveness. With that reconciliation and entering into a right relationship with God comes life in its fullness. Eternal life does not begin after death, but in the present.

I love how this passage ends on a cliff-hanger: will the fig tree bear fruit the following year, or will it be cut down? Perhaps the choice is ours.

COLLECT

Lord, you have taught us
that all our doings without love are nothing worth:
send your Holy Spirit
and pour into our hearts that most excellent gift of love,
the true bond of peace and of all virtues,
without which whoever lives is counted dead before you.
Grant this for your only Son Jesus Christ's sake,
who is alive and reigns with you,
in the unity of the Holy Spirit,
one God, now and for ever.

| *Reflection by* **Chine McDonald**

Psalms 100, 101, 117
Jeremiah 9.23-24
Acts 4.32-end

Tuesday 11 June
Barnabas the Apostle

Acts 4.32-end

'... everything they owned was held in common (v.32)

The radical unity of the early Church described in today's passage sounds a million miles away from the fractured Church we so often hear about today. Rather than being known for being 'one in heart and mind', followers of Christ today divide along many different theological and social fault-lines. We often air our family disagreements on the world's stage and thereby present a Christianity characterised by what tears us apart rather than what brings us together. But there is hope.

On several occasions in the gospel accounts, Jesus' followers are seen to argue about their status, and they respond very differently to Jesus' predictions of his death and his eventual resurrection. Perhaps for a unified Church to emerge, they had to become unified in mission and purpose – something that could only come about through the Holy Spirit once they had witnessed the risen Christ and the truths they had struggled to comprehend fell into place. But fast forward to this scene in Acts and we find some years later a group of Christians living in harmony together. Not only are they one in heart and mind, but they share their possessions, each holding what they have lightly, the less well-off sharing the needs they had and those needs being met by those who sold their possessions to help. May the Church again become a model to the world of radical unity.

Bountiful God, giver of all gifts,
who poured your Spirit upon your servant Barnabas
and gave him grace to encourage others:
help us, by his example,
to be generous in our judgements
and unselfish in our service;
through Jesus Christ your Son our Lord,
who is alive and reigns with you,
in the unity of the Holy Spirit,
one God, now and for ever.

COLLECT

Reflection by **Chine McDonald** | 173

Wednesday 12 June

Psalm 119.57-80
Judges 5
Luke 13.22-end

Luke 13.22-end

'Some are last who will be first, and some are first who will be last'
(v.30)

Today's verses bring back childhood memories of being anxious about my salvation. I had grown up in churches in which the concept of the narrow door and the exclusivity of the Christian faith were the focus. Our critics spoke of the theology of a 'get out of jail free card' that was held by the faithful few who diligently went to church, said their prayers and definitely did not swear. The idea that many of us who call ourselves Christian might be turned away by God, despite us having done all the 'right' things can still strike much fear in many.

There has been much discussion over centuries about the nature of salvation – from whether a few will be saved, to the universalist belief that all will eventually be so. What strikes me, though, in reading today's passage is the idea that the kingdom of God is always surprising, and never predictable. It says to us, 'You thought you knew what it meant to be righteous? Think again. You thought you know who would be first in line? You're wrong.' The kingdom of God is a place in which things are turned upside down. It is a place in which human wisdom is replaced with divine wisdom. It's a place in which the status quo cannot be assumed. It's a place of newness and wholeness, where we will see things as they should be. Thank God for that.

COLLECT

Lord, you have taught us
that all our doings without love are nothing worth:
send your Holy Spirit
and pour into our hearts that most excellent gift of love,
the true bond of peace and of all virtues,
without which whoever lives is counted dead before you.
Grant this for your only Son Jesus Christ's sake,
who is alive and reigns with you,
in the unity of the Holy Spirit,
one God, now and for ever.

174 | *Reflection by* **Chine McDonald**

Psalms 56, **57** (63*)
Judges 6.1-24
Luke 14.1-11

Thursday 13 June

Luke 14.1-11

*'For all those who exalt themselves will be humbled,
and those who humble themselves will be exalted ...' (v.11)*

'Pride goes before a fall, and a haughty spirit before destruction.'
(Proverbs 16.18) Today's parable echoes that warning, with Jesus
cautioning against thinking too much of oneself after seeing guests
take the places of honour at a dinner in the home of a prominent
Pharisee. He warns that those who do this will eventually be
humiliated and moved to lesser seats. Far better to choose for oneself
the lowest place.

Dinner table seating instructions from the Messiah might seem a
little strange. But Jesus' words here reflect the nature of the
kingdom of God. This is a place where the usual rules do not apply.
Humility is what is prized in the upside-down nature of God's
kingdom. This is difficult for so many of us to do. We live in a world
where we are asked to measure ourselves against others, where
pride in ourselves, our achievements and what we have – whether
that is family, a great job or great car – are what matters. Despite
the context in which we find ourselves, it is through the Holy Spirit
that we can humble ourselves rather than exalt ourselves. As we
navigate our way through this day, how might we find ways to exalt
others rather than ourselves? How might we be examples of humility
in a world filled with ego?

Faithful Creator,
whose mercy never fails:
deepen our faithfulness to you
and to your living Word,
Jesus Christ our Lord.

COLLECT

Reflection by **Chine McDonald** | 175

Friday 14 June

Luke 14.12-24

'... none of those who were invited will taste my dinner' (v.24)

I love arranging a party or social event. I get a thrill out of gathering people: planning the logistics, sending out invitations, deciding what people will eat and drink, how I'll greet my guests and what music I'll play. I come from an ethnic group of people for whom gathering around the table with food and drink in abundance is key to cementing relationship and forming community. I often think that for me, it doesn't really matter who I gather around the table, just as long as there are plenty of people there.

I like to believe we can forge relationship and find points of connection with everyone, but while I might think that I'm open to gathering *anyone* around the table, I – like many others – tend to gravitate towards those who are a little like me. When the original guests – the A-listers – made excuses to not attend the host's party in Jesus' parable of the great banquet, others who are on the fringes, whose lives are very different from the host's, are eventually invited in. So often in Jesus's parables, the usual suspects can learn from the example of the unexpected. God invites each and every one of us into the kingdom, but those of us who feel we are on the A-list might take this invitation for granted.

Today, may we find moments to glimpse the kingdom of God among unexpected people in surprising places.

COLLECT

Lord, you have taught us
that all our doings without love are nothing worth:
send your Holy Spirit
and pour into our hearts that most excellent gift of love,
the true bond of peace and of all virtues,
without which whoever lives is counted dead before you.
Grant this for your only Son Jesus Christ's sake,
who is alive and reigns with you,
in the unity of the Holy Spirit,
one God, now and for ever.

| *Reflection by* **Chine McDonald**

Psalm **68**
Judges 7
Luke 14.25-end

Saturday 15 June

Luke 14.25-end

'... if salt has lost its taste ... they throw it away' (vv.34-35)

What difference does it make to be a follower of Jesus? What, if anything, marks us out as distinctive? When I look around, it can be hard to distinguish myself from those around me: my colleagues, friends and family. I have the same concerns as them, the same worries, the same hang-ups, the same anxieties. In the early days of my faith journey, I used to be so committed to making a difference. I wanted to be the salt that seasoned every place I entered, every relationship I made, everything I came into contact with, with the flavour of Christ, with the help of the Holy Spirit.

I am sure I am not alone when I describe the zeal with which I approached my faith and how much I wanted to tell people about it, but if I'm honest, the zeal gave way to the preoccupations of everyday life. Other things got in the way. As the years go by, it can be far too easy for us to lose our saltiness and blend into the background, to be flavoured by the things around us rather than the other way round. In today's passage, Jesus challenges us yet again, warning that the salt will be thrown out if it loses its flavour.

What can we do today to bring the savour of Christ and change the atmosphere around us?

Faithful Creator,
whose mercy never fails:
deepen our faithfulness to you
and to your living Word,
Jesus Christ our Lord.

COLLECT

Monday 17 June

Psalm **71**
Judges 8.22-end
Luke 15.1-10

Luke 15.1-10

'I have found my lost sheep' (v.6)

I saw a cartoon recently depicting this parable. On the edge of the picture the Shepherd was lowering himself precariously over a cliff edge, to reach and lift the lost sheep from the ledge onto which it had strayed. In the centre of the picture were the other ninety-nine, all safe and sound, and looking rather put out, all of them bleating their slogan together: 'All sheep matter!' It was a sharp take on some people's indignant response to 'Black Lives Matter'.

These two parables have so much to give, and at the heart of both of them is God's active love, his restless desire to find us. Augustine says, 'Our hearts are restless till they find their rest in you'. But this is even better, for Jesus tells us that God's heart is also restless until he finds our hearts too. This strong image of a risk-taking, restless shepherd speaks of a God on the move, perhaps alarmingly so.

C.S. Lewis said that it was absurd to speak of religion as 'Man's search for God' and added, 'you might as well talk of the mouse's search for the cat.' But when he pounces on us, we need not fear. We will, in another phrase of Lewis's, be safe 'between the Lion's paws.'

COLLECT

Almighty God,
you have broken the tyranny of sin
and have sent the Spirit of your Son into our hearts
    whereby we call you Father:
give us grace to dedicate our freedom to your service,
that we and all creation may be brought
    to the glorious liberty of the children of God;
through Jesus Christ your Son our Lord,
who is alive and reigns with you,
in the unity of the Holy Spirit,
one God, now and for ever.

| *Reflection by* **Malcolm Guite**

Tuesday 18 June

Luke 15.11-end

'... he ran' (v.20)

It's good to read this almost too familiar parable in its gospel context, for that context may shift our emphasis a little. We call it 'The Parable of the Prodigal Son', but it has as much claim to be called 'The Parable of the Prodigal Father'. And since the last two stories were about a loving God's active search for what is lost, then surely this one continues the theme and suggests we focus as much on the father as on the son.

If prodigality means lavish and imprudent extravagance, then this father is prodigal indeed, prodigal twice over. 'While he was still far off the father saw him ...and he ran'. Those who first heard this parable would have been astonished. For fathers in those days were lords and masters of their households, they kept their dignity, sat in their favourite chair and were waited on. Still today, in parts of the Middle East, self-respecting men do not run. But here is one careless of dignity, careless of precedent, who picks up his skirts and runs, impelled by prodigal love and compassion. And then when the lost son is found and recovered, the father is prodigal a second time: bring the ring, the best robe, the fatted calf – let's have a massive party!

'If you have seen me,' says Jesus, 'you have seen the Father,' and this father's prodigality is not only matched but exceeded by Jesus, from the prodigality of the overflowing wine at Cana, to the gift of his heart's blood from the cross.

God our saviour,
look on this wounded world
in pity and in power;
hold us fast to your promises of peace
won for us by your Son,
our Saviour Jesus Christ.

COLLECT

Reflection by **Malcolm Guite** | 179

Wednesday 19 June

Psalm **77**
Judges 9.22-end
Luke 16.1-18

Luke 16.1-18

'How much do you owe?' (v 5)

In a way this next parable continues the theme of prodigality, indeed the charge of squandering is there at the outset. It's a story full of mischief and humour, but it must certainly be said that the manager is prodigal with his master's money when it comes to giving away the bargains. Black Friday has nothing on it – here's an invoice slashed by 50%!

Perhaps the key to this parable is the manager's initial question to his master's debtors: 'How much do you owe?' This is a parable about debt and it therefore picks up the resonance of that other parable about the two debtors and, even more tellingly, the language of the Lord's Prayer: 'Forgive us our debts as we forgive the debts of others.' If this is also a parable about forgiveness, then prodigality is just what we're after. We have been entrusted as it were with a huge bank of forgiveness, and God wants us to be magnificently prodigal in doling it out. Whatever scores we are keeping against others, this urges us to just go ahead and tear them in half, or cancel them altogether. God is happy to see all these moral debts written off because he himself, in his great prodigality, has already covered them. Black Friday has nothing on it, but Good Friday has everything to do with it.

COLLECT

Almighty God,
you have broken the tyranny of sin
and have sent the Spirit of your Son into our hearts
    whereby we call you Father:
give us grace to dedicate our freedom to your service,
that we and all creation may be brought
    to the glorious liberty of the children of God;
through Jesus Christ your Son our Lord,
who is alive and reigns with you,
in the unity of the Holy Spirit,
one God, now and for ever.

| *Reflection by* **Malcolm Guite**

Psalm **78.1-39***
Judges 11.1-11
Luke 16.19-end

Thursday 20 June

Luke 16.19-end

'... a great chasm' (v. 26)

The political philosophy of Dives, the rich man, was probably summed up in the verse of 'All things bright and beautiful' which we no longer sing:

> The rich man in his castle,
> The poor man at the gate,
> God made them, high or lowly,
> And ordered their estate.

If anyone suggested to him otherwise, or recommended a little social mobility, Dives doubtless replied, 'It's quite out of the question, for in a well-ordered society there is, of necessity, a great chasm fixed between the upper and lower classes.'

Indeed such is the chasm, so ingrained is his sense of entitlement, that even in the clarity of death, even as he lies in Hades, he can't see past it. He can't conceive of people like Lazarus as anything but either wastrels or servants: 'Send Lazarus,' he says imperiously, twice!

Fortunately this is only a story, but it is a story with a point, and that point is directed towards all of us who might turn out to be Dives, or one of his five brothers, rather than Lazarus. As it happens someone has indeed risen from the dead and come to warn us, the question is, will it make any difference?

COLLECT

God our saviour,
look on this wounded world
in pity and in power;
hold us fast to your promises of peace
won for us by your Son,
our Saviour Jesus Christ.

Friday 21 June

Psalm **55**
Judges 11.29-end
Luke 17.1-10

Luke 17.1-10

'... woe' (v.1)

'Occasions for sin' scarcely covers it. The Greek word is *skandalon*, which first meant a trap, and later came to mean a stumbling block; it is the root of our word scandal. We cannot read this without thinking of the enormous scandal, in every sense of that word, of child-abuse, hurting 'these little ones'. It's a scandal made worse when it is clerical abuse, when the very people whose role is to guard and protect have themselves become predators. Jesus does not mince his words, in pronouncing this 'woe.' It is such a grievous thing to become the *skandalon*, the cause of calamity and wounding, the destroyer of faith in another, that it would be better to have been cast into the sea.

But not withstanding these harrowing words of warning, the Church that works in Jesus' name has allowed such things to happen so many times over, that not only are the victims hurt, but also all those who love them and the wider society, rightly scandalised, are losing trust in the Church, and even faith in God.

And still, in spite of everything Christ keeps covenant with us, and will not let us go or cast us off, neither the sinner nor the sinned against. What is to become of those whom he said should be cast into the sea with a millstone round their necks? Only the one who took Jonah as his only sign can answer that.

COLLECT

Almighty God,
you have broken the tyranny of sin
and have sent the Spirit of your Son into our hearts
    whereby we call you Father:
give us grace to dedicate our freedom to your service,
that we and all creation may be brought
    to the glorious liberty of the children of God;
through Jesus Christ your Son our Lord,
who is alive and reigns with you,
in the unity of the Holy Spirit,
one God, now and for ever.

| *Reflection by* **Malcolm Guite**

Psalms **76**, 79
Judges 12.1-7
Luke 17.11-19

Saturday 22 June

Luke 17.11-19

'... and he was a Samaritan' (v.16)

XAnyone in a public facing role, serving a community, whether clergy or lay, knows Christ's experience only too well. Most of their work is hidden: the visits, the offers of all sorts of help, practical and spiritual, the kindly words in season, the sorting and fixing of things behind the scenes. So often there is little thanks, even from those who have been helped, let alone from the congregation, the local body of Christ on whose behalf the person has been ministering. And often it turns out that the one who comes back and says 'thank you' is not a member of the congregation at all, but one of the unchurched, an outsider, a Samaritan. The lepers themselves, we may note, made no such proud distinctions; Jews and Samaritans, sharing a common affliction, formed their own community, whatever their race and creed, drawn together on the margins.

All ten were healed by Christ, whatever their creed, but it is striking that he says to the Samaritan 'your *faith* has made you well'. Technically that was a heretical faith, for Jesus also said to the woman at the well 'salvation is from the Jews', and yet he still healed the leper and the Samaritan woman was still offered the living fountain. Jesus seems less concerned that we should be orthodox, theologically sound, than that we should be faithful, responsive and grateful.

God our saviour,
look on this wounded world
in pity and in power;
hold us fast to your promises of peace
won for us by your Son,
our Saviour Jesus Christ.

COLLECT

Reflection by **Malcolm Guite**   183

Monday 24 June

Birth of John the Baptist

Psalms 50, 149
Ecclesiasticus 48.1-10
or Malachi 3.1-6
Luke 3.1-17

Luke 3.1-17

'We have Abraham as our ancestor' (v.8)

This is a warning about not resting on our religious laurels, especially when those laurels turn out to be someone else's anyway. 'We have Abraham as our ancestor', encapsulates a sense of religious entitlement, which is not confined to this 'chosen people' with their Abrahamic covenant, content to live on the spiritual and moral capital of their ancestors rather than adding to it themselves. This may also apply to us! However far we may have come on our spiritual journey, there is always the temptation to think we have arrived and start taking for granted a faith that must be always new. So John the Baptist' call to bring his own people back to the Jordan may be a call to us to return to the source and make our faith new again. For it was centuries beforehand that Joshua had led the people across the Jordan into the promised land. 'Job done', say the complacent, but John says, 'no one can cross this river on your behalf, you must forsake your sense of entitlement, get close to God in the wilderness as your ancestors did, and then make for yourself the crossing they made.'

In so far as our society still has some compassion, in its institutions, and its individuals, it is drawn from the dwindling stock of moral capital built up by an age of faith. That deposit needs replenishing; John offers many practical suggestions on how to do it.

COLLECT

Almighty God,
by whose providence your servant John the Baptist
    was wonderfully born,
and sent to prepare the way of your Son our Saviour
by the preaching of repentance:
lead us to repent according to his preaching
and, after his example,
constantly to speak the truth, boldly to rebuke vice,
and patiently to suffer for the truth's sake;
through Jesus Christ your Son our Lord,
who is alive and reigns with you,
in the unity of the Holy Spirit,
one God, now and for ever.

| *Reflection by* **Malcolm Guite**

Psalms 87, **89.1-18**
Judges 14
Luke 18.1-14

Tuesday 25 June

Luke 18.1-14

'... this widow keeps bothering me' (v.5)

This extraordinary story of the widow battering away at the door of a lazy or indifferent judge, a story that seems to cast God in such a bad light, nevertheless speaks directly and honestly into our own experience. For we seem so often, as Shakespeare says, 'to trouble deaf heaven with our bootless cries'. And in our daily lives, we often meet those who have given up or are about to give up, who need to hear this word from Christ. For the story is not only about frustration

but also about dogged perseverance. This parable is I think the ultimate source for that phrase in which George Herbert describes prayer as an 'engine against the Almighty'. He is probably thinking of a siege engine, and may also be remembering John Donne's great sermon on the same theme which takes Christ's story of the indignant god-bothering widow, and turns it into an epic siege:

'Earnest prayer hath the nature of Importunity; Wee presse, wee importune God ... Prayer hath the nature of Impudency; wee threaten God in Prayer ... and God suffers this Impudency and more. Prayer hath the nature of Violence; in the publique Prayers of the Congregation we besiege God, saies Tertullian, and we take God Prisoner, and bring God to our Conditions; and God is glad to be straightened by us in that siege.'*

The Sermons of John Donne, ed. Potter and Simpson (Los Angeles, 1953–62) vol V, p. 364

O God, the protector of all who trust in you,
without whom nothing is strong, nothing is holy:
increase and multiply upon us your mercy;
that with you as our ruler and guide
we may so pass through things temporal
that we lose not our hold on things eternal;
grant this, heavenly Father,
for our Lord Jesus Christ's sake,
who is alive and reigns with you,
in the unity of the Holy Spirit,
one God, now and for ever.

COLLECT

Wednesday 26 June

Psalm 119.105-128
Judges 15.1 – 16.3
Luke 18.15-30

Luke 18.15-30

'... a camel to go through the eye of a needle' (v.25)

I'd love to stay with the sayings about the children and the kingdom, but the camel is looking at me awkwardly and I know this is the one I have to tackle. What an astonishing image it is, the camel trying to get through the needle's eye! Is it just memorable rabbinic exaggeration, like being asked to take the log out of your own eye, before you move the speck from your brother's? Or is it, as some scholars say, an allusion to the smallest of the gates into Jerusalem, known locally as 'the Needle's Eye?' A poor person unencumbered could walk through it easily, even someone whose means extended to a modest donkey could squeeze through. But someone rich enough to possess a laden camel was presented with a problem. It could be done, but not without offloading the camel, bringing it to its knees and willing it through, spitting and cursing.

Perhaps those of us, like this 'certain ruler', who are blessed, and burdened with the goods of this world, must, like loaded camels, get on our knees, consent to be unburdened, to sit light to the goods we carry, enter through the little gate, and know ourselves blessed without these things. It may be that we will pick up our goods again, bring them through that searching needle's eye one at a time, but after that they will always and only be detachable extras.

COLLECT

O God, the protector of all who trust in you,
without whom nothing is strong, nothing is holy:
increase and multiply upon us your mercy;
that with you as our ruler and guide
we may so pass through things temporal
that we lose not our hold on things eternal;
grant this, heavenly Father,
for our Lord Jesus Christ's sake,
who is alive and reigns with you,
in the unity of the Holy Spirit,
one God, now and for ever.

| *Reflection by* **Malcolm Guite**

Psalms 90, **92**
Judges 16.4-end
Luke 18.31-end

Thursday 27 June

Luke 18.31-end

'... they understood nothing' (v.34)

It's always comforting to read Luke's editorial asides about how the disciples failed to grasp what Jesus was saying. At least we can feel, as we puzzle over our readings, that we are in good company! It's scarcely surprising, that at this point the disciples are still shocked and uncomprehending as Jesus talks of the appalling fate that awaits him in Jerusalem.

They had anticipated an entirely different story: a triumphal entry into Jerusalem in which the people would at last recognise the Messiah for who he is. And then the revolution: a swift change of government, a proper purging of the temple, and then who knows, the Last Day itself, a general resurrection, a final vindication of Israel, and suitably chastened tributes from the awestruck Gentile world, especially from the Romans, their present oppressors. Surely that was the whole point of their movement and was just what Scripture prophesied.

They have not yet grasped that Jesus' great triumph will be precisely when he enters into the depths of our suffering, when he does our dying for us, when he is made to be sin who knew no sin that we might become the righteousness of God, when he changes everything for all humanity, instead of just leading a local coup. They don't share his vision yet, but perhaps that's why the very next thing Jesus does is to open the eyes of the blind.

Gracious Father,
by the obedience of Jesus
you brought salvation to our wayward world:
draw us into harmony with your will,
that we may find all things restored in him,
our Saviour Jesus Christ.

COLLECT

Reflection by **Malcolm Guite** | 187

Friday 28 June

Psalms **88** (95)
Judges 17
Luke 19.1-10

Luke 19.1-10

'... to seek out and save the lost' (v.10)

Here we see the literal enactment of all those parables about seeking and saving the lost with which Luke has prepared us for this moment: the lost sheep, the lost coins, the lost son. Jesus shows us that these parables are not empty words with no impact on life. On the contrary they are a call to action.

The disciples might be shocked that 'the lost' didn't just mean 'the deserving poor,' or believers who had strayed in their doctrine. No, the lost for whom the Lord is searching turns out to include this odious rich man, a traitor to his own people who has enriched himself by colluding with the occupying power. It's small wonder that Zacchaeus couldn't get to the front of the crowd, he would have been excluded by his indignant neighbours. And so he climbs a tree. In one sense he was already isolated, up a tree from which he imagined he couldn't climb down. Rich, but despised, the object of contempt. The only way back into his community, would be to climb down in every sense, climb down from and undo everything to which greed and sharp practice had prompted him.

In this story he does just that, enabled at last, by a moment of grace in which he grasps that Jesus has already accepted him as he is. Now he has hope and rejoices in doing what he can to give thanks for it.

COLLECT

O God, the protector of all who trust in you,
without whom nothing is strong, nothing is holy:
increase and multiply upon us your mercy;
that with you as our ruler and guide
we may so pass through things temporal
that we lose not our hold on things eternal;
grant this, heavenly Father,
for our Lord Jesus Christ's sake,
who is alive and reigns with you,
in the unity of the Holy Spirit,
one God, now and for ever.

| *Reflection by* **Malcolm Guite**

Psalms 71, 113
Isaiah 49.1-6
Acts 11.1-18

Saturday 29 June
Peter the Apostle

Acts 11.1-18
'... not to make a distinction between them and us' (v.12)

This story of the conversion of Peter, a conversion to the all-inclusive love of God, is just as vital for the Church as the more famous story of the conversion of St Paul. For both of them it involved a *volte-face*, a radical break with a mindset which was not only entrenched but which they thought was God-given. Peter's struggle, as it is told here, is almost comic, as he attempts to correct God himself. He is saying, effectively, 'Surely Lord you must have read your own Scriptures! Let me offer you an expository reading of Leviticus.' But it won't do, and on the third attempt Peter gives in to the radical grace that must often make us set aside our own cherished readings of what we think 'the Bible says'.

And Peter puts that vision of radical grace into action. He rejects the insidious theology of taint, he goes into the house of a Gentile, mixes and joins with those 'outside the law'. Like Paul, he too becomes an 'apostle to the Gentiles'. Perhaps our own church is still stuck with Peter on the rooftop in Joppa. We are presently called on to include all sorts of people whom we have traditionally excluded, with apparent scriptural authority, by distinctions of gender or sexuality. Will we be as courageous as Peter, come down from our high place, and recognise that 'God gave them the same gift that he gave us'?

Monday 1 July

Psalms **98**, 99, 101
1 Samuel 1.1-20
Luke 19.28-40

Luke 19.28-40

'Blessed is the king, who comes in the name of the Lord!' (v.38)

Bethany was home from home for Jesus. He often stayed there with Mary, Martha and Lazarus. So, the borrowing of the donkey may have been quite easy to arrange. But it happens against a backdrop of growing opposition. As with other stories at this stage in Jesus's ministry it is clear he has been making plans without telling others. The precise words and phrases used to obtain the donkey, told twice, all suggest the need for secret arrangements. This will be familiar territory to those who have lived under oppressive regimes – the need to know who can be trusted, the threat of informers and the need for coded speech and actions.

Luke emphasises the royal identity of Jesus throughout these passages. And authoritative initiatives have been all his so far. Now, when the foal comes, 'they set him on it'. The action shifts to his excited followers. It may be that this deliberately highlights the tension in expectations about this king. There was a belief around that this kingdom was imminent (19.11). Surely, this is the moment! He enters the city to wild celebration. The king is coming to his throne. But there will be a significant difference between the throne his followers would 'set him on' and the Kingdom over which he comes to reign. And what kind of king *borrows* what he needs?

COLLECT

Almighty and everlasting God,
by whose Spirit the whole body of the Church
    is governed and sanctified:
hear our prayer which we offer for all your faithful people,
that in their vocation and ministry
they may serve you in holiness and truth
to the glory of your name;
through our Lord and Saviour Jesus Christ,
who is alive and reigns with you,
in the unity of the Holy Spirit,
one God, now and for ever.

| *Reflection by* **David Runcorn**

Psalm **106*** (*or* 103)
I Samuel 1.21 – 2.11
Luke 19.41-end

Tuesday 3 July

Luke 19.41-end

'If you, even you, had only recognized on this day the things that make for peace!' (v.42)

And what are the things that make for peace? 'We pray for peace in the world': is any petition or intercession offered with more frequency and longing? But in the face of unrelenting violence and suffering, these words feel powerless to change much.

Jesus sees the terrible destruction that is coming upon the city and the people he loves and he finds it heart-breaking. But soon after, he is found angrily shattering what 'makes for peace' in the holy temple itself. It seems the peace of God can be established only after the peace of this world, and even its practices of faith, are exposed as false. Perhaps that is why Christian faith is more often marked by conflict than calm. But the Christ we seek is found in the midst of all this, not in some privileged escape from it.

At the end of Christian worship, we are often sent out with the words 'Go in peace'. This is not an invitation to leave 'feeling peaceful'. Go *into* peace. That is what it means. We are being invited to enter some*where*. Go into the place where Christ's reigning love is making possible new ways of living and hoping together, where there will be unexpected possibilities for responding differently, for conversion of life and for entering the ways that make for peace.

COLLECT

Almighty God,
send down upon your Church
the riches of your Spirit,
and kindle in all who minister the gospel
your countless gifts of grace;
through Jesus Christ our Lord.

Reflection by **David Runcorn** | 191

Wednesday 3 July
Thomas the Apostle

Psalms 92, 146
2 Samuel 15.17-21
or Ecclesiasticus 2
John 11.1-16

John 11.1-16

'Let us also go, that we may die with him' (v.16)

There are only a few, brief encounters with Thomas in the gospels. Here, Jesus had just announced he was returning to a region where his life had only recently been seriously threatened. When the appalled disciples fail to change his mind, it is Thomas who says, 'Let us also go, that we might die with him'. What tone of voice do you hear Thomas speaking with? Is this faithful devotion? Or is it exasperation – rolling his eyes at these mad plans of Jesus? On another occasion Jesus confidently tells his disciples, 'You know the way to where I am going.' Thomas flatly contradicts him, 'Lord, we *don't* know! …' (John 14.1-6). Finally, Thomas famously refuses to believe the disciples' account of the resurrection appearance he had just missed.

So, what picture do we get of this man? A blunt, stubborn, down-to-earth character. Like those around him, he is easily confused by what he sees and hears of Jesus, but what stands out is his directness and honesty. Every community needs characters like Thomas. They are the people who are willing to ask the questions that no one else dares to. They are truthful and they keep their friends more truthful too.

Thomas's name is forever attached to 'doubting'. But his last recorded words, before the risen Jesus were, 'My Lord and my God.'

COLLECT

Almighty and eternal God,
who, for the firmer foundation of our faith,
allowed your holy apostle Thomas
    to doubt the resurrection of your Son
till word and sight convinced him:
grant to us, who have not seen, that we also may believe
and so confess Christ as our Lord and our God;
who is alive and reigns with you,
in the unity of the Holy Spirit,
one God, now and for ever.

| *Reflection by* **David Runcorn**

Psalms 113, **115**
1 Samuel 2.27-end
Luke 20.9-19

Thursday 4 July

Luke 20.9-19

'What then will the owner of the vineyard do to them?' (v.15)

Absentee landlords were familiar in the rural economy in Jesus's time. Issues with difficult tenants were not unfamiliar either. In this parable Jesus may well be drawing on an actual local incident, known to his audience.

There are surely echoes here of the creation story in Genesis. There too a garden was created, and its care entrusted to others by the creator. There too we read of a wilful folly, Adam and Eve, like the tenants, trying to claim what was not theirs to own.

Given the escalating violence against his successive messengers, the owner would be expected to exercise his legal right and evict the tenants by force. But the story takes a completely unexpected turn. The owner enforces nothing. Instead, he sends his own son, unarmed. 'Perhaps they will respect him' is better translated 'feel shame before him'. The son stands before them, defenceless. Will they let this gracious response move them to turn back from attempts to possess what is not theirs? They do not. The beloved son is seized and killed.

The sin that is original to this world is always the attempt to live a life that does not actually exist – a presuming to possess what can only be gift. And the abiding tragedy of this mad heist is that it was all gift in the first place. But to claim to own it, you must kill the giver.

Reflection by **David Runcorn** | 193

Friday 5 July

Psalm **139**
I Samuel 3.1 – 4.1*a*
Luke 20.20-26

Luke 20.20-26

'Give ... to God the things that are God's' (v.25)

When are taxes ever popular? There were riots when the Romans imposed them in Jesus' day. But they are among the necessary realities of life lived under governing authorities, foreign or otherwise. The New Testament Church accepted this. 'Let everyone be subject to the governing authorities,' taught Paul. Why? 'For there is no authority except from God, and those authorities that exist have been instituted by God.' (Romans 13.1) Though this teaching too would be tested when those same authorities became manifestly anti-Christ in expression.

The question of taxes was not a serious one though. It was a device to trap Jesus – to force him into a corner with extremists and denounce him. The hostility of the Jewish governing authorities towards Jesus is unabating (and religious groups may not fight any more fairly than anyone else when their interests are threatened). In his response Jesus neatly turns a negative into a positive. Give to both what is their due. Respond out of positive service, not from negative self-interest.

We might note that the religious authorities too had their tax system in place. And not long before, Jesus had been found in the temple furiously overturning what it had become and denouncing the temple itself as a den of thieves.

Caesars come and go. But give to God what belongs to God – and all things will find their proper place.

COLLECT

Almighty and everlasting God,
by whose Spirit the whole body of the Church
    is governed and sanctified:
hear our prayer which we offer for all your faithful people,
that in their vocation and ministry
they may serve you in holiness and truth
to the glory of your name;
through our Lord and Saviour Jesus Christ,
who is alive and reigns with you,
in the unity of the Holy Spirit,
one God, now and for ever.

194 | *Reflection by* **David Runcorn**

Psalms 120, **121**, 122
1 Samuel 4.1*b*-end
Luke 20.27-40

Saturday 6 July

Luke 20.27-40

'He is God not of the dead, but of the living' (v.38)

The Sadducees did not believe in the resurrection. They had a favourite story they believed to expose this belief for the nonsense that it is. A much-widowed woman arrives in heaven with seven husbands waiting to greet her! How absurd! The tone is mocking. This is what happens when texts and stories are read with a kind of wooden literalism rather than the questioning and imagination that living faith call for.

Jesus' response reminds me of the person asked for directions to somewhere. 'Well,' he said, 'if you want to get there, you should not be starting from here'. Jesus carefully meets them on their own terms, though – engaging the scriptures that are important to them. Theological issues need theological responses. His words are persuasive to some of them.

But what will the life of heaven be like? This is a practical concern for those, who have, for example, been married more than once and wonder whether to be anticipating awkward reunions. Jesus speaks of life beyond death that completely transcends existing patterns of relating and committing in this world of time. Addressing the same question, St Paul contrasts this life with the world to come as like the difference between the seed and the great tree it grows into (1 Corinthians 15.35-41). But we are fumbling for words here. The transformation is beyond even our comprehension.

Christian faith is lived out of the future. In our praying and trusting, we are offering what we do not yet see or can yet imagine. Lord, 'I do have faith, but not enough. Help me have more.' (Mark 9.24, GNV)

Almighty God,
send down upon your Church
the riches of your Spirit,
and kindle in all who minister the gospel
your countless gifts of grace;
through Jesus Christ our Lord.

COLLECT

Reflection by **David Runcorn** | 195

Monday 8 July

Psalms 123, 124, 125, **126**
I Samuel 5
Luke 20.41 – 21.4

Luke 20.41 – 21.4

'... this poor widow has put in more than all of them' (v.3)

Jesus is in mid-flow in the temple, as Luke continues to lay the biblical foundations of his identity and mission. Imagine him seated near the temple treasury with those large containers for donations. It would have been busy and noisy, especially when offerings were being made by people concerned to be very public about it. Did he become distracted by it all? Pausing his sermon he offloads unsparing condemnation at the ostentation, selfishness, and abuses of the rich in front of him. They have it coming, he says.

Then he looks up just as a poor widow adds her tiny offering. Did she do it furtively, not wanting to be seen or shamed? No one was less significant in that world. Had he not looked at that moment he would surely not have noticed her. Her two copper coins would fall unheard.

But how often in the economics of Kingdom, the smallest and the least are revealed to be the greatest and most significant. Jesus cannot literally mean the widow had left herself with nothing. The 'all' she has given, symbolised by those tiny coins, is her entire life, faith, devotion and love for God. And it is truly immense!

One of the mysteries of life remains though. Not, why does God allow people to be poor? But, why does God allow the rich not to share?

May the little or plenty in our lives be found in the same immensity of that woman's offering.

COLLECT

Merciful God,
you have prepared for those who love you
such good things as pass our understanding:
pour into our hearts such love toward you
that we, loving you in all things and above all things,
may obtain your promises,
which exceed all that we can desire;
through Jesus Christ your Son our Lord,
who is alive and reigns with you,
in the unity of the Holy Spirit,
one God, now and for ever.

| *Reflection by* **David Runcorn**

Psalms **132**, 133
1 Samuel 6.1-16
Luke 21.5-19

Tuesday 9 July

Luke 21.5-19

'Not one stone will be left upon another; all will be thrown down'
(v.6)

Even today the remains of the temple in Jerusalem are impressive. Some of the surviving stones are so large that archaeologists have trouble understanding how they could possibly have been transported. But when standing in all its original glory it would have been an overwhelming sight for ancient pilgrims. So, it is not surprising to find it commented on in conversations with Jesus. This was the heart of their faith: the very house of God. But Jesus simply refused to treat the temple as physically or theologically significant. In fact, he says, it will all be turned to ruins. There are echoes here of prophets like Jeremiah, warning the people they are fatally over-attached to places and buildings for their security.

And the time was coming, as Jesus foretold, when this vast, validating monument to God's blessing, protection and faithfulness would be reduced to rubble and God's people would go into exile. And there in a strange land they must begin to learn new ways of doing faith, find new words to pray with, seek new understanding of God's presence and ways and of their place in this world.

Centuries later, when a group of Hasidic rabbis was asked the question, 'Where is the dwelling of God?', they simply laughed at the question. The answer was obvious. 'God dwells wherever we let him in' (adapted from Martin Buber, *The Way of Man*, 33).

Creator God,
you made us all in your image:
may we discern you in all that we see,
and serve you in all that we do;
through Jesus Christ our Lord.

COLLECT

Wednesday 10 July

Psalm 119.153-end
I Samuel 7
Luke 21.20-28

Luke 21.20-28

'... stand up and raise your heads' (v.28)

These are terrifying visions. Jesus spares his hearers nothing. Vivid scenes of appalling destruction and violence reveal a cataclysm that is cosmic. Factual details are reported alongside apocalyptic imagery. Desperate refugees flee beneath the turmoil in the heavens. Jesus speaks as if he sees it all happening. And perhaps, with the eye of a prophet, he does.

And how were his hearers to respond to all this? In the midst of it all Jesus utters a bold and unexpected call to faith, 'Raise your heads. Your redemption is drawing near'.

Jesus was foretelling specific events. Jerusalem was destroyed in AD 70. But there are people and places in the world today facing similar terrors and searching for the response of faith in the midst of chaos. They too cry out to a God who sees, who cares, who will ultimately overcome – but does not, yet, prevent.

In the Bible, faith in such times is forged through the prayer of lament. Those raw cries of protest, anger, longing and questioning are signs of faith, not the loss of it. Over two thirds of the psalms start from such places. It is a language more often absent from Christian worship and we need to learn it. Lament has been vividly described as 'dropping our doctrine of God into the furnace of dire experience and find it again as refined gold' (C. Wright, *The Message of Lamentations*, IVP 2015, p.23).

What will you lament today?

COLLECT

Merciful God,
you have prepared for those who love you
such good things as pass our understanding:
pour into our hearts such love toward you
that we, loving you in all things and above all things,
may obtain your promises,
which exceed all that we can desire;
through Jesus Christ your Son our Lord,
who is alive and reigns with you,
in the unity of the Holy Spirit,
one God, now and for ever.

| *Reflection by* **David Runcorn**

Thursday 11 July

Luke 21.29-end

'When you see these things taking place, you know that the kingdom of God is near' (v.31)

'Strange fruit hanging from the trees', sang Billy Holliday. Her iconic song protested the 'strange and bitter crop' of lynchings in the southern states of America. A similar clash of images between death and fruitfulness is found running through the teaching of Jesus as events build towards the bitter crop of his own cross.

What are 'these things' that Jesus refers to? Wars, famine, plagues, persecution and social collapse, no less. What are they signs of? 'The kingdom is near.' Really? Elsewhere, Jesus speaks of the same violent turmoil as the contractions of a world in labour, the birth pangs of an emerging new age.

As he often does, Jesus is employing a familiar rabbinic style of teaching, provocatively setting up collisions of opposites or using clashing images to shock, challenge and awaken new understanding. He warns once again that faith in such a world requires vigilance and discipline. It is active service, so stay alert, pray to endure and be watchful. This needs much more than good intentions.

Through it all, Jesus insists, something else is going on. It is yet to be finally revealed, but it can be utterly trusted. Weaving its way through the midst of the desperate fragility and instability of this world is something utterly enduring. It is the life of the coming Kingdom. Keep watch. Stand firm. You will see it.

COLLECT

Creator God,
you made us all in your image:
may we discern you in all that we see,
and serve you in all that we do;
through Jesus Christ our Lord.

Reflection by **David Runcorn** | 199

Friday 12 July

Luke 22.1-13

'Satan entered into Judas called Iscariot, who was one of the twelve ...' (v.3)

We know almost nothing of what led Judas to act as he did. The shadow of his actions clearly lay heavy upon the first Christian communities. As if to emphasise the abiding shock of it all, Luke reminds readers of what they already know. Judas was 'one of the twelve'. The arrival of Satan into the drama here is unexpected and perhaps disturbing. It might be thought that if Judas was possessed by evil, he surely had no choice? But that is not what the text says. The account treats him as a responsible player throughout this drama. So does Jesus. 'Satan entered him' is a way of expressing the moment his descent into disagreement, disillusionment and, finally, opposition to Jesus becomes a moment of decisive action. There is no other way. He must betray. And so, this tragically confused disciple enters into an unholy conspiracy with unredeemed religion and evil.

The stage is set. It seems that sinful humanity, perverted religion and even Satan himself, must become the means by which Jesus fulfils the work he was destined for. The incarnation was always the divine intention. The glorious union of all things in Christ its goal. Human waywardness means this gift can only be offered through a work of tragic redemption. So it is that our sin and evil itself, draws from God an even greater revelation of divine love.

COLLECT

Merciful God,
you have prepared for those who love you
such good things as pass our understanding:
pour into our hearts such love toward you
that we, loving you in all things and above all things,
may obtain your promises,
which exceed all that we can desire;
through Jesus Christ your Son our Lord,
who is alive and reigns with you,
in the unity of the Holy Spirit,
one God, now and for ever.

| *Reflection by* **David Runcorn**

Psalm **147**
1 Samuel 9.15 – 10.1
Luke 22.14-23

Saturday 13 July

Luke 22.14-23

'Do this in remembrance of me' (v.19)

The longing of Jesus to share this meal with his disciples is tender and moving. He knows this will be their last until the coming Kingdom. It must have felt bitter-sweet and lonely, as his followers remain uncomprehending and increasingly bewildered at the drama unfolding around them. At table, as he approaches his own Passover and Exodus, Jesus blesses and breaks the bread of his own affliction and invites them all to share it 'in remembrance of me'. His followers, in every time and place, have done this ever since.

One of the most insistent challenges in the Bible is to 'remember'. 'Remember me', says God, 'remember Torah', 'remember your story', 'teach your children to remember'. This remembering is not looking back into the past, and it is much more than having a good memory for dates and events. The opposite of re-member is dis-member. Something re-membered is re-connected. Remembering is a call to re-enter the story we are participating in, living now with what makes us who we are. We never leave the past behind in that sense.

We are to hear the words of Jesus at the last supper in the present tense. We are as present in this meal as those first disciples. This story is continually making and remaking who we are. So do this, 'in remembrance of me'. Until Kingdom come.

Creator God,
you made us all in your image:
may we discern you in all that we see,
and serve you in all that we do;
through Jesus Christ our Lord.

COLLECT

Monday 15 July

Luke 22.24-30

'But not so with you...' (v.26)

Just before the words in this text, Jesus celebrated the Last Supper with his disciples and taught them about his sacrifice. It appears as though the disciples hadn't really understood what he had just taught them – otherwise they would not have argued about their relative greatness. I really feel for Jesus faced with his disciples' obliviousness. In this text, Jesus is forced to talk bluntly emphasizing how his teachings are the opposite of the world's teachings. He was absolutely clear that he wanted them to live and behave in a way that was completely different from the culture around them.

If Christianity means being like Christ, it means most of the time behaving and acting differently from how the world expects. Leadership means service that goes beyond any boundaries. That service entailed Christ giving his life to serve the world. The disciples' argument shows that they have not switched to be on the same frequency as that of Jesus, to think the way he thinks. When we switch to this frequency, we see that everything changes: the way we live, the way we think and the way we see life. This reminds me of Paul's words to the Philippians 'In your relationships with one another, have the same mindset as Christ Jesus' (Philippians 2.5) This mindset cannot happen through our own power. We should want to switch but the switch happens through the power of the Holy Spirit.

COLLECT

Lord of all power and might,
the author and giver of all good things:
graft in our hearts the love of your name,
increase in us true religion,
nourish us with all goodness,
and of your great mercy keep us in the same;
through Jesus Christ your Son our Lord,
who is alive and reigns with you,
in the unity of the Holy Spirit,
one God, now and for ever.

| *Reflection by* **Nadim Nasser**

Psalms **5**, 6 (8)
I Samuel 10.17-end
Luke 22.31-38

Tuesday 16 July

Luke 22.31-38

'I have prayed for you that your own faith may not fail...' (v.32)

Jesus is aware that the disciples are divided and lack unity and cohesion among themselves. He therefore warns them of the temptations that will hit them individually. When you are divided, he warns, evil can strike and try to destroy you. We see this happen later with Peter he denies Jesus. However, Jesus doesn't abandon them to this bad news but assures them of his prayers. Even when he is heading towards the cross, he held his disciples in his heart and his prayers: he didn't want to leave them abandoned.

Peter is sincere when he states that he is ready to follow Jesus to his death but Jesus sees beyond this enthusiasm and passion and recognises Peter's weakness and vulnerability. This reminds us that we need to open up to the Lord to strengthen us in our desire to follow him. Jesus knew that Peter would fall, but would ultimately succeed. God accepts us when we fall and challenges us to stand up again. The difference between Judas and Peter is that although they both fell, Peter was open to redemption and did not give up on the Lord. Judas lost faith that Jesus would redeem him and fell into the trap of despair. We must hold on to our faith even when we fall to give room for the Lord to rebuild us.

Generous God,
you give us gifts and make them grow:
though our faith is small as mustard seed,
make it grow to your glory
and the flourishing of your kingdom;
through Jesus Christ our Lord.

COLLECT

Reflection by **Nadim Nasser** | 203

Wednesday 17 July

Luke 22.39-46

'... pray that you may not come into the time of trial' (v.46)

In this significant event, we see Luke connecting Jesus' prayers with how Jesus had taught the disciples to pray 'Lead us not into temptation' (Luke 11.4). Of course, Jesus's ultimate temptation was to avoid the cross. In his prayer to the Father Jesus enables us to stand in front of God, open our hearts and tell him what we really want. Even Jesus stood in front of God and refused to accept his future. This passage shows the full humanity of Jesus and gives us the permission to show our weaknesses and our fears of the future before God. Jesus strongly felt the temptation to refuse the cross and anguished over this temptation praying for the strength to face it, according to the Father's will and not his own.

Jesus encourages us to keep our dialogue with the Father going. In order to face the temptations in our lives, we need to be close to God, to be in a dynamic conversation with God in order to know God's will. The closer I am, the more my will and God's will are the same. Christ was able to face the cross and accept it when his Father's will became his own will. This is the model we should adopt when facing the crosses that we face in life. This prayer unites us with God through the Spirit.

COLLECT

Lord of all power and might,
the author and giver of all good things:
graft in our hearts the love of your name,
increase in us true religion,
nourish us with all goodness,
and of your great mercy keep us in the same;
through Jesus Christ your Son our Lord,
who is alive and reigns with you,
in the unity of the Holy Spirit,
one God, now and for ever.

204 | *Reflection by* **Nadim Nasser**

Psalms 14, **15**, 16
1 Samuel 12
Luke 22.47-62

Thursday 18 July

Luke 22.47-62

'The Lord turned and looked at Peter' (v.61)

After his prayer, Jesus reconciled himself with obeying the will of the Father, so there was no question of his defending himself when the guards came to arrest him. He was heartbroken that one of his disciples had betrayed him, especially with such an intimate gesture as a kiss. His arrest made Peter curious to follow him and see what would happen. Although the fire lit up Peter's face, the hour—and power— of darkness had fallen. Peter first denied knowing Jesus as a person, then he denied the community of Jesus, and finally he denied his own memories and history with him.

Only in Luke's Gospel do we see how Jesus turned to look at Peter. Peter realised that he had behaved exactly as foretold, and the Lord's gaze reminded him of the weakness and fragility behind his passion and enthusiasm. It is wonderful to have this same kind of energy in following Christ but, at the same time, we need to be aware of the power of the darkness that surrounds us, and that evil can strike at any time (cf. 1 Peter 5.8). When Jesus looked at Peter, it was not to condemn him but to express his love for him and to encourage him to be strong. Jesus continues to look with love at each one of us whenever we fall, and give us the strength we need to carry on.

Generous God,
you give us gifts and make them grow:
though our faith is small as mustard seed,
make it grow to your glory
and the flourishing of your kingdom;
through Jesus Christ our Lord.

COLLECT

Friday 19 July

Luke 22.63-end

*'... the assembly of the elders of the people... gathered together,
and they brought him to their council' (v.66)*

Every day we are on trial as believers in Jesus Christ the Son of God.
Jesus' trial, while it ended with the cross, has continued for his
followers in every generation. Jesus attended his trial knowing that
the sentence had already been passed. The chief priests and the
scribes were searching for anything to justify the sentence on which
they had already decided: death Jesus decided to face this travesty of
a trial with the bold assertion that the Son of Man is seated at the
right hand of God. In today's world, the situation is no different and
Christianity is being persecuted around the world. What we need to
hang onto is Jesus's promise that he will be with us and the Holy
Spirit will speak through us. Let's pray and remember those who are
facing death every day for their faith in the Lord of life.

Luke clearly portrays the gathering of the council as a warning of
what we might face when we follow the Lord. Jesus did not lack the
courage to confront the religious leaders of his time, even when he
knew that nothing he said would change their minds. He took this
circus of a court as an opportunity to reveal again his identity as the
Son of God. This courageous act in the face of certain death has
inspired countless Christians around the world to stand up to
injustice and persecution and continues to do so today.

COLLECT

Lord of all power and might,
the author and giver of all good things:
graft in our hearts the love of your name,
increase in us true religion,
nourish us with all goodness,
and of your great mercy keep us in the same;
through Jesus Christ your Son our Lord,
who is alive and reigns with you,
in the unity of the Holy Spirit,
one God, now and for ever.

| *Reflection by* **Nadim Nasser**

Psalms 20, 21, **23**
I Samuel 13.19 – 14.15
Luke 23.1-12

Saturday 20 July

Luke 23.1-12

*'The chief priests and the scribes stood by, vehemently
accusing him' (v.10)*

We see here how the religious leaders were much harsher in their condemnation of Jesus than the political leaders who did not see him as a threat. The chief priests and scribes had already decided that Jesus should be killed. The religious institutions which should have embodied the godly values of justice and mercy decided instead to politicise the case by bringing a false accusation – that Jesus had incited people not to pay their taxes. Both Pilate and Herod, though, interrogated Jesus at length without finding any reason to pronounce him guilty.

Sometimes the Church is much harsher in judging people than the world at large. The religious leaders found Jesus to be a threat more to their power than to their values. Nevertheless they didn't want to dirty their hands with his blood and so tried to manipulate the political powers of the day to have him killed.

This passage could be seen as directed at the Church, warning us not to lose the focus on mercy and justice, nor to judge people too harshly, nor be prejudiced against an individual or group. Sometimes it is too easy, even in the name of God, to demonize others and sentence them, even using the words of the Scriptures to do so. Our role should be the opposite: to support all who are marginalized.

Generous God,
you give us gifts and make them grow:
though our faith is small as mustard seed,
make it grow to your glory
and the flourishing of your kingdom;
through Jesus Christ our Lord.

COLLECT

Reflection by **Nadim Nasser** | 207

Monday 22 July
Mary Magdalene

Psalms 30, 32, 150
1 Samuel 16.14-end
Luke 8.1-3

Luke 8.1-3

'The twelve were with him, as well as some women' (vv.1-2)

Jesus' disciples numbered women and men; both were at the heart of his ministry. The Church has always been slow in recognizing the vital role of women in the life of the body of Christ. Mary Magdalene is a wonderful example of a woman who dedicated her life to serve Christ after he had transformed her heart and mind. She is brave, courageous and loving, putting God at the centre of her life. Sadly, too many churches around the world emain male dominated.. The place of Mary Magdalene in the gospels is a constant reminder that God works in each and every one of us regardless of gender.

Mary Magdalene joins the other women in Luke's gospel who illustrate powerfully the place women held in the heart of Jesus' ministry. We see Mary and Martha, personal friends of the Lord, interacting with him in a way that teaches us lessons of discipleship. We shouldn't forget that Mary Magdalene was one of the women who followed him to the Cross and even to his tomb. Luke goes further in explaining the role of women in the life of the Lord and shows that they were the first to experience his resurrection. These women carried the good news of the resurrection to the disciples and from the disciples to the whole world. They are the origin of our joy at this news that changed the face of history.

COLLECT

Almighty God,
whose Son restored Mary Magdalene to health of mind and body
and called her to be a witness to his resurrection:
forgive our sins and heal us by your grace,
that we may serve you in the power of his risen life;
who is alive and reigns with you,
in the unity of the Holy Spirit,
one God, now and for ever.

| *Reflection by* **Nadim Nasser**

Psalms 32, **36**
I Samuel 15.1-23
Luke 23.26-43

Tuesday 23 July

Luke 23.26-43

'Father, forgive them; for they do not know what they are doing'
(v.34)

Jerusalem, like modern day Damascus, Baghdad and Beirut, has suffered and continues to suffer violence and destruction. Jesus' words resonate with the people of the Near East now more than ever. The scene of the crucifixion, described so vividly by Luke, has been repeated on the streets of these capitals over and over again during recent decades. Coming from that part of the world and reading these words of the Lord makes me think and ask – along with the millions of refugees who have lost loved ones to the violence at home or in the boats escaping across the Mediterranean – how long can we continue to say 'Father, forgive' especially when we know that those who are responsible for the pain and suffering know exactly what they are doing?

Today, as the evil of war has invaded the heart of Europe, to whom do we turn to break the madness that is expanding to engulf every continent? We can only embrace the mystery of the cross and lift our suffering and fragile world to the wounded hands of the crucified and risen Lord. We can only pour out our hearts in prayer that the light of his resurrection may break through the dark hearts of many of our rulers and decision makers. May the Lord who freely accepted the cross help us carry our own cross – and may our hope bloom into a glorious resurrection.

Almighty Lord and everlasting God,
we beseech you to direct, sanctify and govern
both our hearts and bodies
in the ways of your laws
and the works of your commandments;
that through your most mighty protection, both here and ever,
we may be preserved in body and soul;
through our Lord and Saviour Jesus Christ,
who is alive and reigns with you,
in the unity of the Holy Spirit,
one God, now and for ever.

COLLECT

Reflection by **Nadim Nasser** | 209

Wednesday 24 July

Luke 23.44-56*a*

'Jesus, crying with a loud voice...' (v.46)

Even the Lord himself, hanging on the cross between heaven and earth, experienced the loneliness which is a part of the human condition. Where now is his Father, who had said at his baptism 'This is my Son, the Beloved, with whom I am well pleased'? (Luke 3.22) That same Father who spoke at the Transfiguration saying, 'This is my Son, my Chosen; listen to him!' (Luke 9.35). Was Jesus, perhaps, waiting for an encouraging intervention by his Father? At the very moment when he needed this encouragement, all that he got was silence. As the darkness covered the place, this silence became more deafening until Jesus had screamed aloud and surrendered his spirit into the hands of the Father. Who among us hasn't felt at least once this harsh feeling of abandonment at the most difficult time in our lives? Jesus's surrender didn't mean the absence of the Father but reflected the fact that he still felt the presence of the Father and that the Father wanted his Son to face this ultimate challenge on his own.

Today, we hold deep in our hearts those who scream with and who feel the presence of God in their lives even in the midst of silence. We live by faith that we are never abandoned, never forsaken because the risen Lord is with us and his spirit is in us empowering us to face the darkest moments that life can make us experience.

COLLECT

Almighty Lord and everlasting God,
we beseech you to direct, sanctify and govern
    both our hearts and bodies
in the ways of your laws
    and the works of your commandments;
that through your most mighty protection, both here and ever,
we may be preserved in body and soul;
through our Lord and Saviour Jesus Christ,
who is alive and reigns with you,
in the unity of the Holy Spirit,
one God, now and for ever.

| *Reflection by* **Nadim Nasser**

Psalms 7, 29, 117
2 Kings 1.9-15
Luke 9.46-56

Thursday 25 July
James the Apostle

Luke 9.46-56

'... he set his face to go to Jerusalem' (v.51)

James, in his passion and love for the Lord, was ready to ask God to destroy the Samaritan village because people there did not accept Jesus. On one hand, the village being Samaritan (the historic enemies of the Jews) did not receive him; on the other hand, James wanted to show his loyalty towards his master. Unfortunately, James in the heat of his enthusiasm, missed the whole point of Jesus' ministry. Jesus had to correct him, and teach him along with the other disciples the mindset of Easter. On the road to Jerusalem, according to Luke, Jesus did not stop teaching his disciples the ultimate purpose of his time on earth. He wanted to plant in their hearts the seeds of Easter so that later they would remember his teachings.

Today, we – as members of the body of Christ – need constantly to remind ourselves that to be the followers of Christ we must renew in *ourselves* the mindset of Easter. In everything we do or say, the message of Easter should be the heart and soul of our words and deeds. That message is a message of joy and hope: Jesus Christ came into the world to save and not to condemn. Let's remind ourselves of this message when we become like James, quick to judge and to condemn, or when we fail to love people not only as neighbours but as Jesus himself has loved us.

Merciful God,
whose holy apostle Saint James,
leaving his father and all that he had,
was obedient to the calling of your Son Jesus Christ
and followed him even to death:
help us, forsaking the false attractions of the world,
to be ready at all times to answer your call without delay;
through Jesus Christ your Son our Lord,
who is alive and reigns with you,
in the unity of the Holy Spirit,
one God, now and for ever.

COLLECT

Friday 26 July

Psalm **31**
I Samuel 17.31-54
Luke 24.13-35

Luke 24.13-35

'... how he had been made known to them in the breaking of the bread' (v.35)

The Italian Baroque master Caravaggio's magnificent painting *The Supper at Emmaus* illustrates the moment when these two disciples recognise the Lord after he had broken bread with them. We see their astonishment and utter amazement while Jesus stretches out his arm in a gesture of teaching and blessing. Aren't we all expected to live these moments of recognition every time that we break bread? It seems that these disciples' problem was the perspective within which they understood the Scriptures. After the resurrection, we are a new creation. Our eyes interpret the Scriptures in a new way. Once Jesus had explained the Scriptures with reference to himself, the written word came alive in a way that they had never experienced before.

As we celebrate the sacrament of the Eucharist and study the written word, we open our hearts and lives to recognise the risen Christ afresh. We see those disciples becoming restless: they are compelled to report back to the others and share with them what has happened on that walk and around that table. It is, likewise, the mission of the Church and of all followers of Christ, to have this same passion to share the message of the resurrection This is the effect of recognising the risen Lord in our lives and in ourselves.

COLLECT

Almighty Lord and everlasting God,
we beseech you to direct, sanctify and govern
    both our hearts and bodies
in the ways of your laws
    and the works of your commandments;
that through your most mighty protection, both here and ever,
we may be preserved in body and soul;
through our Lord and Saviour Jesus Christ,
who is alive and reigns with you,
in the unity of the Holy Spirit,
one God, now and for ever.

212 | *Reflection by* **Nadim Nasser**

Psalms 41, **42**, 43
I Samuel 17.55 – 18.16
Luke 24.36-end

Saturday 27 July

Luke 24.36-end

'You are witnesses of these things' (v.48)

Three young men in the small Christian city of Malula, near Damascus in Syria, were brutally killed by the terrorist organization ISIS when the city was stormed during the height of the civil war there. The story goes that those young men had refused to deny Christ in public, and because of that they were tortured and killed in order to terrify the whole Christian community, who still speak Aramaic, the language of the Lord himself. A similar event happened on the beach in Libya when ISIS executed 21 Coptic Egyptians because they refused to deny Christ. These stories of martyrdom did not happen in the early Church but in our own century, more than 2,000 years later.

Martyrdom is not a matter of history but is also present in the news today. When we bear witness to the risen Lord, we declare our faith in the bodily resurrection of the man Jesus Christ. We believe that we will also rise bodily to be with him because he has prepared a place for us. Bearing witness to our faith can be costly because the grace of God is far from cheap – as Dietrich Bonhoeffer, a German theologian and pastor killed by the Nazis in prison, teaches us. We are the living witnesses of the resurrection and we share that joy with the whole world that God so loved the world that he did not send an email or a YouTube message but rather came himself to share our humanity and give us a better life.

Lord God,
your Son left the riches of heaven
and became poor for our sake:
when we prosper save us from pride,
when we are needy save us from despair,
that we may trust in you alone;
through Jesus Christ our Lord.

COLLECT

Monday 29 July

Psalm **44**
I Samuel 19.1-18
Acts 1.1-14

1 Samuel 19.1-18

'You saw it and rejoiced ... why then will you sin ...?' (v.5)

This story reminds us of the importance of keeping faith with one another. Loyalty is not only a virtue in itself, it is also an antidote to the vices which plague the human mind. Saul, who was initially so impressed by David, has become a victim of his own envy, driven to distraction by David's youth, talent and success.

Envy is hugely destructive. Even when Saul has promised Jonathan that he will control his murderous rage against David, his resolution proves weak, and violent emotion takes over. The evil spirit that overwhelms Saul is 'from the Lord' suggesting that God makes the judgement that Saul has become incapable of sticking by his promise. As we read this passage, we need to keep in mind that God has plans for David beyond David's own imagining and that he is ultimately safe in spite of the immediate danger. We can benefit from seeing the story both from David's and Saul's perspectives. David encourages us to see ourselves as under God's protection. The outcome of any trials we may face this day are in God's hands. But we can also learn from the tragedy of Saul. We do not retain power and position for ever. Our envy of others may not harm them at all, but it certainly diminishes us.

COLLECT

Almighty God,
who sent your Holy Spirit
to be the life and light of your Church:
open our hearts to the riches of your grace,
that we may bring forth the fruit of the Spirit
in love and joy and peace;
through Jesus Christ your Son our Lord,
who is alive and reigns with you,
in the unity of the Holy Spirit,
one God, now and for ever.

| *Reflection by* **Angela Tilby**

Psalms **48**, 52
1 Samuel 20.1-17
Acts 1.15-end

Tuesday 30 July

1 Samuel 20.1-17

'Show me the faithful love of the Lord ...' (v.14)

David is traumatised by Saul's hatred and is tempted to doubt Jonathan's sincerity. The outcome is a covenant between David and Jonathan, a promise that each will protect the long-term interests of the other. This is a promise which goes beyond feelings. It also has its roots in God's will beyond the expressed love and loyalty of the two friends. Through the covenant, God's intentions towards the house of David are safeguarded for the future.

Caught in our particular moment of time it can be hard for us to see where our own lives may fit into God's redemptive purposes. But we will not go far wrong if we value the loyalty and love of the particular people who cross our paths in life. Friendship and love are among the greatest of God's gifts. They are where we are tested and where we have the opportunity to prove our loyalty. It is no accident that Jesus insisted on calling his disciples 'friends' rather than servants (John 15.15). True friendship is an insight into the nature of God, the non-possessive, outward focused love of the Trinity.

COLLECT

Gracious Father,
revive your Church in our day,
and make her holy, strong and faithful,
for your glory's sake
in Jesus Christ our Lord.

Reflection by **Angela Tilby** | 215

Wednesday 31 July

1 Samuel 20.18-end

'The Lord shall be between me and you ...' (v. 43)

There has been much recent speculation about the nature of David and Jonathan's relationship. We know it was intense, emotional and exclusive and that it was expressed through a personal covenant in the presence of God. Saul suggests that the relationship was 'shameful'. Perhaps he regretted Jonathan's conception (v.30), blaming his son's perversity on his mother. Given our current preoccupations over same-sex relationships we may find ourselves asking whether we are meant to see their love in sexual terms, but scripture does not resolve this issue for us. What it does, though, is to expose the limits of family and tribal relationships. Jonathan cannot be his true self with his father. He recognises that Saul is sick, and dangerous. Saul, for his part, curses Jonathan, who he rightly sees will not carry on his line or his kingdom.

There is a graciousness and humility in the character of Jonathan that can be an inspiration to us. It is hard to accept second place, to know that what you might once have thought to be your privilege and destiny has been given to another. But this is often the Christian way. Ultimately the 'other', the brother, friend and lover for each one of us is Christ, to whom our deepest loyalty belongs. Family, inheritance and tradition help us to understand our identity, but they can also obscure our vocation.

COLLECT

Almighty God,
who sent your Holy Spirit
to be the life and light of your Church:
open our hearts to the riches of your grace,
that we may bring forth the fruit of the Spirit
in love and joy and peace;
through Jesus Christ your Son our Lord,
who is alive and reigns with you,
in the unity of the Holy Spirit,
one God, now and for ever.

| *Reflection by* **Angela Tilby**

Psalms 56, **57** (63*)
1 Samuel 21.1 – 22.5
Acts 2.22-36

Thursday 1 August

1 Samuel 21.1 – 22.5

'He became captain over them' (22.2)

David's behaviour at this stage of the story is far from exemplary. He lies to the priest Ahimelech, wrongfully takes the sacred bread, briefly escapes to Philistine territory, pretends madness, and eventually finds his way to the cave of Adullam where he becomes the leader of a potential revolt of those who are discontented with Saul's reign. But his movements do not go unobserved. As with the anxious Moses and the deceitful Jacob we see with David that God has a habit working his will through those whose characters are flawed. There is no mention of God's intervention in the passage, and yet we know that God will eventually vindicate David. In the cave of Adullam he gathers his family and the beginnings of a rebel army of four hundred discontents. As readers, of course, we know that David is the anointed one and that his cause will prevail.

David's actions raise a host of questions for us. It is always worth asking ourselves whether there are indeed circumstances in which it might be justified to be less than honest, to deceive others in support of a goal to which we feel morally committed. Those who follow David appear to be the dregs of society, people whose rights and freedoms have been neglected under Saul. How aware are we of the needs of those on the margins of our society?

COLLECT

Gracious Father,
revive your Church in our day,
and make her holy, strong and faithful,
for your glory's sake
in Jesus Christ our Lord.

Friday 2 August

Psalms **51**, 54
1 Samuel 22.6-end
Acts 2.37-end

1 Samuel 22.6-end

'I am responsible for the lives of all your father's house.' (v.22)

There is something pathetic about Saul as he holds court at Gibeah, armed and surrounded by his retinue and yet still so full of jealousy and paranoia. He has turned in on himself to such an extent that he has no recognition of his responsibilities, no concern for the needs of others, no conscience. He is an example of what often happens, even in our age, to 'strong man' rulers, who end up detached from reality. All Saul is capable of is the unjustified orgy of killing that he unleashes on the priests and on the city of Nob.

But as Saul falls apart, David is beginning to come into his true status. When he learns that Saul has killed the priests he takes responsibility, owns his part in the disaster and offers Abiathar protection. David shows himself capable of learning from his mistakes in a way that the self-pitying Saul simply cannot. In our daily struggles to walk with integrity before God we should be on guard against defensiveness and brittleness of character. God can use us as long as we allow ourselves to be moulded by the circumstances that come our way. God walks with us, whatever difficulties surround us. But hardness of heart, so often condemned in scripture, is never a strength, but always a refusal to learn.

COLLECT

Almighty God,
who sent your Holy Spirit
to be the life and light of your Church:
open our hearts to the riches of your grace,
that we may bring forth the fruit of the Spirit
in love and joy and peace;
through Jesus Christ your Son our Lord,
who is alive and reigns with you,
in the unity of the Holy Spirit,
one God, now and for ever.

| *Reflection by* **Angela Tilby**

Saturday 3 August

1 Samuel 23

'You shall be king over Israel ...' (v.17)

David's ascent to kingship was never going to be easy while Saul was determined to kill him. Yet as David's problems increased so he learned a deeper readiness to depend on God. And he had human support too, both from the faithful Abiathar and from an unexpected visit from Jonathan who assures him that he will indeed fulfil his calling from God. But enemies remain. At the point when he is finally about to fall into Saul's hands, an unexpected raid from the Philistines distracts the army that is about to track him down. Once again, he escapes.

The wilderness experience is important for David. It is a place of exposure and vulnerability where he learns in the very marrow of his being that God is faithful to him. We often speak of being in the wilderness when we are experiencing illness, bereavement or betrayal. Jesus sought out the wilderness at the beginning of his ministry as a test of his vocation, to discover what it really meant to be Son of God. It is never a comfortable place to be but it is often a portal into a deeper understanding of God's will, and to finding the resources to fulfil it. Consider today where your greatest temptations lie, and the resources you need to resist them.

Gracious Father,
revive your Church in our day,
and make her holy, strong and faithful,
for your glory's sake
in Jesus Christ our Lord.

COLLECT

Monday 5 August

1 Samuel 24

'Then Saul ... left the cave, and went on his way' (v.7)

It would have been so easy for David to interpret Saul's unexpected 'bathroom stop' in the cave as a providential act of God. And he was tempted. All his problems solved with a single blow! He could not resist the small but real violation of cutting off a fragment of Saul's cloak. Yet this action enables David to prove to Saul that he does not have harmful intentions towards him. And Saul seems now to be reconciled to the future and to David's eventual kingship.

It takes time to come to terms with events which seem to conspire against our interests. Saul has set his heart on founding a dynasty and it takes time for him to recognise that his dream is not to be. Today it would be a helpful exercise to look back on your own life so far and see if you aware of things which you once hoped for which never came to be. How reconciled are you to them? Of course there are sometimes second chances. Sometimes our longings and desires change through time. Knowing when to let go of another person or a cherished ambition can be an experience of grace, a genuine release. God's future sometimes requires us to be more flexible than we often wish to be, to be free even in relation to our most cherished desires. In all circumstances, including today, we are invited to pray 'Thy will be done.'

COLLECT

Let your merciful ears, O Lord,
be open to the prayers of your humble servants;
and that they may obtain their petitions
make them to ask such things as shall please you;
through Jesus Christ your Son our Lord,
who is alive and reigns with you,
in the unity of the Holy Spirit,
one God, now and for ever.

| *Reflection by* **Angela Tilby**

Tuesday 6 August
Transfiguration of Our Lord

1 Kings 19.1-16

'... and after the fire a sound of sheer silence' (v.12)

This is one of the most profound passages in scripture, an inspiration and encouragement to all who have felt the anguish of despair. On the Feast of the Transfiguration it reminds us of both the mystery and the closeness of God. God is light, but it is a light that dazzles to the point of darkness. The voice of God is often heard in silence. Elijah's flight through the wilderness is directed by God through the angel and the provisions made for him. Yet when he gets to Mount Horeb, the place of the giving of the law, God does not manifest himself. Only when nature is silenced does he become aware of what an earlier translation called 'a still, small voice'. The Hebrew word can mean 'voice' or 'sound', and 'still, small', or 'sheer silence' is represented by words which sound like a distant murmur, something heard in the background.

The anguish of Elijah is heard by God. The drama of the earthquake, wind and fire, represents the torment of the prophet's spirit, the impossibility of finding rest. The 'dark night of the soul' is a real experience described by the sixteenth-century mystic St John of the Cross. The way through it is not to demand assurance but to plough on in naked faith. God makes himself known as and when he will.

Father in heaven,
whose Son Jesus Christ was wonderfully transfigured
before chosen witnesses upon the holy mountain,
and spoke of the exodus he would accomplish at Jerusalem:
give us strength so to hear his voice and bear our cross
that in the world to come we may see him as he is;
who is alive and reigns with you,
in the unity of the Holy Spirit,
one God, now and for ever.

COLLECT

Wednesday 7 August

Psalm **77**
1 Samuel 28.3-end
Acts 4.13-31

1 Samuel 28.3-end

'Saul ... was afraid, and his heart trembled greatly' (v.5)

The sad story of Saul's attempt to use mediumship to conjure of the spirit of Samuel is intended to warn of the dangers of departing from trust in God. Samuel is indeed brought up from his sleep, but only to condemn Saul and intensify his despair. But between the lines the ghostly encounter is described with a degree of tenderness and sympathy for Saul's plight. The medium's care for Saul in his traumatised state (note that she is not described in v.21 as a medium, but just as 'the woman') contains a hint that though Saul's fate is now sealed, the Lord has not forgotten him. He will always have a part in the history of God's people.

It also reveals how difficult we find it to deal with uncertainty and adversity; how eager we are to blame others and to seek false consolation. Hence the enduring appeal, not least online, of astrology, the Tarot, and other occult routes to knowledge of the future. Our true condition is that we are always mortal and vulnerable, that the future always includes some darkness. The plight of those who feel abandoned by God should not call out condemnation, but recognition, pity and the assurance that we are indeed in God's hands and his ultimate purpose is redemptive.

COLLECT

Let your merciful ears, O Lord,
be open to the prayers of your humble servants;
and that they may obtain their petitions
make them to ask such things as shall please you;
through Jesus Christ your Son our Lord,
who is alive and reigns with you,
in the unity of the Holy Spirit,
one God, now and for ever.

| *Reflection by* **Angela Tilby**

Psalm **78.1-39***
1 Samuel 31
Acts 4.32 – 5.11

Thursday 8 August

1 Samuel 31

'... all the valiant men set out ... and took the body of Saul' (v.12)

Saul's final battle ends in a rout – he and his sons are driven to their deaths by the enemy. It is a terrible end for one who was once chosen by God and anointed as king. Reading this passage today reminds me of current struggles for territory and power where interests clash and whole people are driven into exile or subjugation. Defeat for one nation is victory for another. Yet even as we read of the victory of the Philistines and the dishonouring of Saul's body, we are meant to absorb the deeper truth that God remembers his promises. The 'valiant men' retrieve the bodies and dispose of them decently. There is something of Holy Saturday in this last chapter of the first book of Samuel. We are at one of the low points in the history of God's people, and yet, despite 'earth to earth, ashes to ashes', there remains a sure and certain hope.

For those whose lives are suspended in what seems like total defeat there may be no way forward. But God sometimes asks us to accept the reality of defeat, bury our dead dreams in hope and to wait patiently for a new chapter of life to unfold. None of this is easy. But trials of faith are inevitable in a broken and fallen world while we wait for God's future to unfold.

Lord of heaven and earth,
as Jesus taught his disciples to be persistent in prayer,
give us patience and courage never to lose hope,
but always to bring our prayers before you;
through Jesus Christ our Lord.

COLLECT

Reflection by **Angela Tilby** | 223

Friday 9 August

Psalm **55***
2 Samuel I
Acts 5.12-26

2 Samuel 1

'How the mighty have fallen ...' (v.25)

Even in death, Saul is dishonoured, this time by an enemy soldier hoping to save his own life by pretending to have responded to Saul's request to kill him. David's response is ruthless, a measure of his own still-conflicted emotions about Saul. These are finally poured out in his lamentation for Saul and Jonathan. The lament combines an eloquent tribute to Saul and a passionate farewell to Jonathan, David's beloved, and the friend of his heart. The name 'Jonathan' means 'given by God'. His life has been a gift to David and David acknowledges that his heart is broken.

Christian teaching has sometimes tended towards Stoicism and even encouraged us to move on too quickly for our good when a loved one dies. But Scripture does not suggest we should try to rise above human emotion. Jesus wept for Lazarus. Allowing ourselves to lament is a way of integrating our deepest loves and greatest losses within the love of God.

It is right to be grateful for those friends who know us deeply, those whose love we treasure and depend on, our true partners in life. Lamenting their loss is a way of honouring them in the presence of God, and of bringing healing to our own hearts. Grief, as is so often said, is the price we pay for love.

COLLECT

Let your merciful ears, O Lord,
be open to the prayers of your humble servants;
and that they may obtain their petitions
make them to ask such things as shall please you;
through Jesus Christ your Son our Lord,
who is alive and reigns with you,
in the unity of the Holy Spirit,
one God, now and for ever.

| *Reflection by* **Angela Tilby**

Saturday 10 August

2 Samuel 2.1-11

'... the house of Judah followed David' (v.10)

David's future was still far from assured. Guided by God to base himself in Hebron (where the patriarch Abraham was buried with Sarah his wife) he is anointed king of Judah. His first attempt to extend his kingdom is unsuccessful. Saul's commander Abner arranges for Saul's son Ishbaal to be anointed king of Israel in succession to his father. This sets the scene for a long and brutal war between David and those loyal to Saul. David has seven years as a campaigning war lord before he is able to fulfil his call to be king of Israel. It is a reminder that David was not born to privilege, he was selected by Samuel as the youngest and least significant of his family. And now, even after his victories and successes, he has no choice but to serve a long apprenticeship.

It is tempting for some to crave success and recognition when they are not truly ready for them, and in a culture which idolises youth and celebrity this is a temptation to which it is easy to succumb. Seven years is a long time, but it is a tenth of the Biblical lifespan (Psalm 90.10). It is time for significant change, for new habits to form, for promise to mature. As you reflect on your own life consider areas where you might be feeling impatient and what you might have yet to learn of God's ways and God's will.

Lord of heaven and earth,
as Jesus taught his disciples to be persistent in prayer,
give us patience and courage never to lose hope,
but always to bring our prayers before you;
through Jesus Christ our Lord.

COLLECT

Monday 12 August

Psalms **80**, 82
2 Samuel 3.12-end
Acts 6

2 Samuel 3.12-end

'... powerless, even though anointed king' (v.39)

Grasping political power is rarely a clean business. Today's reading exemplifies that in good measure. There's a tortured knot of problems here. David is on the make. Abner, a leading opponent, sees David as the man to back, and wants to switch sides. Joab, David's nephew, has scores to settle with Abner. In the end, David is faced with a quandary – Abner is assassinated by David's relative and most faithful lieutenant. This casts David in a bad light, a plotter rather than a just king.

David decides to act as honourably as he can. He disassociates himself from the assassination and tries to honour the enemy. We glimpse the future statesman, and the person who seeks to walk in God's ways even amid great murkiness.

Questions for reflection arise quickly from a passage like this: how do we stand up for good, and avoid the pitfalls of politics and personal vengeance? How do we distance ourselves from skulduggery, and from playing situations for self-justification and personal advantage?

In the end, it's a matter of our personal integrity before God who reads the heart. We may not face the dilemmas of a king on the make in an ancient and violent world, but not giving in to self-seeking values remains a challenge in a quiet way for all of us as we negotiate through life. How do we keep God in view?

COLLECT

O God, you declare your almighty power
most chiefly in showing mercy and pity:
mercifully grant to us such a measure of your grace,
that we, running the way of your commandments,
may receive your gracious promises,
and be made partakers of your heavenly treasure;
through Jesus Christ your Son our Lord,
who is alive and reigns with you,
in the unity of the Holy Spirit,
one God, now and for ever.

| *Reflection by* **Gergory Cameron**

Tuesday 13 August

2 Samuel 5.1-12

'... for the sake of his people Israel' (v.12)

David has made it. Not only has he won the support of the people for the top job, he captures a shiny new capital city.

It must have seemed that God was on his side in every sense. Yet David cannot have known what God's providence would make of Jerusalem and its significance as a site of holiness and suffering, as a centre for people's hopes and fears, for spiritual aspiration and exasperation down through the centuries, a physical and spiritual metaphor of God's dwelling place.

There's a subtlety to God's will in this passage. Yes, God manifests a personal interest in David and pours out his blessing upon him, but God is also up to bigger things, lining up the future to be a witness to his ways of working, teaching the world about a faithfulness which endures for centuries, and a vocation to a city and a people to be something larger than they could ever guess, as witnesses to salvation history.

The story of God's people is a symphony of myriad parts. Somehow each individual, each contribution, is important in God's eyes, but the tale we're woven into is also so much larger than ourselves. It's a working out of the Kingdom—the kingship—of God. Thanks be to God for the specificity of his invitation to us, and his grand design for the redemption of the world.

God of glory,
the end of our searching,
help us to lay aside
all that prevents us from seeking your kingdom,
and to give all that we have
to gain the pearl beyond all price,
through our Saviour Jesus Christ.

COLLECT

Wednesday 14 August

2 Samuel 6.1-19

'How can the ark of the Lord come into my care?' (v.9)

Today we're introduced to another of the most potent symbols of God's presence, the Ark of the Covenant. The scriptures recorded its creation in the time of the Exodus, when it was the premier symbol of God's presence, so that God was believed to reside between the two cherubim which adorned its lid.

As David transferred the ark into Jerusalem however, something happened – one of those protecting its journey is slain for daring to touch it. To the modern reader, this sounds savage. Uzzah was trying to steady the ark, not harm it. However, the Scriptures commanded that the ark should be carried on poles, not in a cart, so there is negligence of God's instructions. We have to understand the extraordinary value that the Old Testament writers placed on holiness. In their experience it was something akin to radiation, and unless all the proper precautions were followed, it could contaminate as well as bless.

After this event, it takes three months to persuade David that the ark can be a vehicle of blessing –, during which its new hosts experienced blessing from God. Only then is David truly convinced that the next step is to bring the ark with much celebration to the site set aside for the future temple.

This passage teaches us something of the nature of holiness: it is not something to be trifled with; but properly sought, it will bring blessing, joy and celebration.

COLLECT

O God, you declare your almighty power
most chiefly in showing mercy and pity:
mercifully grant to us such a measure of your grace,
that we, running the way of your commandments,
may receive your gracious promises,
and be made partakers of your heavenly treasure;
through Jesus Christ your Son our Lord,
who is alive and reigns with you,
in the unity of the Holy Spirit,
one God, now and for ever.

| *Reflection by* **Gergory Cameron**

Psalms 98, 138, 147.1-12
Isaiah 7.10-15
Luke 11.27-28

Thursday 15 August
The Blessed Virgin Mary

Isaiah 7.10-15

'… the Lord himself will give you a sign' (v.14)

This Feast of the Blessed Virgin Mary interrupts our journey through stories of King David, shifting our attention from the physical Ark of the Covenant to the one who was the living Ark of the New Covenant, carrying Christ in her womb.

The feast has accrued various layers of meaning through the Christian centuries – as the Dormition (the falling asleep of the Virgin Mary) or the Assumption (the rapturing of Mary's physical presence into heaven), or simply as the feast of the 'BVM', as she is known colloquially to some Christians.

Here is an object lesson on the many layers by which scripture operates. The original context is only one of many theological strata that glisten from a text. Originally, Isaiah offers a sign to King Ahaz that within the period of one child's gestation and weaning, political realities will undergo unexpected upheavals. For the early Christians, however, the text was confirmation of the birth of the Messiah. It does not really matter whether the passage speaks of a 'virgin' or a 'young woman' (both translations are valid); the point is that God becomes incarnate in Mary's child, Immanuel. The early Church saw it as assurance of Jesus' supernatural origin.

This scripture also gave the Church a new icon: 'The Virgin of the Sign', which shows Mary at prayer pregnant with a Christ who rules as King from her womb. It is a call to take the incarnation seriously.

Almighty God,
who looked upon the lowliness of the Blessed Virgin Mary
and chose her to be the mother of your only Son:
grant that we who are redeemed by his blood
may share with her in the glory of your eternal kingdom;
through Jesus Christ your Son our Lord,
who is alive and reigns with you,
in the unity of the Holy Spirit,
one God, now and for ever.

COLLECT

Reflection by **Gregory Cameron** | 229

Friday 16 August

2 Samuel 7.18-end

'... you are God, and your words are true' (v.28a)

David is praying. He had just made up his mind to build a temple for God, but in the first half of this chapter, Nathan the prophet gives the answer, 'No': it is God's will for his son, Solomon, to put that plan into action.

Accepting this, David prays a dynamic prayer of thanksgiving. He begins humbly, recognising that God's choice set him on the path to kingship and that God's strength enabled him to see it through. He recites the history of God's actions down through the centuries, bringing it into the present, and claiming God's promises for the future.

This pattern of the prayer might be familiar, because it occurs in every celebration of the Eucharist. At the heart of the celebration of Holy Communion is a prayer known as 'The Great Thanksgiving'. The celebrant praises God, calling to mind God's gracious acts. As David prayed about the acts of God in Israel's history, we give thanks for God's actions in creation and redemption through Jesus, and invoke God's blessing in our own lives.

Our passage today is an invitation to make thanksgiving a central part of our own prayer. Prayer should not become just a shopping list of requests: it can be a moment to reflect on where we have seen God at work in our lives, and to claim his promises for our future journey of faith.

COLLECT

O God, you declare your almighty power
most chiefly in showing mercy and pity:
mercifully grant to us such a measure of your grace,
that we, running the way of your commandments,
may receive your gracious promises,
and be made partakers of your heavenly treasure;
through Jesus Christ your Son our Lord,
who is alive and reigns with you,
in the unity of the Holy Spirit,
one God, now and for ever.

230 | *Reflection by* **Gergory Cameron**

Psalms 96, **97**, 100
2 Samuel 9
Acts 8.4-25

Saturday 17 August

2 Samuel 9

'Is there anyone remaining of the House of Saul to whom I may show the kindness of God?' (v.3a)

With the controversy of his youth behind him, David is settling old scores – but not in the way you may expect. The scores that David settles are by way of making peace – in this case with the house of Saul. There must have been old and painful reminiscences here. The house of Saul represented both joyous and sorrowful memories for David. He had been a great friend to Jonathan – a friendship so great that the scriptures record that it was 'wonderful, passing the love of women' (2 Samuel 1.26). However, Jonathan's father, King Saul, had been increasingly suspicious of David and jealous of his successes, so much so that Jonathan had to intervene to save David's life on one occasion.

David moves to make amends. He restores to Mephibosheth, Jonathan's son, his ancestral lands, and gives him dining rights at the king's table, a sign of high royal favour.

It is never too late to make peace, or to restore justice. In life, we tend to move on, but David, conscious of God's continuing mercy, seeks to set straight ancient hurts and rivalries. Jesus had things to say along the same lines. 'Be merciful, just as your father is merciful' he preaches in the Gospel according to Luke (6.36), and in Matthew's Gospel, he tells us that even if we are in the middle of worship, and we remember an unresolved wrong, we should leave to make peace first (5.23-24).

God of glory,
the end of our searching,
help us to lay aside
all that prevents us from seeking your kingdom,
and to give all that we have
to gain the pearl beyond all price,
through our Saviour Jesus Christ.

COLLECT

Monday 19 August

2 Samuel 11

'... the thing that David had done displeased the Lord' (v.27b)

The scriptures are more interested in morality than virtually all other ancient texts. Although we are reading through the ancient history of the people of God, the writers of the Old Testament focus upon questions of faith and morality rather than straightforward history. There is no whitewashing here and even the great David slips up in a big way.

Early interpreters of the scriptures tended to see allegory everywhere. For example, St John Cassian, a fourth-century monk and religious teacher, reflected on the seven tribes that Joshua had overcome in conquering the Promised Land in the book named after him, and decided that the best way to understand them was as symbolic of fundamental sinful orientations, from which all other sins could flow, and which the virtuous Christian had to overcome. John thus created the first list of the seven deadly sins.

Amongst them was lust, a root sin, which here ensnares King David, when he indulges in a bit of voyeurism. The voyeurism leads to adultery, and the adultery to murder. One thing leads to another. David sinks into ever deeper water.

Jesus taught his disciples to pray, 'Lead us not into temptation, but deliver us from evil.' One of my theological teachers explained this as, 'When there is opportunity, Lord, spare us the inclination; when there's the inclination, spare us the opportunity.' It would have been a good prayer for David, and remains a good prayer for us.

COLLECT

Almighty and everlasting God,
you are always more ready to hear than we to pray
and to give more than either we desire or deserve:
pour down upon us the abundance of your mercy,
forgiving us those things of which our conscience is afraid
and giving us those good things which we are not worthy to ask
but through the merits and mediation
of Jesus Christ your Son our Lord,
who is alive and reigns with you,
in the unity of the Holy Spirit,
one God, now and for ever.

Reflection by **Gergory Cameron**

Psalm **106*** (*or* 103)
2 Samuel 12.1-25
Acts 9.1-19*a*

Tuesday 20 August

2 Samuel 12.1-25

'You are the man!' (v.7a)

The fallout from David's sin continues. Indeed, the pace of events in this reading comes thick and fast, and many things could draw our attention, not least, the very human story of bereavement in the second part of the reading.

I'd like to focus on the role of the prophet Nathan, however. It must be a very difficult thing to 'speak truth to power', to adopt the widely used Quaker phrase. David has shown himself to be surprisingly unscrupulous, and for Nathan to challenge him must have taken a fair bit of courage. The story Nathan tells might be a difficult one for modern readers, given that we no longer see women as flocks of sheep to be owned, but it is a clever approach – David's instinct for justice is roused before he is revealed as the offender himself. Although we tend to think as prophets as foretelling the future, their main role in the scriptures is quite distinct: they speak the word of God's truth into any situation. It is noteworthy here though that God's judgement is intended as a call to repentance – and a change of direction.

The Church is called to be prophetic in this sense in particular. The scriptures proclaim God's concern for justice in society, and Christians need to develop the skills shown by Nathan to speak into the many contexts of the modern world. Where might your voice be needed?

God of constant mercy,
who sent your Son to save us:
remind us of your goodness,
increase your grace within us,
that our thankfulness may grow,
through Jesus Christ our Lord.

COLLECT

Reflection by **Gregory Cameron**   233

Wednesday 21 August

2 Samuel 15.1-12

'Absalom stole the hearts of the people of Israel' (v.6b)

They say that history repeats itself, and here we find, in the Books of Samuel, a historical drama the like of which seems to have been repeated by all the great dynastic powers down through the centuries. It is the tale of the talented but hot-headed heir of the monarch who gets fed up with waiting to inherit power, and instigates rebellion.

In English history, King Henry II is reported to have painted a mural in his chamber in Winchester Palace of four eaglets attacking their proud golden eagle father, said to represent his own disenchantment with the sons who plotted his overthrow. Here, David faces the rebellion of Absalom, who quietly wins over the favour of the people with the promise of easier justice. Ties of blood seem to exert no loyalty once ambition and power come into play.

This story of David was preserved by the biblical writers because they cherished his memory as the model of a righteous king, but here we see all too human elements at work: jealousy, revenge, subterfuge, and betrayal. They testify to both the reality of the history—even divinely favoured heroes face the messiness of life and family relationships—and David's vulnerability. No-one gets to escape the flaws that accompany life. While we hold our breath to find out what happens next, we can at least pray for all families in which there is estrangement or hurt.

COLLECT

Almighty and everlasting God,
you are always more ready to hear than we to pray
and to give more than either we desire or deserve:
pour down upon us the abundance of your mercy,
forgiving us those things of which our conscience is afraid
and giving us those good things which we are not worthy to ask
but through the merits and mediation
of Jesus Christ your Son our Lord,
who is alive and reigns with you,
in the unity of the Holy Spirit,
one God, now and for ever.

| *Reflection by* **Gergory Cameron**

Psalms 113, **115**
2 Samuel 15.13-end
Acts 9.32-end

Thursday 22 August

2 Samuel 15.13-end

'... go back to the city in peace' (v.27)

David recognises the plight of his position, and decides he must abandon his capital and flee. It speaks volumes for the quality of leadership that he has provided that so many stick with him, however. Recent foreign recruits, led by Ittai the Gittite, remain loyal, as do the priests, Abiathar and Zadok.

What is outstanding, however, is that David cares more for his followers than he does for himself. 'You've barely arrived.' he says to Ittai, 'make your peace with Absalom, and don't get wrapped up in my problems.' 'Keep the ark in Jerusalem,' he says to the priests, 'I am content to let God's will be done.' So we discover there's more generosity, faith and trust in David than recent chapters might suggest. He cares for those around him, even facing great distress himself, and puts all matters into the hands of God. Here's the example that the biblical writers wanted us to witness.

Even so, David keeps his wits about him. He knows that the insightful and intelligent Ahithophel needs to be countered, and so he recruits a spy. It reminds us of the advice of Jesus: 'I am sending you out like sheep into the midst of wolves; so be as wise as serpents [as well as] innocent as doves.' (Matthew 10.16)

Lord God, teach us both what is right and wise in times of difficulty.

God of constant mercy,
who sent your Son to save us:
remind us of your goodness,
increase your grace within us,
that our thankfulness may grow,
through Jesus Christ our Lord.

COLLECT

Friday 23 August

2 Samuel 16.1-14

'It may be that the Lord will look on my distress' (v.12)

They say that you find out who your friends are when you experience great need. Here, David is the one who has fallen on hard times. Ziba remains a friend, but many of his old rivals from the house of Saul seize their chance for payback,or mock the king's misfortune. Mephibosheth shows no gratitude, and Shimei takes the opportunity to gloat.

The good example of David remains steadfast, however. Faced with the anger of his loyal followers, who want to take revenge, David refuses to react violently, and continues to put his trust in God. In great need, or great fortune, the truth of our nature often slips out. The famous poem 'If' by Rudyard Kipling seems to speak into this situation:

'If you can meet with Triumph and Disaster
And treat those two imposters just the same ...'

But perhaps the scriptures speak even more powerfully: 'You keep him in perfect peace whose mind is stayed on you, because he trusts in you' (Isaiah 26.3, ESV).

David becomes the example of the steadfast, suffering servant here. 'Humble yourselves therefore under the mighty hand of God, so that he may exalt you in due time' (1 Peter 5.6). This is not so much the stoicism that Kipling commends, but rather is a trust in God, the sure hope that in life there can be no greater source of comfort and strength than in placing ourselves in God's hands.

COLLECT

Almighty and everlasting God,
you are always more ready to hear than we to pray
and to give more than either we desire or deserve:
pour down upon us the abundance of your mercy,
forgiving us those things of which our conscience is afraid
and giving us those good things which we are not worthy to ask
but through the merits and mediation
of Jesus Christ your Son our Lord,
who is alive and reigns with you,
in the unity of the Holy Spirit,
one God, now and for ever.

236 | *Reflection by* **Gergory Cameron**

Psalms 86, 117
Genesis 28.10-17
John 1.43-end

Saturday 24 August

Bartholomew the Apostle

Genesis 28.10-17

'... this is the gate of heaven' (v.17b)

This reading, for the Feast of St Bartholomew, really needs to be read in conjunction with John 1.43-51, which records the call of the disciples Philip and Nathanael, since the latter is regarded as the same person as Bartholomew, under a different name. In that passage, Jesus is taken by surprise at Nathanael's fervour, and promises him that he will have the same experience as Jacob: he will see 'heaven opened and the angels of God ascending and descending ...'

Jacob's vision causes him to name the location of his dream Bethel (the house of God), and the Genesis story is probably recorded to explain the origin of the placename. However, it becomes for Christians a description of what a church building, a house of God, is intended to be – a place where a ladder is set up between heaven and earth, whose rungs are forged from the prayers, worship and sacraments celebrated in the building over the generations.

Jesus, however, gives this story a new spin. The angels will ascend and descend upon him, and Bartholomew will see heaven opened not in a place, but in the person of Jesus. 'I am the gate,' says Jesus (John 10.9). Both passages call on us to recognise that God is a God who reveals himself, making covenants, solemn binding relationships of love, with those who worship him, and who make a place for him in their hearts.

Almighty and everlasting God,
who gave to your apostle Bartholomew grace
truly to believe and to preach your word:
grant that your Church
may love that word which he believed
and may faithfully preach and receive the same;
through Jesus Christ your Son our Lord,
who is alive and reigns with you,
in the unity of the Holy Spirit,
one God, now and for ever.

COLLECT

Reflection by **Gergory Cameron** | 237

Monday 26 August

2 Samuel 18.1-18

'Deal gently for my sake with the young man Absalom' (v.5)

If I were an army general, what I would learn from this concerns military strategy. Absalom drew up his troops with rough, wooded terrain behind him. When his soldiers retreated their lines were broken and they were picked off as easy targets in the forest. It was the undoing of Absalom himself as he tried to escape, with merciless Joab both judge and executioner.

If I were a head of state, what I would learn from this concerns power. Absalom had rebelled against his own father, had much-publicised sex with his father's concubines, and divided a nation. No matter what was going through David's head, his senior staff Joab, Abishai and Ittai knew that previous attempts at appeasement had failed. This time there no way back.

But I'm neither of those. I'm a middle-aged man whose family relationships sometimes involve clashing priorities, struggles with personalities that I know too well, and grievances I can't let go of. So what I learn from the example of David is altogether more mundane. It's about how loving people can sometimes stop me making tough decisions, or make me unwisely indulgent, or cause me to give in to my emotions in an unhelpful way. I thank God that no one is going to war because I act foolishly toward the people I love. But I can't forget those fractious holidays, those long car journeys, those late nights for which I need to ask forgiveness.

COLLECT

Almighty God,
who called your Church to bear witness
that you were in Christ reconciling the world to yourself:
help us to proclaim the good news of your love,
that all who hear it may be drawn to you;
through him who was lifted up on the cross,
and reigns with you in the unity of the Holy Spirit,
one God, now and for ever.

| *Reflection by* **Peter Graystone**

Tuesday 27 August

2 Samuel 18.19 – 19.8*a*

'Would I had died instead of you, Absalom, my son' (18.33)

'Tell us a tale,' pleaded the children. 'A happy tale or a sad one?' said the storyteller. 'A happy one.' The storyteller began, 'The grandfather died. The father died. The son died.' It was only years later that the crestfallen children understood. There is an order to the way God has organised our world. When it proceeds in the way we expect, we can consider death with equanimity. When it is broken, the grief can be unbearable. If that is part of your family's story, please accept my condolences. To read David's lament over his dead son must have stirred agonising memories.

In my experience, the death of someone can also bring feelings of guilt. 'If only I had spoken before it was too late.' 'If only we had spent more time together.' I wonder whether guilt exacerbated David's grief. His sins against Bathsheba and her husband had unleashed a curse that 'the sword shall never depart from your house' (2 Samuel 12.10). It was Bathsheba's grandfather Ahithophel, driven perhaps by hatred of David for what was done to his granddaughter, who played a key role in this tragedy. His defection triggered Absalom's revolt (2 Samuel 15.12; 17.1-4).

Today I pray for those who mourn, for those who cannot assuage their guilt, for those who minister to the bereaved and for those who, like David, feel they have no choice but to suppress their heartbreak and carry on.

Almighty God,
you search us and know us:
may we rely on you in strength
and rest on you in weakness,
now and in all our days;
through Jesus Christ our Lord.

COLLECT

Wednesday 28 August

Psalm 119.153-end
2 Samuel 19.8*b*-23
Acts 11.19-end

2 Samuel 19.8*b*-23

'Your servant knows that I have sinned' (v.20)

David had received appalling treatment from Shimei. He was from the same clan as Saul, over whom David had been victorious on his way to kingship. So it is understandable that, during the civil war which pitted David against Absalom, Shimei took Absalom's side. At a stage when Absalom had the upper hand, Shimei called down a curse on David and pelted him with rocks and dirt as he rode away from Jerusalem through a valley (2 Samuel 16.5-8).

Now the tide has turned. David is returning triumphant, Shimei is at David's mercy. He flings himself at the king's feet and begs for his life. Against the advice of his generals, David decides to spare him. It is the attitude that Paul later expects of the church in Rome as Christ-like behaviour: 'Do not repay anyone evil for evil, but take thought for what is noble in the sight of all' (Romans 12.17).

I find these narratives of violent excess and nation-changing passion hard to relate to my simple life. But half an hour ago, while this Bible passage was fresh in my mind, I received appalling treatment during a phone call with a utilities company. It would have been entirely deserved if I had raged and shouted. But I decided to be calm and patient until I got the correct result. That was Shimei's gift to me today. It's not much, but it's something.

COLLECT

Almighty God,
who called your Church to bear witness
that you were in Christ reconciling the world to yourself:
help us to proclaim the good news of your love,
that all who hear it may be drawn to you;
through him who was lifted up on the cross,
and reigns with you in the unity of the Holy Spirit,
one God, now and for ever.

| *Reflection by* **Peter Graystone**

Psalms **143**, 146
2 Samuel 19.24-end
Acts 12.1-17

Thursday 29 August

2 Samuel 19.24-end

'Let him take it all' (v.30)

Military victory was only part of what David needed in order to reunite a bitterly divided nation following the civil war. He also needed diplomatic skills, to work to rebuild relationships, and generous kindness.

He made a shrewd political move by appointing the man who had formerly been Absalom's commander-in-chief as the leader of his army (2 Samuel 19.3-15). That gave confidence to those who had taken the side of David's adversary that they would not be oppressed. It wasn't entirely successful because the final verses of today's reading show dissatisfaction not entirely resolved. But it did allow David to make his way safely to his capital city.

It was accompanied by two great compassionate gestures. One was toward the grandson of his former enemy Saul. Mephibosheth was the son of Jonathan and is one of the few examples in the Bible of a disabled person neither healed nor excluded, but honoured for who he is. His servant Ziba had bribed his way into David's approval (2 Samuel 16.1-4). Mephibosheth found his way into David's affections by honest devotion. They both came away rewarded.

People of a great age are, in contrast, always portrayed with respect. Here, in a tender exchange with Barzillai, David shows the compassionate understanding of a man who knows how to make peace as well as how to make war.

Almighty God,
you search us and know us:
may we rely on you in strength
and rest on you in weakness,
now and in all our days;
through Jesus Christ our Lord.

COLLECT

Reflection by **Peter Graystone** | 241

Friday 30 August

Psalms 142, **144**
2 Samuel 23.1-7
Acts 12.18-end

2 Samuel 23.1-7

'One who rules over people justly' (v.3)

These are David's famous last words. Fifty years after the resurrection of Jesus, the last words of the Roman emperor Vespasian were, 'Oh dear, I think I am becoming a god.' One thousand years before Jesus, David's last words were, 'Oh dear God, I have become your exalted one.'

What was so important to David that he wanted people to consider them his final statement to the world? Three things. First, he had discovered that treating people fairly leads to a blessing not only for those on the receiving end of justice, but for those who make it happen. It is as certain as sunrise.

Second, he knows that the faithfulness of God can be relied on utterly, and that he can be at peace about committing himself, his family and their future into God's hands.

Third, his experience is that the way of evil is worthless and short-lived. Evil gives the impression of being as threatening as trying to pick up thorns. But in the ultimate righteousness of God the thorns are just thrown into the fire.

What would I want my final utterance to be? I hope that, like David, it will reflect how enriched my life has been by being aware of the presence of God year after year. It would be hard to better John Wesley's famous last words: 'The best of it is that God is with us.'

COLLECT

Almighty God,
who called your Church to bear witness
that you were in Christ reconciling the world to yourself:
help us to proclaim the good news of your love,
that all who hear it may be drawn to you;
through him who was lifted up on the cross,
and reigns with you in the unity of the Holy Spirit,
one God, now and for ever.

242 | *Reflection by* **Peter Graystone**

Saturday 31 August

2 Samuel 24

'Offerings to the Lord my God that cost me nothing' (v.24)

A memory resurfaces. I'm aged eight and I'm in church. The collection is being taken. Every week my mother reaches into her handbag and passes me sixpence, which I put into the bag. It's an offering to God that costs me nothing. It's precisely what David declined to do, even though Araunah had proffered it out of his generous (or perhaps fearful) heart.

'I will not offer burnt offerings to the Lord my God that cost me nothing.' The challenge that David's decision puts before us is about the priority our worship and our giving is accorded in our lives. Do we set aside time for our devotions in the tired edges of our day, or as a prime time offering to God? Do we give out of what we can spare, or in a sacrificial way?

The decisions we make about this have consequences that we might never be aware of, but which allow God to act in ways we cannot imagine. There was a direct line of consequence in David's actions. It began with suffering and death which, rightly or wrongly, David believed to be caused by his sin. It developed into obedience to God and an act of generosity. It was honoured by answered prayer. And in the future that David did not live to see, the hilltop threshing floor on which the sacrifice was made became the site of the glorious temple (1 Chronicles 22.1).

> Almighty God,
> you search us and know us:
> may we rely on you in strength
> and rest on you in weakness,
> now and in all our days;
> through Jesus Christ our Lord.

COLLECT

Monday 2 September

Psalms 1, 2, 3
I Kings 1.5-31
Acts 13.13-43

1 Kings 1.5-31

'Who should sit on the throne?' (v.27)

In Autumn 2022 power changed hands twice in the UK in contrasting ways. Once it was sombre and orderly, as King Charles III succeeded his mother. Once it was chaotic, as Rishi Sunak was appointed to succeed his short-lived predecessor. But in neither case did it involve the trauma and fear of death that marked the end of David's reign in about 970 BC.

Adonijah, whose good looks had allowed him to get away with shameful behaviour, attempted to enthrone himself while his father David was still on his deathbed. He was the king's son by Haggith, so for another of David's wives, Bathsheba, and those loyal to her this could have been a death sentence.

Adonijah is depicted as opportunistic and ambitious, quick to assert his rights as the eldest surviving son, and divisive in enlisting a powerful team including the high priest Abiathar. The prophet Nathan is portrayed in a contrasting way. His devotion to God had once led him to rebuke the king when David's lust for Bathsheba turned him murderous (2 Samuel 12.1-10). Now it led Nathan to risk intervening on Bathsheba's behalf, prompting David to nominate her son Solomon as his successor.

The power-grabbing here leads me to thank God for political systems that are designed to allow a peaceful transfer of leadership, and to pray for those who live in countries where these fraught and potentially deadly scenes are still recognisable as today's reality.

COLLECT

Almighty God,
whose only Son has opened for us
a new and living way into your presence:
give us pure hearts and steadfast wills
to worship you in spirit and in truth;
through Jesus Christ your Son our Lord,
who is alive and reigns with you,
in the unity of the Holy Spirit,
one God, now and for ever.

| *Reflection by* **Peter Graystone**

Psalms **5**, 6 (8)
1 Kings 1.32 – 2.4; 2.10-12
Acts 13.44 – 14.7

Tuesday 3 September

1 Kings 1.32 – 2.4; 2.10-12

'Keep the charge of the Lord your God' (v.3)

Adonijah, pretender to the throne, feasts in one part of Jerusalem. Meanwhile, in a different part of the city and accompanied by a marching band, another group makes its way to the sacred spring of Gihon. Solomon is on a mule (normal for those riding in state – horses came later). With him is Zadok, one the two high priests, the prophet Nathan, and David's own elite mercenary army. The people acclaim King Solomon so jubilantly that the ground reverberates beneath their stomping feet. The game is up for Adonijah.

David's final words to his successor remind him that conditions are attached to the promise God made him. Solomon and his heirs will prosper if they obey God's Law with all their heart and soul. We will see Solomon compromise and succumb to competing interests, and the irony of these words will become clear.

And what happened to the characters we have met over the past week? In an effort to secure his status, Adonijah over-reached himself and Solomon had him put to death. Abiathar the high priest was deposed and banished. Joab, terrified by what was happening to his fellow-conspirators, sought sanctuary beside the Lord's altar, but Solomon had him killed anyway. Shimei was put under house arrest, but he broke the terms of his sentence and was executed. The account ends, chillingly, 'So the kingdom was established in the hand of Solomon' (2 Kings 2.46).

COLLECT

Merciful God,
your Son came to save us
and bore our sins on the cross:
may we trust in your mercy
and know your love,
rejoicing in the righteousness
that is ours through Jesus Christ our Lord.

Wednesday 4 September

1 Kings 3

'The wisdom of God was in him to execute justice' (v.28)

The book of Proverbs repeatedly speaks of the value of wisdom which is, consistent with Solomon's request, preferable to great wealth or long life: 'Happy are those who find wisdom, and those who get understanding, for her income is better than silver, and her revenue better than gold' (Proverbs 3.11-12). The story of the two mothers, which is told to show Solomon's wisdom in action, has the beguiling quality of a fable. Solomon's wisdom is more than cleverness. It demonstrates even-handedness, imagination and wit – three fine virtues that do not spring to mind as often as they should when godly qualities are being considered.

From the start, however, Solomon shows himself to be a man pulled in different directions. His love of the Lord is explicitly mentioned. But he makes a politically prudent marriage – the start of a series of dalliances with those who worship other gods which will compromise his devotion (11.1). He offers a prayer of touching humility before God, while at the same time making grandiose sacrifices at shrines.

The characteristic of Solomon that I most yearn for is discernment. The collect for Pentecost describes it as 'to have a right judgment in all things'. St Paul longed that his readers would be able 'to determine what is best, so that on the day of Christ you may be pure and blameless' and believed that greater love would mean greater discernment (Philippians 1.10).

COLLECT

Almighty God,
whose only Son has opened for us
a new and living way into your presence:
give us pure hearts and steadfast wills
to worship you in spirit and in truth;
through Jesus Christ your Son our Lord,
who is alive and reigns with you,
in the unity of the Holy Spirit,
one God, now and for ever.

| *Reflection by* **Peter Graystone**

Psalms 14, **15**, 16
1 Kings 4.29 – 5.12
Acts 15.1-21

Thursday 5 September

1 Kings 4.29 – 5.12

'There was peace' (5.12)

The Hebrew word usually translated as peace, shalom, has a much richer meaning and implies wholeness, prosperity and wellbeing. In the case of Solomon's kingdom, in the early days of his reign, it encompasses joy in learning, appreciation of music and literature, and understanding of the place of nature in God's plan for the planet. It takes in neighbourliness, both personally in human relationships and internationally in trade deals and military alliances. When it comes to praying for the good of our own homeland, those five features make an excellent basis for intercessions for our own national life.

However, idyllic though it sounds, this life was under threat. Further south in Egypt, the sole survivor of a clan that Solomon's father had wiped out was angrily waiting for the moment when he would take revenge (1 Kings 11.14-22). And the temple, magnificent though it would be, was not built by a fairly paid workforce, but by forced labourers whom Solomon conscripted – a practice the prophets condemned (1 Kings 5.13-14, Jeremiah 22.13).

If even the glory of Solomon comes with a questionable shadow side, where can we go to find something of true worth? Maybe the garden. Have a look at a flower in bloom and put those worries in perspective. Such is the shalom of the Creator God that 'even Solomon in all his glory was not clothed like one of these' (Luke 12.27).

Merciful God,
your Son came to save us
and bore our sins on the cross:
may we trust in your mercy
and know your love,
rejoicing in the righteousness
that is ours through Jesus Christ our Lord.

COLLECT

Friday 6 September

Psalms 17, **19**
1 Kings 6.1, 11-28
Acts 15.22-35

1 Kings 6.1, 11-28

'I will establish my promise with you' (v.12)

The temple was not as big as we might imagine. If you have a really big back garden, you could accommodate its 40 metres by 15 metres. But it was lavishly beautiful, with wood panelling, gold and carved cedar.

It had four purposes. Firstly, it was a national shrine – the spiritual focus of the people of Israel. Secondly, it was a royal chapel, closely associated with the palace complex. Thirdly, it was the home of the ark of the covenant. This was the acacia wood box which held the stones on which the ten commandments were engraved. Topped with ornate carvings of angels, it occupied a windowless cubic space within the temple.

Fourthly it was 'a house for the Lord's name' and the most sacred sign of the presence of God among his people. So in the heart of the description of the building's architecture the writer inserts a reminder of God's call to Solomon to be obedient. God's promise never to abandon his people Israel was not dependent on how beautiful the building was, but upon how faithfully his ways were followed.

In years to come the Jews would develop a misplaced trust in the temple alone to save them when they were under threat. But it was the justice, compassion and obedience of which the building was a sign that God held dear, not the wood and gold of which it was made (Jeremiah 7.1-7).

COLLECT

Almighty God,
whose only Son has opened for us
a new and living way into your presence:
give us pure hearts and steadfast wills
to worship you in spirit and in truth;
through Jesus Christ your Son our Lord,
who is alive and reigns with you,
in the unity of the Holy Spirit,
one God, now and for ever.

| *Reflection by* **Peter Graystone**

Psalms 20, 21, **23**
1 Kings 8.1-30
Acts 15.36 – 16.5

Saturday 7 September

1 Kings 8.1-30

'The highest heaven cannot contain you' (v.27)

The placing of the ark of the covenant in the temple was a moment which allowed God's people to assert that their wanderings were at an end and an era of stability was intended. The ark had been an affirmation of God's presence, accompanying them on their travels. However, Solomon draws attention to something that we take for granted but was being progressively revealed to the Hebrews. God was not to be found solely within the temple, but 'even heaven and the highest heaven' were not big enough to contain his vastness. This became vitally significant centuries later when the Jews were conquered and taken captive into exile. They were kept from despair by the discovery that God had not perished in the rubble of the destroyed temple, but was with them in Babylon. In fact, God was everywhere. It was during those decades of exile that this book was compiled.

To this omnipresent God Solomon prays. He hallows God with his praise. He asks for God's will to be done. He brings before God the people's needs. And he asks for forgiveness. It is the pattern that Christians follow in the Lord's Prayer. Through Jesus' prayer, we have a direct link back to this moment in Hebrew history. And it is through Jesus that we his followers can rejoice that, when it comes to giving God a home, no building will ever be as large as the human heart.

COLLECT

Merciful God,
your Son came to save us
and bore our sins on the cross:
may we trust in your mercy
and know your love,
rejoicing in the righteousness
that is ours through Jesus Christ our Lord.

Monday 9 September

1 Kings 8.31-62

'… then hear in heaven your dwelling-place' (v.49)

Solomon has built a temple for the Lord and stands up to pray in hope and faith. As he prays his words coalesce into liturgy. He addresses God in his 'dwelling-place,' heaven, and asks that those who, humbly, direct their longing to God through Jerusalem and the temple will receive blessing and favour.

I suspect many of us know the power of holy places. A church building, an altar, a wayside cross can act as a focus for prayer. I have certainly been in church buildings where I have had a heightened sense of God's presence or felt struck by holiness. I was formerly a priest with responsibility for an Art Deco church. It wasn't old, but it filled me with awe. A warden there once said to me, 'This is a place where prayer has left its mark.' I have also spent time on Iona, often described as a 'thin place' – a place where heaven and earth seem to meet. Having been to that island, I can believe it.

Of course, God is never limited by place. God's abundant love saturates and sustains reality. I wonder, however, whether it is a token of our limited humanity that we need something on which to focus. Whether it is a holding cross, or a rosary or even a temple, we pray well when we are close to things which act as holy antennae, connecting us to God.

COLLECT

God, who in generous mercy sent the Holy Spirit
    upon your Church in the burning fire of your love:
grant that your people may be fervent
in the fellowship of the gospel
that, always abiding in you,
they may be found steadfast in faith and active in service;
through Jesus Christ your Son our Lord,
who is alive and reigns with you,
in the unity of the Holy Spirit,
one God, now and for ever.

| *Reflection by* **Rachel Mann**

Tuesday 10 September

1 Kings 8.63 – 9.9

'I have heard your prayer and your plea ...' (9.3)

The house of God is built and, rightly, there are celebrations and feasting. Appropriate sacrifices are made to the Lord. This is a time of promise and hope and the people of God are full of joy. It is in this context that the Lord appears to Solomon for the second time.

The word which the Lord delivers to Solomon offers both comfort and a warning against complacency. God assures Solomon that the temple is hallowed and, indeed, hallowed for all time. There is a covenantal reassurance to Solomon that the Davidic royal line will be blessed with generations of offspring. God does not stop there, however. There is a warning too: if the king and his children lead Israel to depart from the ways of the Lord, then the kingdom will fall and the temple will become a 'heap of ruins'.

Is God's grace somehow dependent on our good behaviour, as if we were children in a school with a strict and demanding headteacher? I don't think so. Rather, when we become over-confident about God's mercy, I suspect we fall readily into complacency. As we become complacent about our place in the ecology of God's love, then we are tempted to lose sight of what really matters. Perhaps prayer and devotion and service become perfunctory. We risk no longer heeding our utter dependence on God.

Lord God,
defend your Church from all false teaching
and give to your people knowledge of your truth,
that we may enjoy eternal life
in Jesus Christ our Lord.

COLLECT

Reflection by **Rachel Mann** | 251

Wednesday 11 September

1 Kings 10.1-25

'... your wisdom and prosperity far surpass the report that I had heard' (v.7)

Power is not the same as prosperity. It is entirely possible to be wealthy without exercising executive power, and those who exercise authority do not always make a great display of wealth. Nonetheless, for most kings, queens, presidents and many politicians, displays of wealth and majesty are crucial for their power games.

The encounter between the Queen of Sheba and Solomon is, at one level, all about the bling. The writer of 1 Kings is at pains to underline that both the Queen of Sheba as well as Solomon and Israel are in the first rank of world powers. The Queen of Sheba is left in no doubt that Solomon is the real deal.

However, as Proverbs 3.14 reminds us, 'Wisdom is worth more than silver; it brings more profit than gold' Flashy palaces and piles of gold may communicate power and offer the illusion that because one is prosperous one has been blessed by God. However, wisdom and discernment are much greater gifts. It is Solomon's wisdom that signals his blessedness in God.

We live in a world where some have an enormous amount of wealth, while others have nothing. Power and authority are too often projected by the world's leaders through displays of conspicuous consumption and threats of war. Just imagine how the world might look if leaders prioritised the display of greater wisdom instead.

COLLECT

God, who in generous mercy sent the Holy Spirit
    upon your Church in the burning fire of your love:
grant that your people may be fervent
in the fellowship of the gospel
that, always abiding in you,
they may be found steadfast in faith and active in service;
through Jesus Christ your Son our Lord,
who is alive and reigns with you,
in the unity of the Holy Spirit,
one God, now and for ever.

| *Reflection by* **Rachel Mann**

Psalm **37***
1 Kings 11.1-13
Acts 17.16-end

Thursday 12 September

1 Kings 11.1-13

'His heart was not true to the Lord his God' (v.4)

It is difficult to have much empathy with a hugely wealthy man who wields unbridled power, and upon whom hundreds of vulnerable women depend for their lives. In our own time, we have witnessed the depressing impact of men who hold power without much responsibility, and those who treat women as sexual playthings.

Certainly, when some people commend the concept of 'biblical marriage' I don't think they think of Solomon. Disconcertingly, I'm not even sure if it is his sheer number of wives and concubines which is the cause of God's censure; it is that Solomon has been drawn away from the living God by those wives who worship foreign gods.

Perhaps this passage is a case study in a life corrupted by power and soiled by compromise. Certainly, I am disinclined to cast the women in this passage as the baddies; in the face of a powerful man they did what they needed to survive. Perhaps their achievement was precisely to persuade Solomon to grant them places to pray to gods who reminded them of better days.

Certainly, the aged Solomon is unattractive. He is far away from the wise clarity of his youth and perhaps he deserves to be judged harshly. At the same time, I remember my own compromises. If not in Solomon's class, have I not been soiled by life? Probably. It is all the more reason to seek after the holy ways of the living God.

Lord God,
defend your Church from all false teaching
and give to your people knowledge of your truth,
that we may enjoy eternal life
in Jesus Christ our Lord.

COLLECT

Friday 13 September

Psalm 31
I Kings 11.26-end
Acts 18.1-21

1 Kings 11.26-end

'... you shall reign over all that your soul desires' (v.37)

Part of the Old Testament's power lies in the fact it is peopled with real human beings, inspired by flashes of holiness and driven by mixed motives and distorted desires. The stories of the likes of Solomon and Jeroboam sometimes read as bronze-age *Game of Thrones* plots as much as stories of heroes of faith.

Jeroboam's motives for rebellion against Solomon are unclear. At one level, his action is simply a response to Ahijah's dramatic oracle. Is his rebellion simply a faithful response to God? Or were other prophecies available? Perhaps Jeroboam was captivated by the idea that he would get to rule over all that his soul desired. Ultimately, years later, when Jeroboam's time to reign arrived, Israel was torn apart and his reign proved to be an ungodly one. Perhaps Jeroboam was corrupted, like one of those kings who become ring-wraiths in *The Lord of the Rings*, by a false promise that by getting to rule he would receive his soul's desire.

We too have seen, not least in the behaviour of many political leaders, how much humans can be corrupted by what we imagine is 'our soul's desire'. None of us is immune to such corruption. It's part of our human frailty. Nonetheless, in the midst of our frailty, God's call is consistent: repent and return to the Lord, the Holy One, our King.

COLLECT

God, who in generous mercy sent the Holy Spirit
    upon your Church in the burning fire of your love:
grant that your people may be fervent
in the fellowship of the gospel
that, always abiding in you,
they may be found steadfast in faith and active in service;
through Jesus Christ your Son our Lord,
who is alive and reigns with you,
in the unity of the Holy Spirit,
one God, now and for ever.

254 | *Reflection by* **Rachel Mann**

Psalms 2, 8, 146
Genesis 3.1-15
John 12.27-36*a*

Saturday 14 September
Holy Cross Day

Genesis 3.1-15

'... your eyes will be opened, and you will be like God' (v.5)

Crucifixion is not simply a means to kill a human being. The Roman Empire had any number of ways of putting someone to death. Crucifixion was used to humiliate and shame. It was, potentially, a slow way to die. It was torture, in which the gradual weakening of the victim's body slowly but surely meant death by suffocation.

It is extraordinary to consider that such a cruel means of death could be transmuted into the defining image of salvation, a symbol of God's love and promise. How on earth could such a thing, a cross, be seen as holy? One of the etymological roots of the word holiness is 'that which is whole, uninjured and unimpaired'. The Holy One who is wounded, transgressed and shamed via an instrument of torture becomes the one who heals. There is profound irony at play. Holy Cross Day takes us into the depths of mystery.

Holiness can also mean 'set aside'. Genesis 3 presents us with another mythic transgression, the very first transgression: taking fruit from a tree which God has set aside in the garden. As Adam and Eve take and eat the fruit, they sully their own holiness. They've failed to recognise their holy simplicity as God's creatures. Perhaps it takes our crucifixion of Jesus, fully human yet fully God, to wake us up. We begin to see who we truly are: not gods, but creatures called to holiness, desperate for redemption.

COLLECT

Almighty God,
who in the passion of your blessed Son
made an instrument of painful death
to be for us the means of life and peace:
grant us so to glory in the cross of Christ
that we may gladly suffer for his sake;
who is alive and reigns with you,
in the unity of the Holy Spirit,
one God, now and for ever.

Reflection by **Rachel Mann** | 255

Monday 16 September

Psalm **44**
I Kings 12.25 – 13.10
Acts 19.8-20

1 Kings 12.25 – 13.10

'... the hand that he stretched out against him withered' (13.4)

As the first ruler of the northern kingdom of Israel, Jeroboam defended himself against the southern kingdom of Judah. Two cultic sites spanned his kingdom. Dan was in the Golan heights. Bethel was north of Jerusalem and of immense significance. Abram built an altar nearby, and it was named by Jacob after his vision of a ladder reaching to heaven (*bēth 'ēl* in Hebrew means house of God).

When installing the golden calves, Jeroboam speaks almost the same words as Aaron, from many years earlier (Exodus 32.4). Some scholars maintain that Jeroboam was misrepresented by the southern, temple tradition: that the calves were cherubim. But whatever the precise details of the conflict, Jeroboam emerges as a self-interested king.

Rulers are often tempted to exploit nationalism to secure their power base. But distrust of the 'other' inevitably leads to further fragmentation: to a perpetual hunt for scapegoats and enemies. Leaders of this type all too easily unleash dark forces that destroy communities and divide nations.

Taking the Jeroboam narrative at face-value, we are given a clear warning against opportunistic leadership. Jeroboam's hand withered as he reached out to restrain the man of God – and he subsequently lost Bethel. But it is not enough to wait for the collapse of unjust and manipulative governments. Church communities are called to speak 'truth to power', like the man of God in this passage. How is this to be done?

COLLECT

O Lord, we beseech you mercifully to hear the prayers
 of your people who call upon you;
and grant that they may both perceive and know
 what things they ought to do,
and also may have grace and power faithfully to fulfil them;
through Jesus Christ your Son our Lord,
who is alive and reigns with you,
in the unity of the Holy Spirit,
one God, now and for ever.

| *Reflection by* **Alan Everett**

Tuesday 17 September

1 Kings 13.11-end

'Then the man of God ... ate food and drank water in his house.' (v.19)

The man of God has challenged King Jeroboam, at considerable personal risk, and is now exhausted and hungry. A fellow prophet arrives with the offer of hospitality, claiming that he has been guided by an angel. The man of God surrenders to temptation; who among us would not?

When facing a challenge that requires single-minded focus, convivial distractions can take us off course. Even so, the man of God's sin hardly seems to merit death by a lion – not least since the deceitful prophet avoids condemnation. Less seems to be expected of him – or perhaps he is doing Yahweh's will, so that the man of God's death can be a sign? The conclusion possibly reflects this viewpoint. The lion stands over his body, either as an act of symbolic prophecy or to ensure it is given a decent burial.

This story resonates with those of us who have let down our guard at the end of a difficult task and have compromised the result. Hence the much-loved prayer:

> Direct us, O Lord, in all our doings with your most gracious favour, and further us with your continual help; that in all our works begun, continued, and ended in you, we may glorify your holy Name, and finally, by your mercy, obtain everlasting life; through Jesus Christ our Lord. (Collect from 'Forms of Prayer to be used at Sea' from the 1662 *Book of Common Prayer*)

We may need to draw on deep reserves of vigilance and stamina, to complete an important piece of work given to us by God.

COLLECT

Lord of creation,
whose glory is around and within us:
open our eyes to your wonders,
that we may serve you with reverence
and know your peace at our lives' end,
through Jesus Christ our Lord.

Reflection by **Alan Everett** | 257

Wednesday 18 September

Psalm **119.57-80**
1 Kings 17
Acts 20.1-16

1 Kings 17

'Go from here ...' (v.3)

As if the appalling rule of Ahab and Jezebel did not inflict enough misery, there is now a terrible drought in Judah. Elijah is told by God to go to a wadi. A raven feeds him until the wadi dries up. He is then sent to Zarephath, to a widow gathering 'a couple of sticks'. He asks for a 'little' water and a 'morsel' of bread. She replies that she has only a 'handful' of meal and a 'little' oil. Elijah requests a 'little' cake.

These diminutive terms speak of life on the verge of extinction. Characters move within a limited compass, trying to conserve energy. Yahweh's deliverance has folktale elements: feeding by a raven, and a miraculously replenished jar and jug. But far from being whimsical, the narrative vividly conveys the slow process of starvation. All that is left is a faint, desperate hope for deliverance. The son's loss of breath is a final fading away. In a strange, intimate ritual, Elijah's restores him to life. At a time of extreme need, new bonds are formed.

We are asked to imagine complete dependence on God, but as we reflect on this passage, do we not also sense an invitation to act? Jesus enraged his fellow Jews by pointing out that Elijah was sent only to outsiders (Luke 4.26). In the face of extreme climate changes, affecting the world's poorest communities, we are also challenged to reach across boundaries. Where is God 'telling us to go' today?

COLLECT

O Lord, we beseech you mercifully to hear the prayers
    of your people who call upon you;
and grant that they may both perceive and know
    what things they ought to do,
and also may have grace and power faithfully to fulfil them;
through Jesus Christ your Son our Lord,
who is alive and reigns with you,
in the unity of the Holy Spirit,
one God, now and for ever.

| *Reflection by* **Alan Everett**

Thursday 19 September

1 Kings 18.1-20

'Is it you, you troubler of Israel?' (v.7)

Obadiah, a head servant at the royal court, helps prepare the way for Elijah's trial against the prophets of Baal and Asherah. But first he reminds Elijah of his role in rescuing one hundred and fifty prophets who have been faithful to Yahweh. Whereas Elijah lives and works outside the political system, Obadiah subverts it from within. His resistance is quietly heroic – and equally risky.

The encounter between Ahab and Elijah is puzzling. Rather than arranging remotely for Elijah's execution, Ahab comes to meet the 'troubler of Israel'. Despite Jezebel's brutal purge, it appears that Elijah still has a privileged place in the Kingdom of Judah.

Ahab is a weak, vacillating ruler, overly influenced by his Phoenician wife – as Solomon had been by his foreign wives (1 Kings 11). It is Jezebel who threatens to kill Elijah (19.2) and who arranges Naboth's execution so that Ahab can possess his land (21.8–13).

Although condemned by Old Testament writers as one of Israel's worst rulers, Ahab's ineffectiveness gives Elijah some room for manoeuvre, enabling the contest which is to follow. Even the most menacing political systems have their fault lines.

Crucially, Elijah reverses the narrative. Ahab is Israel's real 'troubler'. Authoritarian power is invariably self-justifying, while protestors are denigrated for their 'disruptiveness'. The compelling figure of Elijah fortifies those who openly defend an unpopular truth. But as Obadiah shows us, resistance can also be quiet, and hidden.

Lord of creation,
whose glory is around and within us:
open our eyes to your wonders,
that we may serve you with reverence
and know your peace at our lives' end,
through Jesus Christ our Lord.

COLLECT

Reflection by **Alan Everett** | 259

Friday 20 September

1 Kings 18.21-end

'The Lord indeed is God ...' (v.39)

The confrontation on Mount Carmel addresses three audiences: the prophets of Baal, Ahab, and the people of Israel. All 'limp' – either following 'two different opinions' or 'about the altar'. The excitements of a fertility cult and the feverish invocations of Baal are grounded in a disabling illusion. Baal does not exist.

Elijah's serene confidence in Yahweh is apparent throughout. He mocks the prophets, urging them to cry louder. He calmly rebuilds the altar and has it drenched with water. Finally, having predicted rain to end the devastating drought, he prostrates himself in prayer. It is only after the eighth viewing that his servant tells him he sees a little cloud 'no bigger than a person's hand' rising from the sea.

Yahweh's power is repeatedly revealed. First, as fire, upon the sodden altar. Second, as heavy rain. Third, as he enables Elijah to run ahead of Ahab, who is fleeing on his horse. But none of this would have been possible without Elijah's complete trust in the true, hidden God.

Some of us may feel challenged by this passage. While the prophets of Baal are clearly ridiculous, Elijah's single-mindedness seems beyond us. We also limp 'with two different opinions.' It is hard to resist the allure of an appetite driven culture. A degree of asceticism and a capacity for reflection and restraint are needed to build trust and patience. We may need to wait before we discover our hidden God.

COLLECT

O Lord, we beseech you mercifully to hear the prayers
    of your people who call upon you;
and grant that they may both perceive and know
    what things they ought to do,
and also may have grace and power faithfully to fulfil them;
through Jesus Christ your Son our Lord,
who is alive and reigns with you,
in the unity of the Holy Spirit,
one God, now and for ever.

| *Reflection by* **Alan Everett**

Psalms 49, 117
1 Kings 19.15-end
2 Timothy 3.14-end

Saturday 21 September

Matthew, Apostle and Evangelist

1 Kings 19.15-end

'Then he set out and followed Elijah, and became his servant.'
(v.21)

Superficially, Elijah appears more lenient to Elisha than Jesus to the man who wants to say goodbye to his family (Luke 9.61). But Elisha is merely given a grace period to perform a ritual of severance. There is no suggestion that he is like those whom Jesus encounters on his final, urgent journey to Jerusalem. Elisha gives no sign of wanting to put his hand to the plough and look back (Luke 9.62). On the contrary: he slaughters a yoke of oxen for others to eat, as a final farewell.

Elisha's purposeful response strengthens a shattered older prophet. But it is really Yahweh who has provided Elijah with the support he now needs – along with the prospect of eventual release. The future is in Yahweh's hands, not Elijah's.

We read about Elisha's call on the feast day of Matthew, who immediately left his tax-collector's booth and followed Jesus (Matthew 9.9). The call to discipleship demands a firm decision, but as the experience of Elijah indicates, it is also time limited.

However important our tasks may be, in due time we must surrender them. Those at the beginning of their working life, or whose identity is tied to a job, may find this idea difficult. But for others, it is a relief. As we plan for our succession, God mercifully and gently lifts our burdens from our shoulders. We can begin to let go.

COLLECT

O Almighty God,
whose blessed Son called Matthew the tax collector
to be an apostle and evangelist:
give us grace to forsake the selfish pursuit of gain
and the possessive love of riches
that we may follow in the way of your Son Jesus Christ,
who is alive and reigns with you,
in the unity of the Holy Spirit,
one God, now and for ever.

Reflection by **Alan Everett** | 261

Monday 23 September

Psalm **71**
I Kings 21
Acts 21.37 – 22.21

1 Kings 21

'Give me your vineyard ...' (v.2)

Royal power is to the fore in the first half of this chapter. Ahab wants Naboth's vineyard, and Jezebel gets it for him, by any means necessary. When Elijah comes onto the scene, it sets up a clash between king and prophet, between idolatry and true faith. Ahab and Jezebel use their status to possess and kill. Naboth and Elijah stand in the tradition that says the land belongs to the Lord, and to his people as an inheritance (Leviticus 25). It cannot be sold or seized at will: the law seeks to avoid the situation where some are indebted or enslaved while others' estates grow ever larger.

Naboth, owner of the vineyard, is a sign of faithful Israel – often likened to a vineyard in the Bible. Ahab, who wants to turn the vineyard into a vegetable garden (the word is used only once elsewhere in the Old Testament, in Deuteronomy 11.10 to refer to Egypt) represents faithless Israel: a king who would turn the people back to slavery and idolatry. But as the royal couple discover, there is a power greater than theirs at work in Israel. Elijah is God's prophet, and through his voice God refuses Ahab's demand that Naboth give him his vineyard. He might come into possession of the particular plot of land, but he cannot possess the vineyard that is the Lord's. The faithful can trust in God's faithfulness.

COLLECT

Almighty God,
you have made us for yourself,
and our hearts are restless till they find their rest in you:
pour your love into our hearts and draw us to yourself,
and so bring us at last to your heavenly city
where we shall see you face to face;
through Jesus Christ your Son our Lord,
who is alive and reigns with you,
in the unity of the Holy Spirit,
one God, now and for ever.

Reflection by **Anna Matthews**

Psalm **73**
I Kings 22.1-28
Acts 22.22 – 23.11

Tuesday 24 September

1 Kings 22.1-28

'Inquire first for the word of the Lord' (v.5)

Again we see the prophetic word set against royal desire. Ahab wants prophets who will confirm him in his plans and tactics, and a God who will grant him success. Jehoshaphat, neighbouring king of the southern kingdom of Judah, is not so easily swayed by the prophetic consensus and seeks a prophet of the Lord, rather than a tamed mouthpiece of the king. Micaiah, the true prophet, initially tells Ahab to go up into battle (God has, remember, already pronounced judgement against Ahab – chapter 21), and when pressed further speaks words of judgement. The people will be scattered, without a shepherd: a foretelling of the exile that will come, and the end of the monarchy.

Ahab prefers the prophets who are more interested in his plans for making Samaria great again than they are in listening for the true word of the Lord. He seeks to silence Micaiah, but he cannot stop the word of the Lord from accomplishing that which he purposes (see Isaiah 55.11) – and that purpose in this instance is the end of Ahab's own rule.

As you reflect on this passage, how do you inquire for the word of the Lord? From where or from whom do you hear God's voice of truth? And whose are the voices that are silenced, and how might you attend to them?

Gracious God,
you call us to fullness of life:
deliver us from unbelief
and banish our anxieties
with the liberating love of Jesus Christ our Lord.

COLLECT

Wednesday 25 September

Psalm **77**
1 Kings 22.29-45
Acts 23.12-end

1 Kings 22.29-45

'I will disguise myself' (v.30)

Ahab's accommodating prophets had spurred him on in his plans to go to war. They had encouraged him to believe he could evade the word of the Lord spoken through Micaiah which had indicated that this was a trap. Yet Ahab does not ride into battle in full, attention-drawing royal armour, but disguised as a peasant. The disguise is not enough, however, to thwart the true prophetic word, which is that Ahab will die, and that in the place where Naboth's blood had been spilt, dogs will lick up the blood of Ahab (21.19). Ahab's disguise may hide his death from the Arameans for a time, but it is not enough to hide him from God's purposes, which are to deliver his people from Ahab's idolatrous and corrupt rule.

God does not simply assent to royal schemes or bless political ambition. His prophetic word brings the counsels of kings, and our own plans, under his scrutiny. The God from whom no secrets are hidden will not be deceived by the disguises we put on to evade his gaze or escape his judgement. His truthful word will, if we let it, confront us, unsettle us, and draw us more fully into his purposes which are, as in this passage, that his people should be free to love, worship and serve him.

COLLECT

Almighty God,
you have made us for yourself,
and our hearts are restless till they find their rest in you:
pour your love into our hearts and draw us to yourself,
and so bring us at last to your heavenly city
where we shall see you face to face;
through Jesus Christ your Son our Lord,
who is alive and reigns with you,
in the unity of the Holy Spirit,
one God, now and for ever.

| *Reflection by* **Anna Matthews**

Psalm **78.1-39***
2 Kings 1.2-17
Acts 24.1-23

Thursday 26 September

2 Kings 1.2-17

'Is it because there is no God in Israel ...?' (v.3)

The passage opens with a sick king ruling over a sick kingdom. Ahaziah, the son of Ahab, follows in his father's bad practices, as we see with clarity when he sends messengers to enquire of Beelzebub about his recovery. In this narrative it is only God who has power to heal and give life. Ahaziah acts as though there is no God in Israel. He is functionally atheist, even if he pays lip service to God and his messengers. So he sends messengers to summon Elijah, who answers to a higher authority and is unmoved by the royal command.

It is a stand-off between royal power seeking security and success in alliance with Baal, and the justice and righteousness of God shown in covenant faithfulness. Ahaziah does not trust God for Israel's future, so seeks help elsewhere. Elijah's words and actions show that there is indeed a God in Israel, who is deeply concerned for his people's plight.

For all its strangeness, this passage asks a similar question of us: do we trust in the God of Israel, whose ways are shown in justice and righteousness, in mercy and in love? Or do we hedge our bets, doubting his power, and seek our security elsewhere? What are the modern day 'gods of Ekron' to whom we are tempted to turn when we doubt that there is a God in Israel?

Gracious God,
you call us to fullness of life:
deliver us from unbelief
and banish our anxieties
with the liberating love of Jesus Christ our Lord.

COLLECT

Friday 27 September

Psalm **55**
2 Kings 2.1-18
Acts 24.24 – 25.12

2 Kings 2.1-18

'Please let me inherit a double share of your spirit' (v.9)

With his rolled-up mantle Elijah strikes the Jordan and the waters part. We are meant to remember the exodus, and Moses' parting of the Red Sea. Where Moses handed on authority to Joshua for the conquest of the promised land, Elijah's authority falls on Elisha, who asks for a double share of his spirit. Divine imagery surrounds Elijah's ascension as he is drawn into heaven: what is left is his spirit, and his work continues through Elisha.

After a three-day search, the company of prophets concedes that Elijah is not dead, nor lost, but has been taken up into heaven. As we read this, the remembering works forwards, too: after three days in the tomb, disciples begin to be convinced that Jesus has been raised from the dead. He is taken up into heaven, and pours upon his Church the fire of his Spirit at Pentecost. That puts the Church in the position of Elisha: inheritor of the Spirit to continue the work that has been begun.

As in Elisha's ministry we see parallels with Elijah's, so in the book of Acts we see the apostles ministering in the same way and with the same power as Jesus did. As baptism gives us a share in Jesus' Spirit, we might ask how we are joining in with Jesus' work, and being drawn into his ministry?

C O L L E C T

Almighty God,
you have made us for yourself,
and our hearts are restless till they find their rest in you:
pour your love into our hearts and draw us to yourself,
and so bring us at last to your heavenly city
where we shall see you face to face;
through Jesus Christ your Son our Lord,
who is alive and reigns with you,
in the unity of the Holy Spirit,
one God, now and for ever.

266 | *Reflection by* **Anna Matthews**

Psalms **76**, 79
2 Kings 4.1-37
Acts 25.13-end

Saturday 28 September

2 Kings 4.1-37

'Go outside, borrow ... empty vessels and not just a few' (v.3)

A poor widow and a rich woman both face economic precarity: the widow because she is in debt; the rich woman because she has no son. For both women, through the action of Elisha, God creates a future. In the case of the rich woman, this is a twofold action: first in the birth of a son, and second in his being restored to life.

Elisha functions as a sign of God's presence in the story: the person through whom release from debt is enacted, abundance flows, life is given and death overcome. In the history of the kings it is a scrappy prophet with a band of followers ministering away from the centre of royal and religious power who stands for God's covenant faithfulness. The misrule of the kings has left the land unproductive and the poor exploited, but the God whose Law urges care for the widow and who makes the barren woman a joyful mother (Deuteronomy 24; Psalm 113) still acts to restore, to release, to make new.

This is the character of God, who through empty vessels, full stops and dead ends still acts to create a future. What parts of your life might God want to fill with his grace? Where might he want to act to restore you and make you new?

Gracious God,
you call us to fullness of life:
deliver us from unbelief
and banish our anxieties
with the liberating love of Jesus Christ our Lord.

COLLECT

Monday 30 September

2 Kings 5

'Go, wash ... and you shall be clean' (v.10)

Naaman arrives with all the trappings and arrogance of power. As the chapter opens, his credentials are there for all to admire. But despite his military prowess and reputation, he is a man with leprosy, facing social stigma and isolation. Desperate enough to listen to the counsel of a young Israelite servant girl who tells of a prophet in Samaria who can heal him, he approaches first the king (the assumed centre of such power) and then Elisha, ready to impress them with his wealth and standing.

Elisha's counsel is insulting: wash in the river Jordan. Naaman's pride almost makes him storm off, but his servants' wisdom prevails. He washes, and is healed and made clean. The proud general is humbled. But more than that. A foreigner is healed in Israel. An enemy is made a worshipper of God.

Naaman's healing prefigures the salvation of the Gentiles, and God's reconciliation of people to each other and himself through the cross of Christ. And just like Naaman, through going down into the waters (of baptism) we are reconciled, joined into one body, and raised to newness of life. Naaman, whose skin has regained a youthful innocence, responds to God's action with gratitude and worship. What response do you want to give God for the grace he has given you?

COLLECT

Almighty and everlasting God,
increase in us your gift of faith
that, forsaking what lies behind
and reaching out to that which is before,
we may run the way of your commandments
and win the crown of everlasting joy;
through Jesus Christ your Son our Lord,
who is alive and reigns with you,
in the unity of the Holy Spirit,
one God, now and for ever.

| *Reflection by* **Anna Matthews**

Tuesday 1 October

2 Kings 6.1-23

'Open his eyes that he may see' (v.17)

Elisha restores a lost, borrowed axe-head: a minor wonder in the scheme of things, but considering the value and scarcity of iron, one through which he saves his fellow prophet from potential debt or slavery. Elisha restores the man to life and a future.

God's promise of new life is present also through Elisha's interventions between the kings of Aram and Israel. Playing with the metaphor of sight, the story subverts the usual operation of power. Aram sets forth a show of force against the ragtag collection of prophets. But for those who can truly see, the power of God surrounds Elisha and is at work in him. For those who walk by faith, not by sight (2 Corinthians 5.7), the world looks different: strength lies in the undefended prophet of God, not in Aram's chariots, the Creator is born as a baby, God hangs on a cross. And this sight unfolds new possibilities: instead of killing the captured Arameans, Elisha invites them to a feast. As they eat and drink together, enemies, for a while, become friends. Hostility turns to peace. A new future opens up.

Here we see prefigured the feast set at the Lord's table, where God invites his enemies and feeds us with Living Bread, making us friends of God and one another. What might it mean to ask God to open your eyes more fully to this reality? How might that shape how you live?

God, our judge and saviour,
teach us to be open to your truth
and to trust in your love,
that we may live each day
with confidence in the salvation which is given
through Jesus Christ our Lord.

COLLECT

Wednesday 2 October

2 Kings 9.1-16

'I anoint you king over Israel' (v.12)

Israel already has a king when Elisha acts to ensure Jehu is anointed. This is not an accession according to any laws of royal succession but a revolutionary act designed by God to bring about his purposes. The prophet who anoints makes this explicit: Jehu is to be the one to enact God's action against Ahab and Jezebel by destroying their house and lineage.

The abuse of royal power does not go unchecked: through this divinely-anointed coup God pronounces his judgement on the idolatrous, greedy, murderous regime of Ahab and his successors. Naboth's blood, along with the blood of the prophets, still cries for vengeance (1 Kings 21), as the faithful of Israel cry for deliverance. Identified now with all that is opposed to God's law and purposes, Ahab's house is doomed. Royal power cannot withstand the sovereign, anointing Spirit of God. The newly anointed and acclaimed King Jehu has cloaks laid out before him – as later, just before he cleanses the temple, the Lord's anointed one will enter Jerusalem over the cloaks laid on the road by those who acclaim him as king (Luke 19.36).

Judgement is an aspect of salvation: it is God's refusal to let sin have the final word. Where might God's sovereign Spirit be at work now, drawing you into God's purposes and vindicating the abused and oppressed?

COLLECT
|
Almighty and everlasting God,
increase in us your gift of faith
that, forsaking what lies behind
and reaching out to that which is before,
we may run the way of your commandments
and win the crown of everlasting joy;
through Jesus Christ your Son our Lord,
who is alive and reigns with you,
in the unity of the Holy Spirit,
one God, now and for ever.

| *Reflection by* **Anna Matthews**

Thursday 3 October

2 Kings 9.17-end

'Is it peace?' (v.18)

Prophecy is fulfilled: Naboth's death is avenged on the ground on which he was killed, and Jezebel's remains are eaten by dogs (1 Kings 21.20ff). In quick succession Jehu kills Joram of Israel and Ahaziah of Judah, and instigates the death of Jezebel, the queen mother. The violent account is the very opposite of the 'peace' (*shalom*) Joram and Jezebel enquire about as Jehu arrives. Any peace already enjoyed by the royal household, however, is a false peace because built on idolatry and oppression, it is a peace secured at the expense of their people and the prophets. Jehu, God's newly-anointed king, will not be complicit in this false peace. He arrives as the agent of God's judgement on royal sin and unrepentance.

For the authors of 1 and 2 Kings, there is no peace for Israel while the people worship foreign gods, and while their leaders deal in oppression and violence. True *shalom* comes with the return to the covenant and the worship of Israel's God – a peace that will prove elusive as their history unfolds. 'Is it peace?' is the question posed to our worship, our plans, our politics: do they lead us to the relationship with God and others he intends for us? Do they share in and speak to others of the *shalom* of God?

God, our judge and saviour,
teach us to be open to your truth
and to trust in your love,
that we may live each day
with confidence in the salvation which is given
through Jesus Christ our Lord.

COLLECT

Friday 4 October

2 Kings 12.1-19

'Let them repair the house' (v.5)

The narrative's attention shifts from the Northern Kingdom to the Southern, where the glorious temple built by Solomon has fallen into disrepair, and where the Arameans threaten at the borders. The temple's sorry state indicates the extent to which the people and their leaders have neglected the true worship of God: it reflects the state of the covenant relationship between God and his people.

Jehoash sets about repairing the temple, an act of piety as well as a political move: in aligning the monarchy with the temple he aligns himself with the God whose presence dwells in the temple. But the repair of the building is not enough, on its own, to repair the faith of Judah: when the Arameans loom, Jehoash swiftly plunders the temple's coffers to pay off the threat. In his weakness, he does not trust the God whose house he has been repairing. It is not the temple that will guarantee the security of God's people, but the faithfulness of God. While the physical temple will be plundered by the Babylonians, and the second temple by the Romans, God will come and dwell among his people in flesh, making a temple of living stones to his glory (1 Peter 2.5).

How do you respond to the idea that you are a dwelling place for God? How might he be building you up into a spiritual house? Where might that house need some repairs?

COLLECT

Almighty and everlasting God,
increase in us your gift of faith
that, forsaking what lies behind
and reaching out to that which is before,
we may run the way of your commandments
and win the crown of everlasting joy;
through Jesus Christ your Son our Lord,
who is alive and reigns with you,
in the unity of the Holy Spirit,
one God, now and for ever.

| *Reflection by* **Anna Matthews**

Saturday 5 October

2 Kings 17.1-23

'They ... became false' (v.15)

With a great litany of their sins, this chapter narrates the end of the Northern Kingdom. Persistent idolatry and disobedience to the law, through which Israel becomes like the surrounding nations, leads to crushing defeat and deportation: indistinguishable from the nations by their behaviour in the promised land, Israel is now absorbed into the nations.

Israel has rejected the covenant made at Sinai, where they promised to worship God alone. They have not trusted in God. They have ignored the repeated warnings of the prophets. Now God gives them over to their unfaithfulness. They have worshipped falsehood and therefore have become false, or unreal themselves – they vanish from the map. The list of sins is the narrator's response to the apparent abandonment by God of his people: it is Israel that has forsaken God. And God, ultimately, does not forsake his people. On the far side of exile a new life will dawn, not just for Israel but for the nations, as God himself takes on their forsakenness (Mark 15.34), bears their sins, and raises Jew and Gentile alike to new life in his Son.

People may become false, but God's character remains true: even faced with the end of Israel, the story of God's people is not over. New life can stir even in the places of our sin and desolation, as God acts to make us his.

God, our judge and saviour,
teach us to be open to your truth
and to trust in your love,
that we may live each day
with confidence in the salvation which is given
through Jesus Christ our Lord.

COLLECT

Monday 7 October

Psalms **98**, 99, 101
2 Kings 17.24-end
Philippians 1.1-11

Philippians 1.1-11

'... sharing in the gospel from the first day until now' (v.5)

Paul means at least three things by 'sharing in the gospel'. The first we should note is that the gospel is something we receive: it is a gift, a matter of grace, something that God shares with us. The second sense of sharing is that the gospel is a way of life and community, bringing membership of a new family. Paul's sense of fellowship, and indeed of spiritual fatherhood, is on show everywhere in his letters. The third angle of sharing is that the gospel also comes to us as a task: it is a message to be spoken, an invitation to be extended, a community to be tended and cared for.

In all of this, we encounter the abundance of God's grace: first, that it raises us from sin, and rescues us from estrangement from God, second, that it grants us the blessing of a new family and kingdom in within the body of the Church, and third, that it enables us by the call to be 'fellow workers' not only with Paul (like the characters in Colossians 4.7; Philemon 1.24) but even a fellow worker with God (1 Corinthians 3.9; 2 Corinthians 6.1; 1 Thessalonians 3.2). This is truly 'grace upon grace' (John 1.16).

COLLECT

O God, forasmuch as without you
we are not able to please you;
mercifully grant that your Holy Spirit
may in all things direct and rule our hearts;
through Jesus Christ your Son our Lord,
who is alive and reigns with you,
in the unity of the Holy Spirit,
one God, now and for ever.

| *Reflection by* **Andrew Davison**

Psalm **106*** (*or* 103)
2 Kings 18.1-12
Philippians 1.12-end

Tuesday 8 October

Philippians 1.12-end

'... whether out of false motives or true' (v.8)

Queen Elizabeth I is famed for having said, 'I have no desire to make windows into men's souls.' (Whether or not she did say it is less clear.) The idea is about wanting to uphold a church where profession of belief was taken in good faith, and the practice of piety and a shared life of worship was seen as more important than settling differences of theology and biblical interpretation once and for all. Paul might profess more insight into the hearts of others ('others proclaim Christ out of selfish ambition'), but he anticipated the first great Queen Elizabeth with his emphasis on the objective over the subjective, and his gladness at what is achieved, as ultimately more important than motives.

Motives are significant, but it's generally better to get on with the objectively good thing, and work on your motives later, than to wait for your motives to be perfect before acting at all. That way, at least the gospel is proclaimed, the hungry fed, and so on. We might even be transformed inwardly by the effect of doing the right thing. Motives are often difficult to discern anyway: even our own. They can be a fruitful topic for discussion with a spiritual director, or similar, but it's best to leave that alone when it comes to the motives of others, and instead join Paul in rejoicing in whatever good is done, rather than casting judgement on what lies beyond our scrutiny.

Faithful Lord,
whose steadfast love never ceases
and whose mercies never come to an end:
grant us the grace to trust you
and to receive the gifts of your love,
new every morning,
in Jesus Christ our Lord.

COLLECT

Wednesday 9 October

Psalms 110, 111, 112
2 Kings 18.13-end
Philippians 2.1-13

Philippians 2.1-13

'Any sharing in the Spirit, any compassion and sympathy' (v.1)

This passage presents us with one of the great hymns to Christ in the New Testament. To my mind, only Colossians 1.15-20 is its rival: 'He is the image of the invisible God, the firstborn of all creation...' For that reason, it is easy to jump straight to this magnificent outpouring about Christ, and pass over an important reference to the Holy Spirit, 'If then there is... any sharing in the Spirit, any compassion and sympathy... be... in full accord and of one mind.'

In the famous invocation from 2 Corinthians 13.14, which we often call 'the grace' ('The grace of our Lord Jesus Christ...'), Paul writes of the 'fellowship of the Holy Spirit'. The Greek is identical, whether typically translated 'fellowship' there, or 'sharing' here. The connection is profound. We have fellowship with the Spirit, and that is found and expressed in sharing with others.

The relation of the believer and the Church to the Spirit sometimes calls for poetry and metaphor (streams of living water, a temple, fruits of the Spirit), and deep analysis, but it is also profoundly practical: being about 'compassion and sympathy.' That is deeply demanding. Being 'of the same mind... in full accord' comes with difficulty for us, as it did, no doubt, for the Philippians, but it is both part of our calling, and ultimately part of God's blessing.

COLLECT

O God, forasmuch as without you
we are not able to please you;
mercifully grant that your Holy Spirit
may in all things direct and rule our hearts;
through Jesus Christ your Son our Lord,
who is alive and reigns with you,
in the unity of the Holy Spirit,
one God, now and for ever.

| *Reflection by* **Andrew Davison**

Thursday 10 October

Philippians 2.14-end

'... shine like stars in the world' (v.15)

Paul probably had the Book of Daniel in mind here, where we read about the wise shining like stars in the coming age of God's kingdom (Daniel 12.3). (The parallel is even stronger in the Greek translation of this part of Daniel.) There may also be something of Daniel's apocalyptic vision at work here in Paul, with its angels of the nations and so on. In that case, 'shining in the world' would not only be a matter of offering a good witness to other people, but also part of reordering the cosmos and the world of angelic powers. Ephesians offers a similar thought, 'that through the church the wisdom of God in its rich variety might now be made known to the rulers and authorities in the heavenly places' (Ephesians 3.10).

That's all grand and stirring, but the way it's shown is arrestingly mundane, 'Do all things without murmuring and arguing.' That might grate against contemporary sensibilities. We don't like telling people to 'put up and shut up,' and the Church should find nothing here to justify stifling protest against injustice, or calling out evil. In another way, however, there's something entirely contemporary about it. We know how easy it is to gripe, to criticise and to belittle, especially in a world of anonymous online interactions. Practice restraint on Twitter, then, and amaze an angel.

Faithful Lord,
whose steadfast love never ceases
and whose mercies never come to an end:
grant us the grace to trust you
and to receive the gifts of your love,
new every morning,
in Jesus Christ our Lord.

COLLECT

Friday 11 October

Philippians 3.1 – 4.1

'I regard them as rubbish, in order that I may gain Christ' (v.8)

A tension runs through Christianity when it comes to earthly identities: creation is God's good gift, and for us that always means belonging to some groups in ways that we don't belong to other. Nonetheless, our truest worth lies in Christ. In the final chapter of the Bible, the 'kings of the earth' bring their 'glory' into the New Jerusalem, which seems an endorsement of much that is particular about cultures and places, and yet they do also bring it all to Christ.

Elsewhere, Paul has plenty to say about the inestimable gifts that God has given the world through his own Jewish tradition and history. In today's passage, however, Paul presses the other side, that nothing is to be compared to Christ and 'being found in him' (v.9). Paul's great list here is of everything about his identity before his conversion ('circumcised on the eighth day…'), but that is no longer what matters for him.

In a world where 'identity' is so central, our passage makes for arresting reading. Paul tends to prefer the clash of opposites, rather than synthesis or resolution. Paul is right. We can't rest in anything other than Christ and his redeeming work. Grace is everything. But, as Aquinas wrote, more emolliently, 'Grace does not abolish nature, but perfects it.' Grace, in the end, is everything, but it also does not make any of God's good gifts less good.

COLLECT

O God, forasmuch as without you
we are not able to please you;
mercifully grant that your Holy Spirit
may in all things direct and rule our hearts;
through Jesus Christ your Son our Lord,
who is alive and reigns with you,
in the unity of the Holy Spirit,
one God, now and for ever.

| *Reflection by* **Andrew Davison**

Psalms 120, **121**, 122
2 Kings 20
Philippians 4.2-end

Saturday 12 October

Philippians 4.2-end

'... if there is any excellence and if there is anything worthy of praise, think about these things' (vv.8-9)

Paul is a great writer of lists. We might think of the fruit and gifts of the Spirit, or of some magnificent writing in 2 Corinthians about his hardships. Here we have an exhortation to think about whatever is true, honourable, just, pure, pleasing, commendable, excellent, and praiseworthy. That is a principle in spiritual direction or formation across the centuries: that what we think about, dwell upon, and chew over shapes who we are, how we live, and how we see. Simple though it may seem, making some adjustments in what we expose ourselves to makes a difference, ideally accentuating whatever accords with Paul's list, and dialling down what doesn't. There is spiritual and moral progress to be made with 'subscribe' and 'unsubscribe' buttons, 'follow' and 'unfollow'.

The point, however, is not only about what we think about, or meditate upon, but also what we do. In the next verse, Paul pairs the 'think about these things' with 'practise these things'. He is probably not dividing 'these things': some into a group to think about, and others to do. In any case, Paul's list of admirable qualities applies to both thoughts and deeds.

Monday 14 October

Psalms 123, 124, 125, **126**
2 Kings 21.1-18
I Timothy 1.1-17

1 Timothy 1.1-17

'... so that... Jesus Christ might display the utmost patience' (v.16)

Given how often God is described as patient in the Bible (Exodus 34.6; Psalm 86.15; 103.8; Nahum 1.3; 9.17; 1 Peter 3.20; 2 Peter 3.9, 15, for a start) this attribute of God does not seem to be discussed very often. We come across the idea again today, this time shown by God in Christ, towards Paul.

Patience is there among the characteristics that God would have grow in us – seen in perhaps the two greatest lists of such characteristics in the New Testament, the qualities of love or charity in 1 Corinthians 13 (where the list of adjectives opens 'love is patient'), and the fruit of the Spirit in Galatians 5.

In one of the great books on the Christian life of the twentieth century, Josef Pieper, in his *Four Cardinal Virtues*, described patience as willingness to suffer for the sake of the good, combined with an expectant eye for when one could seek to 'pounce upon' evil and to bar its way, if this can reasonably be done.'

In 1 Timothy, and in relation to God, the emphasis is on waiting for someone to turn from sin and turn back to God. The English Puritan theologian Stephen Charnock (1628–80) wrote rather beautifully that 'Goodness sets God upon the exercise of patience, and patience sets many a sinner on running into the arms of mercy.'

COLLECT

God, the giver of life,
whose Holy Spirit wells up within your Church:
by the Spirit's gifts equip us to live the gospel of Christ
    and make us eager to do your will,
that we may share with the whole creation
    the joys of eternal life;
through Jesus Christ your Son our Lord,
who is alive and reigns with you,
in the unity of the Holy Spirit,
one God, now and for ever.

| *Reflection by* **Andrew Davison**

Tuesday 15 October

1 Timothy 1.18 – end of 2

'... that we may lead a quiet and peaceable life in all godliness and dignity' (v.2)

We find a seamless connection in the reading today between a desire for a dignified and just order to the world and a missionary concern for the transformation of nature by grace ('God... who desires everyone to be saved and come to the knowledge of the truth'). Although cruelly persecuted, and even tortured, by the very political order for which Paul instructed them to pray (v.1), the early Christians were eloquent in arguing that they too sought the common good, and the well-being of those among whom they lived. The Christian is, or should be, 'the soul of the world', we read in the early Letter to Diognetus (possibly the earliest text we have defending Christianity), holding the earthly city together, however much it might hate them.

Throughout Christian history, there have been those who have witnessed to the saving love of God in spectacular ways: miracle workers, charismatic preachers, those who bore witness by giving up their lives to martyrdom. But a humbler way has also proved to be eloquent for the gospel: a way of kindness and solicitude, of being an exemplary neighbour, after the example of the Good Samaritan. After all, the Greek word behind 'to be saved' – what God so desires, we read – refers to healing as well as rescue from danger. There is more to the gospel than kindness and healing, but few things commend it more eloquently.

COLLECT

God, our light and our salvation:
illuminate our lives,
that we may see your goodness in the land of the living,
and looking on your beauty
may be changed into the likeness of Jesus Christ our Lord.

Wednesday 16 October

Psalm **119.153-end**
2 Kings 23.4-25
1 Timothy 3

1 Timothy 3

'... a bishop must be above reproach' (v.2)

When it comes to who to appoint as a bishop or overseer, and how such a person ought to live, the author of our letter lays on his strictures thickly, but he also tells us why it matters. The Church is 'the pillar and bulwark of the truth.' Those whose role is to guard and tend the Church, and who end up in some sense as its representatives, have quite a task to fulfil. Indeed, according to another way of translating this passage, it is Timothy and other leaders who are that 'pillar and bulwark'.

It is all too easy to associate the character of the Church with its current leaders, and all too easy to pray for 'the church' in our services and (bizarrely) only then mean or mention ordained people. That is a mistake. But the churches have also long exhorted their members to remember their leaders in their prayers, and today's reading underlines why that is so. The Book of Common Prayer thinks it wise to address its daily prayer along these lines to 'Almighty and everlasting God' as the one who 'alone workest great marvels' (not exactly a vote of confidence in the capacities of the clergy!). And yet, that is also not only a prayer for bishops and priests, but for 'all congregations committed to their charge'.

COLLECT

God, the giver of life,
whose Holy Spirit wells up within your Church:
by the Spirit's gifts equip us to live the gospel of Christ
    and make us eager to do your will,
that we may share with the whole creation
    the joys of eternal life;
through Jesus Christ your Son our Lord,
who is alive and reigns with you,
in the unity of the Holy Spirit,
one God, now and for ever.

| *Reflection by* **Andrew Davison**

Psalm **143**, 146
2 Kings 23.36 – 24.17
1 Timothy 4

Thursday 17 October

1 Timothy 4

*'... nothing is to be rejected, provided it is received
with thanksgiving' (v.4)*

What is the domain of the Christian? What is her area of interest and investment? It is not a narrow one. We are to concern ourselves not only with some specifically 'Christian' subset of the life of the world.

We read in Philippians that we are to be occupied – in mind and action – by whatever is true, honourable, just, pure, pleasing, commendable, excellent, and praiseworthy (Philippians 4.8). It is therefore no rejection of the faith to recognise and celebrate all that is good in what God has created, wherever it is to be found. All such things, like food and marriage in the passage today, are to be received and recognised in a Christian way, with 'word and prayer', with reflection and thankfulness.

'Nothing is to be rejected, provided it is received with thanksgiving'. That is not a recipe for immorality, nor is it a 'get out of jail free card' that excuses us from spiritual discernment. But it is a reminder of that great Pauline theme of freedom, and of the great biblical teaching that God's creation is good – 'everything created by God is good' – with a goodness that might be defaced by sin, but is never erased.

God, our light and our salvation:
illuminate our lives,
that we may see your goodness in the land of the living,
and looking on your beauty
may be changed into the likeness of Jesus Christ our Lord.

COLLECT

Reflection by **Andrew Davison** | 283

Friday 18 October

Luke the Evangelist

Luke 1.1-4

'... to write an orderly account for you, most excellent Theophilus'
(v.3)

As commentators have noted, there is hardly a single word in Luke's prologue that scholars have not argued over. Few such commentaries are more delightful, or playful, than the one offered by Origen in the third century in a homily on this passage.

From this prologue, Origen notes, we can tell that Luke has really put in his homework, writing only 'after investigating everything carefully from the very first' (v.3). For that, Origen writes, 'Luke is the only gospel writer to be praised in scripture for his Gospel writing.' (If Luke is, indeed, the person Paul has in mind in 2 Corinthians 8.18. The Church of England's Collect for St Luke's Day assumes he is. Scholars today are less sure.)

And who is this 'Theophilus', for whom Luke wrote his Gospel? A specific person, most commentators would say today. But, faced with this name, which means 'friend of God', Origen let his imagination run riot. 'You are people whom God can love so', he told his congregation, and with these words addressed also to you, 'you therefore also are made to be a 'Theophilus'. And anyone counted as a 'friend of God' is therefore also 'excellent', like this Theophilus. It may not be what Luke meant, but it's true all the same.

COLLECT

Almighty God,
you called Luke the physician,
whose praise is in the gospel,
to be an evangelist and physician of the soul:
by the grace of the Spirit
and through the wholesome medicine of the gospel,
give your Church the same love and power to heal;
through Jesus Christ your Son our Lord,
who is alive and reigns with you,
in the unity of the Holy Spirit,
one God, now and for ever.

| *Reflection by* **Andrew Davison**

Psalm **147**
2 Kings 25.22-end
1 Timothy 5.17-end

Saturday 19 October

1 Timothy 5.17-end

'The sins of some people are conspicuous and precede them to judgement, while the sins of others follow them there.' (v.24)

Timothy is reminded that part of the load that rests upon the shoulders of a pastor is a responsibility for discernment and judgement, and what is said here about church leadership applies in large measure to all. We are all to treat others in a careful way, acting fairly or, as we read here, 'without partiality'. That means reading people and situations accurately, and judging ourselves and our motives scrupulously. Sometimes, for church leaders, there will be difficult situations where adjudication of the deeds and character of another person will be necessary. We are told to do this in an open way, a way that is open, therefore, to assessment, and is an act of the whole community, rather than an individual judgement.

The final couple of verses today are striking, but can seem to float a little free. Perhaps they are a reassurance that God's perfect judgement will one day make everything clear. Perhaps they are a warning to Timothy to be careful in judgement, because one day his assessments will be judged by God's own. Or perhaps they are an elaboration of 'keep yourself pure': Timothy is to keep himself pure (or 'holy') – as are we – because one way or another everyone's sins become evident in the end, as do their good deeds.

God, the giver of life,
whose Holy Spirit wells up within your Church:
by the Spirit's gifts equip us to live the gospel of Christ
and make us eager to do your will,
that we may share with the whole creation
the joys of eternal life;
through Jesus Christ your Son our Lord,
who is alive and reigns with you,
in the unity of the Holy Spirit,
one God, now and for ever.

COLLECT

Reflection by **Andrew Davison** | 285

Monday 21 October

1 Timothy 6.1-10

'We brought nothing into the world so that we can take nothing out of it' (v.7)

The instructions Paul (or the writer of these letters) gives Timothy, are not always easy to read, much less to accept, unless interpreted both in their most accurate historical context, and in the deepest spiritual context too. The opening of this passage is a case in point. It is an inalienable truth that it is wrong for one human being to buy and sell another. The commodification of human beings is blasphemous according to any possible interpretation of the doctrine of Creation or the teaching of Christ. Yet here, Paul, as elsewhere, accepts household slavery as normal, and therefore to be used in illustration of Christian teaching as readily as, say, the tax system, the legal system, or the culture of sport.

Contemporary readers will rightly shudder at this instruction for slaves to regard their masters as worthy of honour, given the horrors of the transatlantic slave trade and the estimated 50 million people living in slavery today. The deepest point that Paul makes is challenging, though. The abuse of power, not least in religion, can make people rich. The fledgling Christian communities must be on the lookout for this false teaching in themselves and in others as their churches form, and as structures and hierarchies are worked out and set up. Loving money is something anyone can fall into if we are not careful and faithful. Paul's challenge is to remain alert to the demands of true discipleship, whoever we are.

COLLECT

Grant, we beseech you, merciful Lord,
to your faithful people pardon and peace,
that they may be cleansed from all their sins
and serve you with a quiet mind;
through Jesus Christ your Son our Lord,
who is alive and reigns with you,
in the unity of the Holy Spirit,
one God, now and for ever.

| *Reflection by* **Lucy Winkett**

Psalms **5**, 6 (8)
Judith 5.1 – 6.4
or Exodus 29.38 – 30.16
1 Timothy 6.11-end

Tuesday 22 October

1 Timothy 6.11-end

'Take hold of the eternal life to which you were called' (v.12)

This is Paul the poet, in similar vein to his writing about love in his first letter to the Corinthians. The 'unapproachable light' (v.16) and the beautiful urging to anyone who will listen that we, along with Timothy, are to 'take hold' of the eternal life that we have been called to, puts all the money-grabbing exploitation of yesterday's reading into perspective. Paul is a realist about human nature (he himself is guilty of persecution, violence and murder) and while holding that knowledge close, he is still capable of trusting completely in the God who he describes as the one 'whom no one has ever seen, or can see' (v.17).

Paul's writing is often emotional, wearing his heart on his sleeve. He seems to be more magnanimous today towards those who are rich in money, simply asking them to be rich in deeds, and to be ready always to share what they have. This in order for them, even them, to join Timothy in that lovely phrase again used in verse 19, in being able to 'take hold of the life that really is life'. Paul's instruction is to guard what we know we can trust in, keep the deepest possible perspective on life, and avoid the endless distractions of contemporary life. This sounds thoroughly modern, and from one friend to another, Timothy and Paul's conversation speaks into our circumstances today.

Almighty God,
in whose service lies perfect freedom:
teach us to obey you
with loving hearts and steadfast wills;
through Jesus Christ our Lord.

COLLECT

Reflection by **Lucy Winkett** | 287

Wednesday 23 October

Psalm **119.1-32**
Judith 6.10 – 7.7 *or* Leviticus 8
2 Timothy 1.1-14

2 Timothy 1.1-14

'Guard the good treasure entrusted to you' (v.14a)

Having established Timothy's credentials in the first letter, here Paul opens his reflections by calling him 'beloved'. The whole of this letter is written in love with an air of self-knowledge: Paul knows he is close to his final days. The closeness between Timothy and Paul is evident as this letter begins. Paul refers to the memory of Timothy's tears, perhaps the last time they saw each other, or perhaps reminiscent of an emotional goodbye similar to the tearful farewell recorded in Acts 20 when Paul left the community at Ephesus for the last time.

The mention of Timothy's grandmother and mother Lois and Eunice is striking. The faith has been passed down through generations, and our presumption must be that Timothy's father isn't mentioned because he was pagan not Christian (Acts 16.1-3). Paul addresses Timothy both as a beloved friend and also a fellow community leader in a dangerous situation. So he encourages him (v.8) not to be ashamed, despite the stigma of state execution surrounding Jesus and the stigma of prison surrounding Paul. He tries to encourage Timothy to rely on the power of God in this precarious and perilous time. We are witnessing Paul's theology developing before our eyes as he insists (here as elsewhere) that it is not by works but by grace that salvation comes (v.9).

COLLECT

Grant, we beseech you, merciful Lord,
to your faithful people pardon and peace,
that they may be cleansed from all their sins
and serve you with a quiet mind;
through Jesus Christ your Son our Lord,
who is alive and reigns with you,
in the unity of the Holy Spirit,
one God, now and for ever.

| *Reflection by* **Lucy Winkett**

Thursday 24 October

2 Timothy 1.15 – 2.13

'The word of God is not chained' (2.9)

It is the particulars in this section of the letter that are so memorable and striking. Paul is upset with some individuals – Phygelus and Hermogenes – but remains grateful for Onesiphorus and his household for standing by him. The vivid details of who stays and who falls by the wayside gives a strong indication of the level of flux – chaos even – in the first fledgling Christian communities. The precariousness and preciousness of the whole enterprise is laid bare in Paul's allusions, even in his complaining or expressions of regret, just as much as his elevated prose. And his prose soars out of these individual reflections. It's almost as if he finds himself mired in the everyday worries of individual decisions, especially who's stood by him and who's let him down.

But then he pulls himself together, through the insistence that his allegiance is to Christ; these worries then seem to fall away. We get Paul at his very best, declaring that although he himself is chained, the word of God is not chained, and that he will endure 'everything' for the sake of the gospel and for love of Jesus Christ who was raised from the dead. The classic Pauline balance of poetry and prose is inspiring as he declares himself ready to be so closely associated with Jesus that he is willing to die with him, knowing that he will also live with him in eternity.

Almighty God,
in whose service lies perfect freedom:
teach us to obey you
with loving hearts and steadfast wills;
through Jesus Christ our Lord.

COLLECT

Friday 25 October

Psalms 17, **19**
Judith 8.9-end *or* Leviticus 16.2-24
2 Timothy 2.14-end

2 Timothy 2.14-end

'But God's firm foundation stands' (v.19a)

Paul builds on his theme of shame, and the relationship between hard practical work and the power of words. He is directive here, warning and cautioning against Timothy becoming embroiled in controversies and wranglings as the new communities of faith work out how to build themselves up and organise their meetings. His warnings, rooted in the correction of individual people such as Hymenaeus and Philetus, feel thoroughly contemporary and widely applicable, as church leaders over centuries have become exhausted or dispirited by the politics of the institution.

These verses are so human and humane, they are encouraging for any who find the collective expression of faith tricky, without relying on bland agreement or repressive orthodoxy to build a unified and loving Church community. He is fierce in his direction to Timothy to avoid senseless controversies that breed quarrels, reminding him that to be the servant of Christ means being a peacemaker, kindly to everyone, with a style characterised by gentleness not agitating others. His analogy of people being different sorts of utensils speaks to his underlying theology of the relationship between works and grace: he calls all disciples, especially leaders, to work hard but to work hard to build up, not tear down, and ultimately always to rely on the grace of God which calls for repentance in leadership as well as warm words.

COLLECT

Grant, we beseech you, merciful Lord,
to your faithful people pardon and peace,
that they may be cleansed from all their sins
and serve you with a quiet mind;
through Jesus Christ your Son our Lord,
who is alive and reigns with you,
in the unity of the Holy Spirit,
one God, now and for ever.

| *Reflection by* **Lucy Winkett**

Psalms 20, 21, **23**
Judith 9 *or* Leviticus 17
2 Timothy 3

Saturday 26 October

2 Timothy 3
'All scripture is inspired by God' (v.16a)

Another way of translating the Greek phrase describing Paul's meditation on Scripture (by which he means the Hebrew Scriptures) is that it is 'God-breathed'. And this goes for this letter too. Paul, self-evidently, didn't know at the time that he was writing Scripture. He was writing a letter, to a specific person in specific circumstances. And so this phrase 'inspired by God' or 'God-breathed' is helpful especially when handling the more puzzling or infuriating aspects of Paul's personality, opinions or views. As a woman, it's difficult to read Paul's comments that some 'silly women' will be 'captivated' by what he deems false teaching (v.6). In letters that assume an uncritical attitude towards household slavery, or remarks about women and how he thinks they behave, which have caused untold suffering to women and girls in Christian communities, it's important to have a devotional reading style that takes the context seriously, at the same time as praying for the underlying wisdom to be revealed.

Paul's focus is there in verse 17. All he wants, in all this advice, is more effectively to equip and strengthen Timothy and, through him, others in the faith, so that they are empowered to do even more than Paul has been able to do. Paul displays a strong reliance on forgiveness, not finding fault for the sake of it, and a discerning spirit when faced with damaging opinions or assumptions. As modern readers, this dynamic is important to us too.

Almighty God,
in whose service lies perfect freedom:
teach us to obey you
with loving hearts and steadfast wills;
through Jesus Christ our Lord.

COLLECT

Monday 28 October
Simon and Jude, Apostles

Psalms 116, 117
Wisdom 5.1-16
or Isaiah 45.18-end
Luke 6.12-16

Luke 6.12-16

'He spent the night in prayer to God' (v.12)

It seems to have been Jesus' practice to withdraw in prayer, not only as part of his regular spiritual discipline, but also at key times of discernment and change. To remain close to the purposes of God when day comes (v.13), in the light and activity of human society, there has to be preparation alone in the shadows of night. This relationship between private and public prayer, contemplation and action, is a key feature of Jesus' teaching, not only what he said but also how he behaved. The choosing of these close disciples was going to be an important part of spreading his message , and while Simon and Jude, whom we celebrate today, are neither the most famous nor the most active of the twelve, the fact that their names are written in Scripture and that their ordinariness was marked out by Jesus as useful to him, is an encouragement for us.

Simon, the Zealot, was part of a political movement that argued for the overthrow of the Roman occupiers, if necessary by force. This movement would become stronger after Jesus's death, but for now, even to have Simon in the same group as Matthew, who by collecting taxes was collaborating with the Romans, would have made for lively political and social debate at meal times, if nothing else. Jesus chose a diverse and lively crew, with different jobs, life circumstances and opinions. So he does the same today.

COLLECT

Almighty God,
who built your Church upon the foundation
  of the apostles and prophets,
with Jesus Christ himself as the chief cornerstone:
so join us together in unity of spirit by their doctrine,
that we may be made a holy temple acceptable to you;
through Jesus Christ your Son our Lord,
who is alive and reigns with you,
in the unity of the Holy Spirit,
one God, now and for ever.

| *Reflection by* **Lucy Winkett**

Psalms 32, **36**
Judith 11 *or* Leviticus 23.1-22
2 Timothy 4.9-end

Tuesday 29 October

2 Timothy 4.9-end

'Do your best to come to me before winter' (v.21)

This is one of the longest final sections of all the pastoral letters. Paul, writing through what we assume is one of his secretaries or friends, is again very particular about the individuals who have stood by him or let him down, before issuing invitations to his 'beloved' Timothy to come and see him. We get the sense that he suspects he's close to the end, broken as he is by several imprisonments, and aware of the cost that his teaching will inevitably bring. His protestations reveal a loneliness that comes with what is often now called change leadership. Where some abandon the task before it's finished, others get scared, others sabotage either the whole enterprise or themselves in the process. But the leader relying on the Lord who 'stood by' Paul will be rescued from the lion's mouth and every evil attack, in order to live for ever in heaven.

It is a poignant end to a letter that has been unsparing in its tone but inspirational in its encouragement. In verse 22, Paul gives the Church a greeting used countless times in its liturgy: 'The Lord be with you: and with thy spirit'. This is a direct quotation from the end of this letter, that Christ Jesus, raised as Paul has insisted, from the dead, will be with the spirit of all who read it, through the particular lens of first century Mediterranean Christianity. A gift beyond price.

Blessed Lord,
who caused all holy Scriptures to be written for our learning:
help us so to hear them,
to read, mark, learn and inwardly digest them
that, through patience, and the comfort of your holy word,
we may embrace and for ever hold fast
the hope of everlasting life,
which you have given us in our Saviour Jesus Christ,
who is alive and reigns with you,
in the unity of the Holy Spirit,
one God, now and for ever.

COLLECT

Reflection by **Lucy Winkett** | 293

Wednesday 30 October

Titus 1

'My loyal child in the faith we share' (v.4)

If Timothy was 'beloved', then Titus is addressed as 'loyal' at the beginning of this short letter. Again, though almost certainly not written by Paul personally, it is absolutely in the 'voice' of Paul, articulating his concerns and themes as the Church grows and develops. The Church's structure is becoming more evident. Elders are appointed by the authority of Paul himself, who leaves behind emissaries such as Titus to select them.

Hospitality is a key attribute of these 'overseers,' or as we would know them, 'bishops'. Also a freedom from addictions (Paul singles out wine, but the point is wider), an ability to control themselves and above all, a 'firm grasp' of the truth of Christ so that whatever they say can be rooted in him. This is a picture of a person able to remain free of underlying anxieties, dependencies and a need for approval (Titus is urged to find people who can refute those who contradict the truth), but instead places their talent for speaking, for teaching or for welcome, at the feet of Christ who will direct their thoughts and guide their actions.

Such sharp words are used in this letter that reveal the strength of feeling towards those who are deliberately disrupting or corrupting the new community. What is longed for is communities of peace, good works and generous welcome. For this vision to be realised, leaders strong in gentleness and self-control are needed then as now.

COLLECT

Blessed Lord,
who caused all holy Scriptures to be written for our learning:
help us so to hear them,
to read, mark, learn and inwardly digest them
that, through patience, and the comfort of your holy word,
we may embrace and for ever hold fast
    the hope of everlasting life,
which you have given us in our Saviour Jesus Christ,
who is alive and reigns with you,
in the unity of the Holy Spirit,
one God, now and for ever.

| *Reflection by* **Lucy Winkett**

Psalm **37***
Judith 13 *or* Leviticus 24.1-9
Titus 2

Thursday 31 October

Titus 2

'Let no one look down on you' (v.15)

These instructions, aimed at different categories of person in the community, are difficult to read for a modern Church. If each sentence is taken literally at its word, then the structure of the Church and behaviour of its members starts to look overly hierarchical, and indefensibly, accepting of a system of household slavery. But the spirit of this section of the letter can be helpful for a contemporary readership when we remember the fundamental instruction is to encourage one another, build each other up, and let no one look down on us. There is a seriousness about the exhortations that is inspiring, if sometimes sounding a little worthy, and a key theme is that of self-control.

One of the fruits of the Spirit, self-control is a way of expressing a temperate nature, not abusing whatever power it is that we have, not becoming enslaved to addictions to work, approval, or such modern drugs of any kind. At the centre of all these instructions is a reminder of the glory of Jesus Christ, who 'gave himself for us'. This in order for us to be redeemed from these thoroughly human compulsions and obsessions, to be free to do all the good we can in all the ways we can think of (v.14).

Titus is encouraged to be a person that tirelessly declares this way of life to be true and honourable. The same for all who read it today.

Merciful God,
teach us to be faithful in change and uncertainty,
that trusting in your word
and obeying your will
we may enter the unfailing joy of Jesus Christ our Lord.

COLLECT

Friday 1 November
All Saints' Day

Psalms 15, 84, 149
Isaiah 35.1-9
Luke 9.18-27

Isaiah 35.1-9

*'If any want to be my followers, let them deny themselves,
take up their cross and follow me' (v.23)*

Today, All Saints Day, inspired by this practical, challenging, life-changing teaching, we should banish from our minds any images of ossified stained-glass unreachable figures and inhabit instead the electrifying teaching of Christ that overturns priorities, upturns established orders and invites believers to join the communion of saints. This communion is irreducibly baked into the life of Church. Into the winter months bursts a riot of colour, noise, chatter, robes, bravery beyond belief, courage beyond measure – the communion of saints – the stories of human lives lived to the full; the awkward squad, the outspoken lot, the colossally unwise-if-you-want-to-stay-alive crowd. Sometimes courageous or foolhardy, obstinate as well as inspiring, saints are human beings who somehow have an irreducible desire to travel towards the centre of things, close to the dwelling place of God.

Like a journey to the centre of the earth, saints will come close to the heat and the dust of living at the core. Anyone is capable of living this life, and Jesus's exhortation as he describes himself in one of his favourite phrases, the 'Son of Man', emphasises this. It will not be everyone's calling to die, he insists but it is everyone's calling to live close to the core love that is at the heart of the universe and the heart of God. And this will inevitably bring pain and love in equal measure.

COLLECT | Almighty God,
you have knit together your elect
in one communion and fellowship
    in the mystical body of your Son Christ our Lord:
grant us grace so to follow your blessed saints
in all virtuous and godly living
that we may come to those inexpressible joys
that you have prepared for those who truly love you;
through Jesus Christ your Son our Lord,
who is alive and reigns with you,
in the unity of the Holy Spirit,
one God, now and for ever.

| *Reflection by **Lucy Winkett***

Psalms 41, **42**, 43
Judith 15.14 – end of 16
or Numbers 6.1-5, 21-end
Philemon

Saturday 2 November

Philemon

'... you will do even more than I say' (v.21)

Paul is more certainly the personal author of this short letter. He writes from prison, although it's not clear where he is being held. Contemporary scholarship has Paul incarcerated in Ephesus, about 100 miles from where Philemon is in Colossae, which makes the suggested visit between them plausible.

Ostensibly a personal and private letter, this begs the question why it was included in the canon of Scripture. It concerns the return of a freed slave, Onesimus, to Philemon from Paul. As previously commented, it is repugnant to contemporary Christians that the system of slavery persisted in churches not only in this period but for 1800 years afterwards. But while he doesn't challenge the system, there is some progression in Paul's thinking here which could indicate a distinctive Christian theology of personhood developing that future abolitionists such as Wilberforce and Equiano would take inspiration from. Paul feels that the slave Onesimus is a son to him, and a brother to Philemon, which, if taken seriously, would be a transformational change in their relations, all as freemen. And mysteriously, hopefully, Paul points Philemon in an even more radical direction perhaps, encouraging him in his dealings with Onesimus to 'do even more than I say'. The familial language emphasises Paul's conviction that in Christ, all are heirs not slaves, and this adoption of human beings as free children of God is a theme that has resonated across centuries whether in this life, enslaved or free.

Blessed Lord,
who caused all holy Scriptures to be written for our learning:
help us so to hear them,
to read, mark, learn and inwardly digest them
that, through patience, and the comfort of your holy word,
we may embrace and for ever hold fast
the hope of everlasting life,
which you have given us in our Saviour Jesus Christ,
who is alive and reigns with you,
in the unity of the Holy Spirit,
one God, now and for ever.

COLLECT

Monday 4 November

Daniel 1

'In the third year...' (v.1)

When it comes to historical accuracy, I am more or less in the 'who cares?' camp. As it happens, Nebuchadnezzar did not take Jerusalem in the third year of Jehoiakim's reign. Nor was it Jehoiakim who fell into the Babylonian's power, but his son and heir, Jehoiachin (see 2 Kings 24). But does anyone really care? How much does it matter?

Of course, in one sense, it matters a great deal. Rightly, we set great store by exactitude. But we need to be careful not to identify exactitude with the truth. For many years I was a screenwriter specialising in historical drama. I wrote for the BBC, Channel 4, the History Channel and many others. There was always a tension in the development of scripts between factual correctness and dramatic truth. Did that *really* happen? Did she *really* say that? And does it matter?

The author of the Book of Daniel is writing historical drama. While the narrative is set at the start of the Babylonian Exile (early sixth century BC), the text was written centuries later, during the Maccabean revolt in the middle of the second century BC. The book of Daniel is – partly – a coded commentary on that conflict.

The text we know as 'Daniel' is generally characterised as an example of 'apocalyptic' writing, from the Greek *apokálupsis*, meaning 'revelation' or 'unveiling'. The truth is not on the surface, found in the facts, but requires 'insight', 'wisdom and understanding.'

COLLECT

Almighty and eternal God,
you have kindled the flame of love in the hearts of the saints:
grant to us the same faith and power of love,
that, as we rejoice in their triumphs,
we may be sustained by their example and fellowship;
through Jesus Christ your Son our Lord,
who is alive and reigns with you,
in the unity of the Holy Spirit,
one God, now and for ever.

| *Reflection by* **Colin Heber-Percy**

Tuesday 5 November

Daniel 2.1-24

'... the desire to understand' (v.3)

Nebuchadnezzar's magicians, enchanters and sorcerers turn out to be mere politicians. Challenged, they stick to techniques of 'trying to gain time' and declaring what they already know.

The French novelist, Marcel Proust recognises this as being the essence of political discourse when he says, 'to repeat what everyone else was thinking was, in politics, the mark not of an inferior but a superior mind.' These magicians, enchanters and sorcerers, with their 'superior' minds, know what they are doing. Their aim is not to 'satisfy the desire to understand', but to understand the desire, and harness it to their own ends: 'gifts and rewards and great honour'. Think of those soundbites, slogans and manifesto promises. Just 'lying and misleading words ... until things take a turn'.

Daniel's approach is different. He prays, thanking and praising God. He is not one of the 'wise men'; instead, he is faithful. Wisdom and power are not his, ultimately, but God's. For Daniel, religious faith is not a matter of knowing, but of needing. So he places himself humbly before God, the source and ground of all knowledge.

Today, politicians and business leaders tell us we should be fostering a 'knowledge-based economy'. As well as being horrible English, this is just a terrible idea. What we really need is an *ignorance*-based economy. Ignorance and awareness of how little we know is the engine of science, of all creative thinking, and of religious faith. Paradoxically, knowing we start from not knowing is vital.

God of glory,
touch our lips with the fire of your Spirit,
that we with all creation
may rejoice to sing your praise;
through Jesus Christ our Lord.

COLLECT

Wednesday 6 November

Psalms **9**, 147.13-end
or **119.57-80**
Daniel 2.25-end
Revelation 2.12-end

Daniel 2.25-end

'... tell the king the interpretation' (v.25)

That the world is fundamentally mysterious and requires interpretation is Daniel's starting point. According to the British philosopher, Alfred North Whitehead, all rational enquiry is a matter of interpretation. 'If we desire,' he says, 'a record of uninterpreted experience, we must ask a stone to record its autobiography'. Surely, this is a tad excessive. Dreams, like Nebuchadnezzar's, might be open to interpretation, but not *everything*. Can we not at least be certain of ourselves and our immediate, waking experience?

In Book Ten of his *Confessions*, St Augustine worries that '*mihi quaestio factus sum*'. The line is often translated as, 'I have become a question to myself'. But actually the words are better rendered as, 'I am *made* a question to myself'. By God's will, we are open to question, open to interpretation. The openness is essential.

Nebuchadnezzar wants Daniel's interpretation to bring closure, to answer his questions definitively. Like him, we tend to interpret away our dreams and uncertainties. Interpretations aim at being answers. But if Augustine is right and we have been *made* as questions not as stones, then answers are our closing, our ending, our petrification.

We cannot 'show to the king the mystery.' It is God in heaven who 'reveals mysteries.' For Daniel, the dream is not an answer to the dreamer's questions, nor a Freudian window onto his subconscious, but a revelation of the will of God. But then, what if *everything* is? Stay open.

COLLECT

Almighty and eternal God,
you have kindled the flame of love in the hearts of the saints:
grant to us the same faith and power of love,
that, as we rejoice in their triumphs,
we may be sustained by their example and fellowship;
through Jesus Christ your Son our Lord,
who is alive and reigns with you,
in the unity of the Holy Spirit,
one God, now and for ever.

Reflection by **Colin Heber-Percy**

Thursday 7 November

Daniel 3.1-18

'... these pay no heed to you, O king' (v.12)

Nebuchadnezzar's faith in Daniel's 'God of gods and Lord of kings' (Daniel 2.47) proves short-lived. Now he commands that all fall down and worship a golden idol. The original readers of this text would have recognised 'Nebuchadnezzar' as representing Antiochus IV Epiphanes, ruler of the Seleucid Empire who desecrated the Temple in Jerusalem and demanded all his subjects worship Zeus.

Confronted by this story today, we readily take it as a prompt to reflect on our own idols: wealth, power, recognition, and so on. But there is a danger here of falling into privileged abstraction. The fact is there are countless Shadrachs, Meshachs and Abednegos all over the world right now, being persecuted for their faith 'more precious than gold' (1 Peter 1.7). Christians in Nigeria, Uyghur Muslims in Xinjiang, and many more. If we enjoy the freedom to ask what it is we live for, they must confront the question of what it is they are prepared to die for.

And as Daniel's co-religionists recognise, there is 'no need to present a defence in this matter.' No need, and no point. Their defence (God) is precisely the issue at stake. And their steadfastness is the cry of those persecuted for their faith, 'We will not serve your gods and we will not worship the golden statue you have set up.'

Faith is not a defence; it is the furnace. That for which many are tested, and by means of which all are delivered.

God of glory,
touch our lips with the fire of your Spirit,
that we with all creation
may rejoice to sing your praise;
through Jesus Christ our Lord.

COLLECT

Reflection by **Colin Heber-Percy** | 301

Friday 8 November

Psalms **16**, 149 *or* **51**, 54
Daniel 3.19-end
Revelation 3.14-end

Daniel 3.19-end

'I see four ...' (v.25)

On the evening of 18 November 1987, a fire broke out under one of the wooden escalators at King's Cross underground station in London. The resulting blaze killed thirty-one people and injured many more. For years, one body remained unidentified, the victim known only as 'Michael' or 'body 115' after the mortuary tag number.

When Shadrach, Meshach and Abednego are brought out unsinged from Nebuchadnezzar's furnace, the mysterious fourth man is nowhere to be seen. He remains unidentified, a 'Michael'. Unlike Daniel's friends, the victims of the King's Cross disaster did not come out of the furnace alive. But they were not alone. 'Michael' was with them.

Thanks to the persistence of his daughters, 'body 115' was finally, after painstaking forensic investigation, found to be that of Alexander Fallon, a Scottish man who had been living rough in the city, heartbroken after the death of his wife.

The ones with names, the one whom 'the king promoted' may be delivered from the flames. But the unidentified, the nameless, they remain, bearing witness eternally. There are angels, Michaels, in our midst. Not by forensic pathologists but by the God who promises that 'even the hairs of your head are all counted' (Matthew 10.30), each of us is identified, known, and loved by a love hotter than any furnace. Wherever we are, and however intense the flames, there is always one more person in the fire with us.

COLLECT | Almighty and eternal God,
you have kindled the flame of love in the hearts of the saints:
grant to us the same faith and power of love,
that, as we rejoice in their triumphs,
we may be sustained by their example and fellowship;
through Jesus Christ your Son our Lord,
who is alive and reigns with you,
in the unity of the Holy Spirit,
one God, now and for ever.

| *Reflection by* **Colin Heber-Percy**

Psalms **18.31-end**, 150 *or* **68**
Daniel 4.1-18
Revelation 4

Saturday 9 November

Daniel 4.1-18

'... a tree at the centre of the earth' (v.10)

A morning walk in Savernake Forest, near where I live, is fresh in my mind. At this time of year, the paths through the trees are littered with acorns and chestnuts, and the leaves are all red and gold and sulphur yellow.

Nebuchadnezzar's dream draws on the shamanic mythology of ancient Eurasia, according to which a World Tree or Cosmic Tree unites earth and heaven and sits at the 'navel' of the world. And the tree is a potent symbol in all faith traditions. Think of the Tree of Knowledge of Good and Evil in the garden of Eden, or *Yggdrasil*, the sacred tree in Norse cosmology, or the Lote Tree in the Quran at the border of the seventh heaven, beyond which even angels cannot pass. Or the Buddha gaining enlightenment under the Bodhi tree.

It is easy to see why the tree is a dominant feature in our sacred texts. The tree is 'great and strong'; it is 'beautiful, its fruit abundant'; it provides a shelter and home for the creatures living under and around it.

Sometimes, however, the tree is not a boundary, a place or a cosmic symbol, but ourselves. In the Psalms, those whose 'delight is in the law of the Lord' are 'like trees planted by streams of water, which yield their fruit in its season' (Psalm 1.2-3).

May you be a tree planted by streams of the 'living water' (John 4.10). And bear good fruit.

God of glory,
touch our lips with the fire of your Spirit,
that we with all creation
may rejoice to sing your praise;
through Jesus Christ our Lord.

COLLECT

Monday 11 November

Daniel 4.19-end

'You have grown great and strong' (v.22)

In our different ways, I imagine we will spend the day walking on the roofs of our palaces and looking out over 'magnificent Babylon'. Like Nebuchadnezzar, we take pride in the lives we have constructed for ourselves. We feel safe and secure. We enjoy it here.

In 2008 and 2009, a group of prominent atheists, with the support of the British Humanist Association, paid a hundred and fifty thousand pounds for an advertising campaign to go on the side of London buses. The slogan read, 'There's probably no god. Now stop worrying and enjoy your life.'

The buses rolled through Babylon.

But look again. The number 94 or the 52, or whatever, passes a homeless person, a foodbank, a prison that is too full, a group of trafficked and exploited refugees washing cars, a woman going to a doctor's appointment for her test results.

In one respect the atheists are right. God causes us to worry, to question, and to be fearful. Far from being a crutch, a salve, or a panacea, God goads us and stings us, pricks our consciences, opens our hearts. In fourth-century Athens, Socrates saw himself as a gadfly, 'sent to the city' by God, 'to attack it ... rousing, and exhorting, and reproaching each one of you all day long'.

God forces us to recognise the contingency of our Babylon lives, our dependence on him, and calls us to truth, justice, and mercy.

COLLECT

> Almighty Father,
> whose will is to restore all things
> in your beloved Son, the King of all:
> govern the hearts and minds of those in authority,
> and bring the families of the nations,
> divided and torn apart by the ravages of sin,
> to be subject to his just and gentle rule;
> who is alive and reigns with you,
> in the unity of the Holy Spirit,
> one God, now and for ever.

| *Reflection by* **Colin Heber-Percy**

Psalms **21**, 24 *or* **73**
Daniel 5.1-12
Revelation 6

Tuesday 12 November

Daniel 5.1-12

'... a thousand of his lords' (v.1)

In the 1890s, Mrs Caroline Astor's New York town house boasted a ballroom with a capacity for four hundred guests. To be invited to a ball at the Astors' was to *belong*. You had arrived. And 'The Four Hundred' became a way of referring to the fashionable and prominent in New York City at that time.

Belshazzar's 'great festival' is a festival of belonging. How important and privileged the invitees must have felt! And as Belshazzar understands, belonging presupposes a border between the invited and the not invited, those on the inside and those left outside. Belshazzar marks this border by display and desecration. The gold and silver vessels from the house of God in Jerusalem are used for carousing. Belonging has triumph and success built in. For *us* to be victorious, *they* must be defeated.

Ultimately, the status of Belshazzar's lords, and the prestige of the 'Four Hundred' rests not on how fashionable and powerful the invitees are, but on how unfashionable and insignificant the rest of us are.

A sense of belonging is vital in any community. But for Christians, this sense of belonging cannot afford to become cosy or clubbable or code for accomplishment. In Matthew's Gospel, Jesus compares the kingdom of heaven to a wedding banquet, and he urges us to 'Go into the main streets and invite everyone you find' (Matthew 22.9).

You are invited. But so is everyone else. The capacity is Christ.

God, our refuge and strength,
bring near the day when wars shall cease
and poverty and pain shall end,
that earth may know the peace of heaven
through Jesus Christ our Lord.

COLLECT

Wednesday 13 November

Daniel 5.13-end

'... even though you knew all this' (v.22)

Shakespeare has Mark Antony reply to Cleopatra that 'there's beggary in the love that can be reckoned.' Reckoning is how we navigate, and calculate our position, how we weigh things up and balance the books, how we hold others to account. When we love we lose this capacity for reckoning. We love unreasonably. From love's perspective, all reckoning is dead reckoning.

In a navigable, accountable world of reckoning, knowledge is currency. Of course, we can invest this currency wisely or foolishly. Belshazzar knows the history of Nebuchadnezzar but he fails to 'capitalise' on that knowledge. And now a price must be reckoned.

But whether or not we spend the currency of knowledge prudently or profligately, we are still accounting, calculating, and reasoning. Antony seems to recognise that when it comes to loving, our currency of knowledge has no real exchange value. And Daniel recognises this too. 'Let your gifts be for yourself, or give your reward to someone else!'

For Martin Luther, on account of the Fall, human beings are irremediably dominated by their egos, and slavishly pursue their satisfaction at all costs. We are born reckoners. Yes, we have knowledge and reason, but this currency is debased because we always reckon it for our own ends. The articles of our faith on the other hand, while not against reason are, as Luther puts it, 'outside, under, above, below, around and beyond it'. Beyond reckoning. There is another currency: love.

COLLECT

Almighty Father,
whose will is to restore all things
in your beloved Son, the King of all:
govern the hearts and minds of those in authority,
and bring the families of the nations,
divided and torn apart by the ravages of sin,
to be subject to his just and gentle rule;
who is alive and reigns with you,
in the unity of the Holy Spirit,
one God, now and for ever.

Reflection by **Colin Heber-Percy**

Psalms **26**, 27 *or* **78.1-39***
Daniel 6
Revelation 8

Thursday 14 November

Daniel 6

'So that the king might suffer no loss' (v.2)

Here is one of the most familiar stories in all scripture, a Sunday School perennial. Reading it again, the story of Daniel in the lions' den has a familiar ring. Not only because we know it so well, but because it closely echoes the earlier story of Daniel's being denounced by Nebuchadnezzar's jealous advisers for not worshipping a golden idol (Daniel 3). And the pattern of the story has a deeper resonance; we recall Jesus' standing trial before a vacillating Pilate on charges brought against him by the threatened religious authorities.

As leader of the Persian Empire, Darius has everything to lose. As a faithful servant of God, Daniel has nothing to lose. Curiously, their opposed positions put them on a par. They share a relationship to loss. And in this sharing is an understanding, a mutual recognition.

What separates Darius and Daniel, what separates Jesus and Pilate, are the satraps and Pharisees – who have everything *to gain*.

The satraps and Pharisees of our own day often appear to be gaining ground. They look for angles and levers, jockeying for position 'among lions that greedily devour human prey' (Psalm 57.4). They know how to turn any situation to their political or social gain by conforming themselves to the world.

But their gaining the world is loss beyond loss, for 'what shall it profit a man, if he shall gain the whole world, and lose his own soul?' (Mark 8.36, KJV).

COLLECT

God, our refuge and strength,
bring near the day when wars shall cease
and poverty and pain shall end,
that earth may know the peace of heaven
through Jesus Christ our Lord.

Friday 15 November

Psalms 28, **32** *or* **55**
Daniel 7.1-14
Revelation 9.1-12

Daniel 7.1-14

'As I watched ...' (v.9)

What sounds mythical in this passage is more political than may at first appear. The four beasts represent kingdoms or empires: the Babylonian, Median, Persian, and worst of all, the Hellenistic or Seleucid empire that assumed control after the death of Alexander the Great in 323 BC. The ten horns of this last beast are the Seleucid kings, and the last horn with 'a mouth speaking arrogantly' stands for Antiochus Epiphanes himself who had desecrated the temple in Jerusalem and against whom the Jewish people had risen in revolt.

So the passage can be decoded, rendered safe. It may be of interest to historians and biblical scholars, but not to us. And yet this is scripture, a text we are called not only to decode and understand but to accept as revelation. There is a truth here that cannot be reduced to historical facts or data.

In our own time, are we free from these ramping beasts, 'terrifying and dreadful and exceedingly strong'? Clearly not. They are with us still, cruel and careless as ever. And we too watch for a kingdom that is not bestial but blessed by the Ancient One and that shall 'never be destroyed'.

Like Daniel, we await an end to worldly tyranny and the coming of one 'with the clouds of heaven'. Daniel's dream does not express a particular hope at a particular time but a universal longing for justice and righteousness to reign forever.

COLLECT

Almighty Father,
whose will is to restore all things
in your beloved Son, the King of all:
govern the hearts and minds of those in authority,
and bring the families of the nations,
divided and torn apart by the ravages of sin,
to be subject to his just and gentle rule;
who is alive and reigns with you,
in the unity of the Holy Spirit,
one God, now and for ever.

| *Reflection by* **Colin Heber-Percy**

Psalms **33** *or* **76**, 79
Daniel 7.15-end
Revelation 9.13-end

Saturday 16 November

Daniel 7.15-end

'... and the time arrived' (v.22)

We are approaching Advent: a season of expectation, of looking forward to the arrival of a saviour, a Prince of Peace who will reign 'with justice and with righteousness from this time onwards and for evermore' (Isaiah 9.7).

Daniel's dream is fulfilled, but not in the way the writer of this text anticipated. We still live in a kingdom that devours the whole earth, that tramples it down and breaks it to pieces. And yet, in the coming of Christ, the ultimate victory of this earthly power is denied. Not by strength and might, but by perfect weakness (2 Corinthians 12.9), because the victory does not come in the form of a great king in his palace, but as a child in a stable. And the 'everlasting kingdom' is proclaimed not to assembled lords and satraps on the battlefield, but to shepherds on a hillside.

Daniel's apocalyptic is full of hope, but his vision unfolds in a context of power play. Empire gives way to empire and the final victory of Israel, 'the people of the holy ones of the Most High' is still expressed in terms of kingship and dominion.

Our Saviour, when he comes, does not have kingship and power and dominion as his end. Instead, he puts an end to 'every ruler and every authority and power' (1 Corinthians 15.24). And he does this, not by gaining victory but by giving himself. For us all.

COLLECT

God, our refuge and strength,
bring near the day when wars shall cease
and poverty and pain shall end,
that earth may know the peace of heaven
through Jesus Christ our Lord.

Monday 18 November

Psalms 46, **47** *or* **80**, 82
Daniel 8.1-14
Revelation 10

Daniel 8.1-14

'For how long is this vision?' (v.13)

Early prophets expected people to understand their message at once, and to be perturbed by its threat of divine judgement. By contrast, later writers such as the author of Daniel, long after the Exile to Babylon, often described mysterious visions that no one could decipher unless they were given a 'key' by God – usually through an angel. Today we read about battles between the two great world powers of the day in the Middle East, based respectively in Egypt and Syria. But they are encoded in the image of a battle between a goat and a ram.

Without the angel's explanation, which we shall read tomorrow, the vision makes little sense. Few nowadays would cloak a description of world events in animal imagery – though we do meet it in cartoons, where we're still familiar with Russia as a bear, and the American Republican party often appears as an elephant. The first readers of Daniel knew they were caught up in conflicts between the powers that struggled to assert themselves as the rightful successors to Alexander the Great – conflicts over which they correctly felt they had no control. They were merely pawns. Most of us feel the same about global politics today. The Bible claims that in the end God is in control of world events. But that end seems to delay, and for most of us, as for the readers of Daniel, it is hard to share the book's confidence. Sometimes it is necessary to press on in faithfulness to God's call even though we don't see much light on the path ahead.

COLLECT

Heavenly Father,
whose blessed Son was revealed
    to destroy the works of the devil
and to make us the children of God and heirs of eternal life:
grant that we, having this hope,
may purify ourselves even as he is pure;
that when he shall appear in power and great glory
we may be made like him in his eternal and glorious kingdom;
where he is alive and reigns with you,
in the unity of the Holy Spirit,
one God, now and for ever.

| *Reflection by* **John Barton**

Psalms 48, **52** *or* 87, **89.1-18**
Daniel 8.15-end
Revelation 11.1-14

Daniel 8.15-end

'The vision is for the time of the end' (v.17)

Now the meaning of the imagery in verses 1-15 is revealed. It refers to events in the second century BC. The 'little horn' of verse 9 stands for a 'king of bold countenance' (v. 23). This must be Antiochus IV Epiphanes (who reigned 215–164 BC), the king based in Syria who unleashed the furious, but unsuccessful persecution of the Jews recounted in 1 Maccabees – the Jewish victory still commemorated today at the festival *Hanukkah*. Daniel is presented as foreseeing these events, and also prophesying Antiochus' downfall at the hand of God alone.

In the story Daniel is meant to be living during the Jewish exile to Babylon, in the sixth century BC, so the events he foretells lie far in the future for him. Consequently he is told to 'seal up the vision': a prediction to be accessed long afterwards. We know, however, that the author was really living in the second century BC, in what he calls 'the time of the end'. He was writing about what for him were contemporary events: like the ancient prophets, his concern was for his own day. By ascribing his comments to the ancient seer Daniel, he suggests that Daniel was predicting the remote future; some Christians accordingly think these predictions are still awaiting fulfilment. But more likely they were validated when Antiochus' armies were defeated. In any case, we must ask ourselves whether we can really see God's hand at work in geopolitical events today, as this writer did.

Heavenly Lord,
you long for the world's salvation:
stir us from apathy,
restrain us from excess
and revive in us new hope
that all creation will one day be healed
in Jesus Christ our Lord.

COLLECT

Wednesday 20 November   Psalms **56**, 57 *or* **119.105-128**
Daniel 9.1-19
Revelation 11.15-end

Daniel 9.1-19

'To the Lord our God belong mercy and forgiveness' (verse 9)

There are three great prayers of confession in the Old Testament, easily remembered as all are in chapter 9 of their respective books: Ezra, Nehemiah and Daniel. They all have a similar style, and share much with later Jewish prayers that are still used in synagogue services today. Most of Daniel's prayer on behalf of his people is a confession of national sin. It is the people's own fault, he says, as well as the fault of their ancestors, that led God to punish them. He allowed (or even caused) the Babylonians to invade and carry off many of the people, and especially the leaders, exiling them to Mesopotamia (now Iraq), in 598 and 587 BC.

The beauty and poetic quality of the prayer can mask difficult questions for a modern Christian. Does God really use invasion and exile as punishment? We don't usually think in these terms now when one country invades another. Is there such a thing as 'national sin' at all? Are ordinary people really implicated in the wrongdoing of their rulers, whom they may not be able to control? Yet at the same time, the prayer also promises forgiveness and restoration for those who repent. Daniel implores God to intervene quickly, 'for your own sake, O my God' (v.19), for he believes God himself is affected by his people's suffering – a great theme in the Old Testament, as it is in much Christian thought.

COLLECT

Heavenly Father,
whose blessed Son was revealed
    to destroy the works of the devil
and to make us the children of God and heirs of eternal life:
grant that we, having this hope,
may purify ourselves even as he is pure;
that when he shall appear in power and great glory
we may be made like him in his eternal and glorious kingdom;
where he is alive and reigns with you,
in the unity of the Holy Spirit,
one God, now and for ever.

| *Reflection by* **John Barton**

Thursday 21 November

Daniel 9.20-end

'To put an end to sin and to atone for iniquity' (v.24)

The angel Gabriel appears to Daniel and tells him God has heard his prayer. Jeremiah had prophesied that the exile of the Jews would last for seventy years (v.2), but Gabriel says this is going to mean seventy 'weeks' of years: seventy times seven, that is 490 years. So the prophecy is going to come true in the very period when the book was written. Once again the concern is not really for a distant future, but for the second century BC – the days of the Maccabees, when the actual writer of Daniel was living. This would have been distant for the Daniel of the story, but it was *now* for the real author and for his readers. God's forgiveness would be shown in concrete changes to the national situation. In particular the Temple, defiled by Antiochus by placing there an idol (an 'abomination that desolates', v.27) was to be restored. This is the restoration Jews celebrate at *Hanukkah*. It reminds us that religious belief and practice often can't be separated from a hallowed place of worship.

The Bible, in both Testaments, is clear that God can be worshipped anywhere. Temples and shrines can even become 'idols' themselves if they are attempts to tie God down. Yet human beings are *local*, and need somewhere to focus their engagement with God. That is why most Christians similarly value and revere their place of worship.

Heavenly Lord,
you long for the world's salvation:
stir us from apathy,
restrain us from excess
and revive in us new hope
that all creation will one day be healed
in Jesus Christ our Lord.

COLLECT

Friday 22 November

Psalms **63**, 65 *or* **88** (95)
Daniel 10.1 – 11.1
Revelation 13.1-10

Daniel 10.1 – 11.1

'No breath is left in me' (v.17)

Chapters 10 and 11 tell us in detail about coming wars, but the main interest for us is that here we learn more about angels than anywhere else in the Old Testament. The angel who appears to Daniel is unnamed, but is far from what many today might expect an angel to be like. This angel is 'in human form' (v.16), a male, warrior-like figure, who seems made of bronze and precious stones, with torches for eyes. He is evidently a kind of angelic national guardian ('prince') alongside the archangel Michael, and is just returning from fighting a battle, with Michael's help, against the angel-guardians of Persia and Greece. This seems to be an Israelite version of the belief that every nation has its own god, as its representative or defender in heaven (cf. Psalm 82). But being monotheistic, Israelites described these superhuman beings as angels rather than gods.

One thing that distinguishes them sharply from the 'angels' we see in nativity plays and in some western art, is that they are absolutely terrifying. The angel comes benignly, in answer to Daniel's prayer for his people. Yet Daniel is still literally floored by the sight, and his companions run away even though they've seen nothing. Many people today believe in angels – some surveys suggest more even than believe in God, but often as comforting figures. In the Bible they induce fear and trembling, even though they always remind humans that they are neither divine nor sent to inspire terror deliberately.

COLLECT

Heavenly Father,
whose blessed Son was revealed
    to destroy the works of the devil
and to make us the children of God and heirs of eternal life:
grant that we, having this hope,
may purify ourselves even as he is pure;
that when he shall appear in power and great glory
we may be made like him in his eternal and glorious kingdom;
where he is alive and reigns with you,
in the unity of the Holy Spirit,
one God, now and for ever.

| *Reflection by* **John Barton**

Psalms **78.1-39** *or* 96, **97**, 100
Daniel 12
Revelation 13.11-end

Saturday 23 November

Daniel 12

'Many of those who sleep in the dust of the earth shall awake' (v.2)

At the end of the events described in complicated symbolic forms in chapter 11, this last chapter of Daniel moves from ordinary human history into the end-time, when earthly and heavenly realities start to interact.

The archangel Michael makes another appearance, together with two other presumably angelic figures. From the sayings of the angels we learn, for the first and only time in the Old Testament, about the ultimate post-mortem fate of the righteous and the wicked. Verses 1-3 speak of a book that records those who will be saved out of the coming afflictions. They, the supremely good, with their opposites, the exceptionally wicked, will be raised to new life: 'many who sleep in the dust of the earth shall awake' (v.2). For the first, there will be 'everlasting life'; for the second, 'shame and everlasting contempt'. Nothing is said about the fate of the mediocre majority! ('Everlasting' may mean 'very long-lasting' – the English translation is not an exact equivalent of the Hebrew.) Nevertheless, the common claim that 'the Old Testament says nothing about life after death' is plainly not true – these verses can refer to nothing else.

Compared with the rich material about resurrection in the New Testament, however, and the teaching that God raises the dead in rabbinic Judaism and in Jewish liturgy, the Old Testament has, very little to say on the subject. Neither faith seems have found this to be a major problem – which may be rather surprising. It is a reminder that there are differences of emphasis in different parts of the Bible – its books do not speak with a single voice, even on a theme as important as this.

Heavenly Lord,
you long for the world's salvation:
stir us from apathy,
restrain us from excess
and revive in us new hope
that all creation will one day be healed
in Jesus Christ our Lord.

COLLECT

Reflection by **John Barton** | 315

Monday 25 November

Psalms 92, **96** *or* **98**, 99, 101
Isaiah 40.1-11
Revelation 14.1-13

Isaiah 40.1-11

'Comfort, O comfort my people, says your God' (v.1)

In the week preceding Advent we read from Isaiah, chapters 40 – 55, often thought to come from the sixth century BC, a couple of centuries after the prophet Isaiah himself, when many Jews were living in exile in Babylonia (now Iraq). These chapters are among the most-loved parts of the Old Testament in Christian circles, while in the liturgy of the synagogue far more of the readings that follow the weekly section from the Torah are taken from them than from any other prophecies. They foretell a glorious restoration of Jerusalem, which was destroyed by the Babylonian army, and peace and joy for the community there. This community would be made up of those who were going to return from Babylonia, reunited with the many who had remained in the land and eked out a living from it. The prophet imagines Jerusalem seeing the exiled people returning across a desert landscape flattened to make their journey easier, with God himself leading them home like a shepherd guiding a flock.

Christians have seen this passage, originally meant for those suffering under the yoke of Babylon, as a message of liberation for faithful believers in every age. It was particularly salient in the mission of John the Baptist, presented in the New Testament as the 'voice crying in the wilderness.'

COLLECT

Eternal Father,
whose Son Jesus Christ ascended to the throne of heaven
    that he might rule over all things as Lord and King:
keep the Church in the unity of the Spirit
and in the bond of peace,
and bring the whole created order to worship at his feet;
who is alive and reigns with you,
in the unity of the Holy Spirit,
one God, now and for ever.

| *Reflection by* **John Barton**

Psalms **97**, 98, 100 or **106*** (or 103)
Isaiah 40.12-26
Revelation 14.14 – end of 15

Isaiah 40.12-26

'It is he who sits above the circle of the earth' (v.22)

When we're concerned with God as the creator of the world in the Bible, we immediately think of the opening chapters of Genesis. But this section of Isaiah is equally important. It emphasizes that God alone made the universe, with no assistance from any other being or power: all the rhetorical questions in verses 12-14 are intended to convince the reader that God required no advice, help, or information from outside himself, but was wholly self-sufficient – a central theme of Jewish and Christian theology and philosophy. What's more, the created world, vast as it is (and we have a far better knowledge than Isaiah's audience of just how vast), when compared with God is less than the dust left on scales when grain is being sold (v.15).

The God who created the world is incomparable in power and wisdom, so worshipping any substitute in the form of an 'idol' – a mere wooden image (vv.19-20) – is ridiculous. The creator, unlike such a man-made 'god', is not part of the world, but sits above 'the circle of the earth'. In ancient Israel the earth was apparently thought of as a flat disc resting on water. God, seated in heaven, was therefore literally above it – see the account of the creation in Proverbs 8.27, 'when he [God] drew a circle on the face of the deep'. This passage in Isaiah lies at the root of Jewish and Christian emphasis on the utter 'transcendence' of God: the belief that God is beyond everything that exists.

God the Father,
help us to hear the call of Christ the King
and to follow in his service,
whose kingdom has no end;
for he reigns with you and the Holy Spirit,
one God, one glory.

COLLECT

Reflection by **John Barton** | 317

Wednesday 27 November

Isaiah 40.27 – 41.7

'I, the Lord, am first, and will be with the last' (41.4)

The possibility of the exiles returning to Jerusalem depended on the defeat of the Babylonians by the Persian king, Cyrus the Great (c. 600–530 BC), in 540 BC. He is mentioned by name in Isaiah 44.28 and 45.1. Isaiah 41.2-4 refers to him, though unnamed, as 'a victor from the east' and describes his rapid advance on Babylon ('scarcely touching the path with his feet'). But this is not said in order to glorify Cyrus. Instead, his military success is ascribed to the God of Israel, who is using him to make possible the liberation of his own people. Isaiah himself, back in the eighth century, had seen the Assyrian conquest of Israel as possible only because the Assyrian king (Sennacherib) was a tool used by God to punish his own people (Isaiah 10.5).

Now, in the new age God was inaugurating, a foreign king was again God's instrument, only this time for their liberation and well-being, rather than for destruction. In the modern world, this understanding of God as moving the pieces on the chessboard of the world is problematic, for Christians as for agnostics. It rightly stresses the weakness and subordinate position of even the greatest empire when compared with God, who is both 'first and last' (this brings to mind Revelation 22.13, 'the Alpha and Omega' – as we might say, 'the A to Z'). But it can also encourage us to identify God's hand at work in the rise and fall of nations, which is a difficult task. How can we take the prophetic message seriously, while avoiding over-simple judgements about world politics?

T	Eternal Father,
C	whose Son Jesus Christ ascended to the throne of heaven
E	that he might rule over all things as Lord and King:
L	keep the Church in the unity of the Spirit
L	and in the bond of peace,
O	and bring the whole created order to worship at his feet;
C	who is alive and reigns with you,
	in the unity of the Holy Spirit,
	one God, now and for ever.

Reflection by **John Barton**

Psalms **125**, 126, 127, 128
or 113, **115**
Isaiah 41.8-20
Revelation 16.12-end

Thursday 28 November

Isaiah 41.8-20

'I will make the wilderness a pool of water' (v.18)

In a country with large areas of parched ground, thirst was a more familiar, frequent, and threatening experience than it commonly is in many modern cities, especially in temperate climates. Provision of superabundant water was therefore a natural image for divine care for people, as well as an obvious example of literal salvation from death. Verses 17-20 here are one of the most vivid illustrations of this theme in the Bible. Abundant water also means that trees can take root and flourish. In the new order the prophet envisages, this will happen even in the desert!

In ancient Israel it must have seemed that only a miracle could plant, for example, cypress trees in barren land. How far did the prophet think of these predictions as literal, how far as symbolic of 'spiritual' blessing? Perhaps both, though Christian readings sometimes gloss over the literal meaning of passages like this too readily. The prophet speaks about an actual return to the land, and its (divinely-given) enhancement to provide for an enormously expanded population (Isaiah 49.19-23). This continues to resonate with the Christian hope for a new world order: perhaps what it will be like when God creates 'new heavens and a new earth' (Isaiah 65.17, also Revelation 21.1). But it is important to recognize that the Bible also thinks of concrete physical reality, of significant change in the political realm, and even in the natural world, as part of God's work in renewing the world he has made.

God the Father,
help us to hear the call of Christ the King
and to follow in his service,
whose kingdom has no end;
for he reigns with you and the Holy Spirit,
one God, one glory.

COLLECT

Friday 29 November

Isaiah 41.21 – 42.9

*'The former things have come to pass, and new things
I now declare' (42.9)*

The prophet ridicules the 'gods' worshipped by other peoples for being unable to foretell the future. Israel's God, by contrast, had 'declared to Zion' the rise of 'one from the north' (that is, Cyrus), and had correctly predicted his conquests. This is the difference between the true God and the other 'gods'. After this the writer launches into the first of what are sometimes called the 'Servant Songs'(42.1-7) – passages within Isaiah that can be lifted out as originally (perhaps) free-standing poems. There is no agreement among biblical scholars about the identity of the 'servant'. It may have been the exiled king, Jehoiachin; maybe a contemporary leader, conceivably even the prophet himself; maybe the personified corporate body of the exiles, or even of those who had *not* been exiled; maybe even Cyrus, which is just about conceivable, given that in 45.1 he is described, amazingly, as God's 'anointed one' (*mashiah*, the word we know as 'messiah').

Christian tradition has seen all the 'Servant Songs' as prophecies of the sufferings and vindication of Jesus. This one portrays a 'servant' who is a 'light to the nations'. Christians saw this as fulfilled in the mission to the Gentiles that St Paul undertook in the name of Jesus (see Romans 15). Whatever the original intention of the Song, it is difficult as a Christian not to feel that it resonates with such a theme, and this impression is enhanced when all four Songs are read in Holy Week.

COLLECT

Eternal Father,
whose Son Jesus Christ ascended to the throne of heaven
 that he might rule over all things as Lord and King:
keep the Church in the unity of the Spirit
and in the bond of peace,
and bring the whole created order to worship at his feet;
who is alive and reigns with you,
in the unity of the Holy Spirit,
one God, now and for ever.

| *Reflection by* **John Barton**

Psalms 47, 147.1-12
Ezekiel 47.1-12
or Ecclesiasticus 14.20-end
John 12.20-32

Saturday 30 November
Andrew the Apostle

Ezekiel 47.1-12

'Water was flowing from below the threshold of the temple' (v.1)

Today is the feast of St Andrew, the apostle of Jesus and brother of Simon Peter, and this is one of the readings appointed for his day – though the reason for this is not clear. It does, however, pick up the theme of life-giving water found in an earlier reading this week (Isaiah 41.8-20). Ezekiel sees water flowing into the Dead Sea and miraculously desalinating it, so that it becomes a habitat for fish like those of the 'Great Sea' (the Mediterranean), and fishermen start to spread their nets in it. Just as in Isaiah's prophecy barren land begins to yield crops and to support trees because God irrigates it, so what with good reason we call the 'Dead' Sea will become fresh and life-giving. The trees along its banks will be exceptionally fruitful, yielding their fruit not just annually, but every month. Even their leaves will have medicinal properties. All this is because the water originates from under the threshold of the renewed temple: it is holy water, therefore, that blesses whatever it touches.

Though the picture conjured up is a strange one to most modern readers, the inner meaning is clear. God will again bless his people, and give them fruitfulness instead of sterility. Once again this has potentially both a physical and a symbolic meaning, and we do well to attend to both: as usual in the Old Testament, blessings are seldom 'purely spiritual', but normally have a concrete, down-to-earth dimension too.

Almighty God,
who gave such grace to your apostle Saint Andrew
that he readily obeyed the call of your Son Jesus Christ
and brought his brother with him:
call us by your holy word,
and give us grace to follow you without delay
and to tell the good news of your kingdom;
through Jesus Christ your Son our Lord,
who is alive and reigns with you,
in the unity of the Holy Spirit,
one God, now and for ever.

COLLECT

Seasonal Prayers of Thanksgiving

Blessed are you, Sovereign God of all,
to you be praise and glory for ever.
In your tender compassion
the dawn from on high is breaking upon us
to dispel the lingering shadows of night.
As we look for your coming among us this day,
open our eyes to behold your presence
and strengthen our hands to do your will,
that the world may rejoice and give you praise.
Blessed be God, Father, Son and Holy Spirit.
Blessed be God for ever.

Blessed are you, Sovereign God,
creator of heaven and earth,
to you be praise and glory for ever.
As your living Word, eternal in heaven,
assumed the frailty of our mortal flesh,
may the light of your love be born in us
to fill our hearts with joy as we sing:
Blessed be God, Father, Son and Holy Spirit.
Blessed be God for ever.

Blessed are you, Sovereign God,
king of the nations,
to you be praise and glory for ever.
From the rising of the sun to its setting
your name is proclaimed in all the world.
As the Sun of Righteousness dawns in our hearts
anoint our lips with the seal of your Spirit
that we may witness to your gospel
and sing your praise in all the earth.
Blessed be God, Father, Son and Holy Spirit.
Blessed be God for ever.

Blessed are you, Lord God of our salvation,
to you be glory and praise for ever.
In the darkness of our sin you have shone in our hearts
to give the light of the knowledge of the glory of God
in the face of Jesus Christ.
Open our eyes to acknowledge your presence,
that freed from the misery of sin and shame
we may grow into your likeness from glory to glory.
Blessed be God, Father, Son and Holy Spirit.
Blessed be God for ever.

Blessed are you, Lord God of our salvation,
to you be praise and glory for ever.
As a man of sorrows and acquainted with grief
your only Son was lifted up
that he might draw the whole world to himself.
May we walk this day in the way of the cross
and always be ready to share its weight,
declaring your love for all the world.
Blessed be God, Father, Son and Holy Spirit.
Blessed be God for ever.

Blessed are you, Sovereign Lord,
the God and Father of our Lord Jesus Christ,
to you be glory and praise for ever.
From the deep waters of death
you brought your people to new birth
by raising your Son to life in triumph.
Through him dark death has been destroyed
and radiant life is everywhere restored.
As you call us out of darkness into his marvellous light
may our lives reflect his glory
and our lips repeat the endless song.
Blessed be God, Father, Son and Holy Spirit.
Blessed be God for ever.

Blessed are you, Lord of heaven and earth,
to you be glory and praise for ever.
From the darkness of death you have raised your Christ
to the right hand of your majesty on high.
The pioneer of our faith, his passion accomplished,
has opened for us the way to heaven
and sends on us the promised Spirit.
May we be ready to follow the Way
and so be brought to the glory of his presence
where songs of triumph for ever sound:
Blessed be God, Father, Son and Holy Spirit.
Blessed be God for ever.

From the day after Ascension Day
until the Day of Pentecost

Blessed are you, creator God,
to you be praise and glory for ever.
As your Spirit moved over the face of the waters
bringing light and life to your creation,
pour out your Spirit on us today
that we may walk as children of light
and by your grace reveal your presence.
Blessed be God, Father, Son and Holy Spirit.
Blessed be God for ever.

From All Saints until the day before
the First Sunday of Advent

Blessed are you, Sovereign God,
ruler and judge of all,
to you be praise and glory for ever.
In the darkness of this age that is passing away
may the light of your presence which the saints enjoy
surround our steps as we journey on.
May we reflect your glory this day
and so be made ready to see your face
in the heavenly city where night shall be no more.
Blessed be God, Father, Son and Holy Spirit.
Blessed be God for ever.

The Lord's Prayer and The Grace

Our Father in heaven,
hallowed be your name,
your kingdom come,
your will be done,
on earth as in heaven.
Give us today our daily bread.
Forgive us our sins
as we forgive those who sin against us.
Lead us not into temptation
but deliver us from evil.
For the kingdom, the power,
and the glory are yours
now and for ever.
Amen.

(or)

Our Father, who art in heaven,
hallowed be thy name;
thy kingdom come;
thy will be done;
on earth as it is in heaven.
Give us this day our daily bread.
And forgive us our trespasses,
as we forgive those who trespass against us.
And lead us not into temptation;
but deliver us from evil.
For thine is the kingdom,
the power and the glory,
for ever and ever.
Amen.

The grace of our Lord Jesus Christ,
and the love of God,
and the fellowship of the Holy Spirit,
be with us all evermore.
Amen.

An Order for Night Prayer (Compline)

The Lord almighty grant us a quiet night and a perfect end.
Amen.

Our help is in the name of the Lord
who made heaven and earth.

A period of silence for reflection on the past day may follow.

The following or other suitable words of penitence may be used

Most merciful God,
we confess to you,
before the whole company of heaven and one another,
that we have sinned in thought, word and deed
and in what we have failed to do.
Forgive us our sins,
heal us by your Spirit
and raise us to new life in Christ. Amen.

O God, make speed to save us.
O Lord, make haste to help us.

Glory to the Father and to the Son
and to the Holy Spirit;
as it was in the beginning is now
and shall be for ever. Amen.
Alleluia.

The following or another suitable hymn may be sung

Before the ending of the day,
Creator of the world, we pray
That you, with steadfast love, would keep
Your watch around us while we sleep.

From evil dreams defend our sight,
From fears and terrors of the night;
Tread underfoot our deadly foe
That we no sinful thought may know.

O Father, that we ask be done
Through Jesus Christ, your only Son;
And Holy Spirit, by whose breath
Our souls are raised to life from death.

The Word of God

One or more of Psalms 4, 91 or 134 may be used.

Psalm 134

1   Come, bless the Lord, all you servants of the Lord, ◆
    you that by night stand in the house of the Lord.

2   Lift up your hands towards the sanctuary ◆
    and bless the Lord.

3   The Lord who made heaven and earth ◆
    give you blessing out of Zion.

**Glory to the Father and to the Son
and to the Holy Spirit;
as it was in the beginning is now
and shall be for ever. Amen.**

Scripture Reading

*One of the following short lessons or another suitable
passage is read*

You, O Lord, are in the midst of us and we are called by
your name; leave us not, O Lord our God.

Jeremiah 14.9

(or)

Be sober, be vigilant, because your adversary the devil is
prowling round like a roaring lion, seeking for someone
to devour. Resist him, strong in the faith.

1 Peter 5.8,9

(or)

The servants of the Lamb shall see the face of God, whose
name will be on their foreheads. There will be no more night:
they will not need the light of a lamp or the light of the sun,
for God will be their light, and they will reign for ever and
ever.

Revelation 22.4,5

Into your hands, O Lord, I commend my spirit.
Into your hands, O Lord, I commend my spirit.
For you have redeemed me, Lord God of truth.
I commend my spirit.
Glory to the Father and to the Son
and to the Holy Spirit.
Into your hands, O Lord, I commend my spirit.

Or, in Easter

Into your hands, O Lord, I commend my spirit.
    Alleluia, alleluia.
Into your hands, O Lord, I commend my spirit.
    Alleluia, alleluia.
For you have redeemed me, Lord God of truth.
Alleluia, alleluia.
Glory to the Father and to the Son
and to the Holy Spirit.
Into your hands, O Lord, I commend my spirit.
    Alleluia, alleluia.

Keep me as the apple of your eye.
Hide me under the shadow of your wings.

Gospel Canticle

Nunc Dimittis (The Song of Simeon)

Save us, O Lord, while waking,
and guard us while sleeping,
that awake we may watch with Christ
and asleep may rest in peace.

1   Now, Lord, you let your servant go in peace:
     your word has been fulfilled.

2   My own eyes have seen the salvation
     which you have prepared in the sight of every people;

3   A light to reveal you to the nations
     and the glory of your people Israel.

Luke 2.29-32

**Glory to the Father and to the Son
and to the Holy Spirit;
as it was in the beginning is now
and shall be for ever. Amen.**

**Save us, O Lord, while waking,
and guard us while sleeping,
that awake we may watch with Christ
and asleep may rest in peace.**

Prayers

Intercessions and thanksgivings may be offered here.

The Collect

Visit this place, O Lord, we pray,
and drive far from it the snares of the enemy;
may your holy angels dwell with us and guard us in peace,
and may your blessing be always upon us;
through Jesus Christ our Lord.
Amen.

The Lord's Prayer (see p. 325) may be said.

The Conclusion

In peace we will lie down and sleep;
for you alone, Lord, make us dwell in safety.

Abide with us, Lord Jesus,
for the night is at hand and the day is now past.

As the night watch looks for the morning,
so do we look for you, O Christ.

[Come with the dawning of the day
and make yourself known in the breaking of the bread.]

The Lord bless us and watch over us;
the Lord make his face shine upon us and be gracious to us;
the Lord look kindly on us and give us peace.
Amen.

Index of readings

REFLECTIONS FOR DAILY PRAYER
App

Make Bible study and reflection a part of your routine wherever you go with the Reflections for Daily Prayer App for Apple and Android devices.

Download the app for free from the App Store (Apple devices) or Google Play (Android devices) and receive a week's worth of reflections free. Then purchase a monthly, three-monthly or annual subscription to receive up-to-date content.

REFLECTIONS FOR SUNDAYS (YEAR B)

Reflections for Sundays offers over 250 reflections on the Principal Readings for every Sunday and major Holy Day in Year B, from the same experienced team of writers that have made *Reflections for Daily Prayer* so successful. For each Sunday and major Holy Day, they provide:

- full lectionary details for the Principal Service
- a reflection on each Old Testament reading (both Continuous and Related)
- a reflection on the Epistle
- a reflection on the Gospel.

This book also contains a substantial introduction to the Gospels of Mark and John, written by Paula Gooder.

£16.99 • 288 pages
ISBN 978 1 78140 030 2

Also available in Kindle and epub formats

REFLECTIONS ON THE PSALMS

£16.99 • 192 pages
ISBN 978 0 7151 4490 9

Reflections on the Psalms provides original and insightful meditations on each of the Bible's 150 Psalms.

Each reflection is accompanied by its corresponding Psalm refrain and prayer from the *Common Worship Psalter*, making this a valuable resource for personal or devotional use.

Specially written introductions by Paula Gooder and Steven Croft explore the Psalms and the Bible and the Psalms in the life of the Church.